CRAFTING EXPOSITORY ARGUMENT

PRACTICAL APPROACHES TO THE WRITING PROCESS FOR STUDENTS AND TEACHERS

Michael Degen, Ph.D.

TELEMACHOS
PUBLISHING

Dallas, Texas

Fifth Edition
First Printing 2012

Telemachos Publishing
PO Box 460387
Garland, TX 75046-0387
www.telemachospublishing.com

Library of Congress Catalog Card Number: 2012935699

ISBN: 978-0-9853849-0-6

For my teacher and friend

Sarah Greer Bush

who not only taught me how to write, to examine language,
and to admire well-crafted prose, but also taught me how to
teach students—working with young writers individually, showing
them how to improve sentences, paragraphs, and papers.
Each time I meet with a student I remember Sarah's gift—
hours at her kitchen table and office desk explaining, guiding,
and shaping my knowledge of prose.

TABLE OF CONTENTS

FOREWORD TO TEACHERS

ARGUMENTS AND APPROACHES

Definition of Expository Argument

Expository argument is nonfiction prose that contains an introductory paragraph with a thesis statement—a THESIS STATEMENT being A SENTENCE ASSERTING A CLAIM THAT MUST BE DEMONSTRATED OR PROVEN—body paragraphs that illustrate and corroborate the elements of the thesis statement, and a concluding paragraph.

Quick Overview: What This Book Is About

These are the beliefs that inform this book.
- Writing well is a difficult and complex task, one that demands more than one year of concentrated study.
- Students do not become better writers merely by reading.
- Students do not become better writers by completing a series of writing assignments with little teacher feedback and no option for revision.
- Students learn to write better if the teacher models the assignment, states directions clearly, offers opportunities for students to practice the skills necessary to achieve high expectations, provides specific feedback toward improvement, and requires students to revise written work after thoroughly instructing them in the revision process.
- The teaching of writing has been made more complex because of academic and social distractions. One academic distraction includes English curricula that emphasizes the quantity of material studied rather than the quality. One social distraction includes our media-driven culture that supports instant gratification and little self-discipline.
- Almost all English teachers battle time restraints because they must teach both literature and composition in one course.
- Serious writers revise; serious teachers expect revision.
- Research demonstrates that teaching grammar without applying it to writing assignments does not improve student writing, but the teaching of writing with simultaneous instruction in the specifics of grammar usage and sentence structure will produce writers skillful in using language. THEREFORE, EVERYONE USING CRAFTING EXPOSITORY ARGUMENT SHOULD EXPECT TO INCORPORATE CHAPTER FIVE, "CRAFTING THE SENTENCE," INTO ALL INSTRUCTION OF THE WRITING PROCESS.

Four Key Teaching Concepts

This manual/resource book is in response to the aforementioned assertions. Moreover, it focuses on four key concepts with regard to teaching secondary students expository argument.

• Clear directions

Write down for students all expectations for written work: whatever length requirements you wish students to achieve, position of topic sentences, location of thesis statement, type of introduction, minimum number of direct quotations, particular types of grammatical structures, etc.

• Repetition

Use consistent directions for each paper all year. For the majority of major writing assignments, require (for a paper) a thesis statement located near the end of the introduction or (for an essay test question) a topic sentence positioned as the first sentence in the paragraph.

• Revision

Each major writing assignment should provide a revision option.

• Modeling

Use class time to model the steps of the writing process: generating a topic, drafting, revising, editing. Use class time to model examples of introductions, thesis statements, topic sentences, body paragraphs, and conclusions. The effectiveness of modeling has been discussed by Janet Emig and Robert Zoellner, who advocate "that instructors demonstrate writing to their students by composing aloud while writing on the blackboard...composing a draft of an assignment at least once and discussing your writing process with the class for fifteen to twenty minutes" (qtd. in Connors and Glenn 106). Other researchers have also emphasized the importance and efficacy of using models to improve student writing, among them Charney, Carlson, and Stolarek. Charney states that "models do influence the content and organization of students' texts. Reading models seems to have reminded writers of concepts that they otherwise would not have included in their texts" (111).

Teaching Expository Argument

At the secondary level there exists an urgency for ensuring that students can write cogent, concise, and coherent exposition. After all, when students leave the classroom, they will be asked in almost any profession to write exposition, to move from data to conclusion with clarity and sophistication. Throughout students' lives they will be frequently asked to draw conclusions from facts, to reorder information, to argue from information, to explain and to describe, whether they be preparing a legal brief, an argument to an insurance company to pay for medical treatment, a proposal to corporate executives, or a computer instruction manual. Moreover, students must learn to write on topics that are not particularly appealing, for they will discover that we do not always have a choice of topics. As Robert Connors and Cheryl Glenn write in *The St. Martin's Guide to Teaching Writing*, "Composition teachers today must turn out students who can write on assigned subjects and demonstrate their engagement with a topic" (154).

Fortunately, research clearly demonstrates that students can learn these skills and that teacher instruction plays a significant role in improving student writing. Studies completed by Sandra Perl demonstrate that student writing improves in classrooms where writing is taken more seriously (19). Not only does writing improve, but also students' general level of self-confidence increases when they see they can perform these critical thinking skills with competence.

• It is not enough to assign the five-paragraph essay.

The urgency exists for educators to become more aggressive in the teaching of expository argument. First, many teachers underestimate the complexity of writing expository argument and hence merely assign a "five-paragraph essay" without providing students instruction in the composing process. For some reason, many believe that, by high school, students should have developed these skills, a belief affirmed by research completed by A.N. Applebee, who found teachers too often making a writing assignment without providing students the tools for being successful at the task. Applebee writes about one such situation, where "only three minutes elapsed from the time the teacher began explaining a writing topic until the time students were expected to begin to write"(102). Perhaps this myth may be due in part to the inaccurate belief that writing is merely talk recorded. Jane Emig points out, in her essay "Writing as a Mode of Learning," that writing is not recorded talk and that writing is a skill emanating "from different organic sources and represents quite different, possibly distinct, language functions"(123).

Perhaps the reason why some teachers assign essays without teaching students how to write the essay and how to improve it is a more personal one— many teachers are not sure how to teach writing or are intimidated by the detail such teaching may require. *Because writing expository argument is a complex process, developing skills takes time; it is something learned through practice and feedback and more practice, not during one year, but year after year through direct teaching by the educators responsible for such instruction.* It is learned as well through interaction among the student writers themselves under the guidance of teachers who not only provide feedback but also offer numerous opportunities for such practice after they have shown students how to write exposition and how to continue to increase the sophistication of their writing. By the ninth grade, students are running out of time. It is naïve to think that a high school student can quickly learn how to write effective expository argument after a few assignments.

Moreover, though the narrative, reflective, and descriptive types of writing (journaling, personal experience writing, the short story, poetry) are important elements of good expository composing and are effective exercises in creativity and thinking, an emphasis or reliance on these types of writing will not teach a student the complex task of expository argument. To think otherwise is unfortunate, for it fails to recognize the complexity and arduousness of helping a young person respond intelligently to an essay test or essay topic.

Teacher's Role

English teachers greet students who have a vast range of writing skills. Few students are truly competent, even by the twelfth grade. This challenge is presented in August or September. With a 50-minute class that meets on average four to five days a week until May or June, a teacher must sandwich a curriculum filled with literature and a host of sundry objectives plus attempt to help students write a skillfully-constructed, compelling argument. It is a daunting task. Little help comes from 400-page writing textbooks that categorize a myriad of forms and sequences. Too much material. Where does a teacher start? And if one started from the beginning, working from writing assignment to writing assignment, would students have time to master any one form? Or should we work on the short story? The poem? Journal writing?

• Focus on the expository form.

With little time and an extensive curriculum guide, it seems wise to keep it simple. Focus primarily on one form, the form most useful and practical—the EXPOSITORY ARGUMENT. If the teacher keeps assigning and explaining the same form all year, mere repetition will affect even the most intellectually withdrawn students. My experience teaching writing suggests that I can be most effective if I primarily teach students throughout the year how to argue a simple but clear thesis, if I teach repeatedly the creation process of the expository paragraph and essay, and if I require the same directions for the composing process. When the expectations stay high and consistent, even the most reluctant students will develop specific writing skills. For those on task and ready to plunge into each assignment, their skills will quickly move beyond competence; some of their essays will sparkle and amaze readers.

Another benefit to this procedure is that it becomes easier to hold students accountable for performance. Grading becomes more accurate because it is based on specific skills being taught and specific expectations being met. It becomes more difficult for a student to cry, "I don't know what you want. I don't know what you mean by blending."

For these reasons this manual focuses on the expository argument. It assumes that most expository nonfiction writing contains a thesis and body paragraphs that illustrate the thesis. Instead of introducing the classification essay, the compare/contrast essay, or the definition essay as separate units, we discuss these as methods for organization once students have narrowed topics and have begun to formulate thesis statements.

• Demonstrate the writing process repeatedly.

Perhaps the most salient element of this manual is that teachers must show their students how to create each part of the paragraph and each part of the essay. Students need to see how to write a topic sentence, how to write a thesis statement, how to make paragraphs more coherent. Teachers must take time in class to show examples, to work with student papers in a positive, constructive, caring fashion in front of the class, so students can see how one improves writing.

Research completed by Steven Graham, Karen Harris, and the University of Maryland faculty demonstrates that teaching students writing strategies in a deliberate manner "increases the number of revisions and results in a much longer, better-quality final product" (Pressley and Woloshyn 169). In their study of helping learning disabled students improve writing skills, they emphasize a series of steps all writing teachers should implement: 1) discuss and model the writing strategy repeatedly; 2) practice repeatedly the steps with the students;

3) provide repeated opportunities for independent practice of the strategy. This research is further supported by Hillocks, Brown, Lave, Williams, Smagorinsky, Raphael, Flower, and Cheng, all of whom advocate the explicit teaching of writing strategies.

Unfortunately—and I did this, too—too many teachers merely assign a paper, provide little instruction over the methods for achieving expectations, and scream while grading "these terrible essays." Simply because students are in the ninth, tenth, eleventh, or even twelfth grade, we can no longer assume that they know how to select and think about a paper topic, craft a thesis, organize a paper, and construct paragraphs. I don't even assume, when assigning the sixth or eighth or tenth paper of the year, that I can simply pass out the instructions and move onto the literature.

We often forget that "the ability to communicate through writing develops at a much slower rate than does the ability to communicate through speech and requires much more formal instruction" (Connor and Glenn 111–112). Even after a year's instruction, there may remain a handful of students who need me to go through one part of the process or another once again. To keep assigning papers without teaching how to write them is professional negligence.

Lesson Plans That Lead Toward Exposition

The lesson plans are available online at www.telemachospublishing.com. Bear in mind that the "Suggested Lesson Planning Sequence" is a type of blueprint that explains the basic approach toward the teaching of writing as well as how to integrate successfully practical grammar instruction that students will employ in their writing. It is a *flexible blueprint*. The grammar instruction, focusing on sentence structures and syntax (see chapter five), may be woven into the fabric of the writing process by you at a different pace than I have approached it here

The WRITING TO SHOW exercises use the modes of description and narration to teach *universal writing skills* of elaboration, concrete diction, vivid verb usage, and sentence variety. These exercises develop a positive, enjoyable foundation and environment for writing instruction that continues throughout the year, a foundation for writing that significantly improves student outcomes, as illustrated by research done by Frank Pajares and Margaret Johnson. Later, when you begin writing about literature, students will, with your guidance, apply these WRITING TO SHOW skills to their expository compositions.

INTRODUCTORY REMARKS TO STUDENT WRITERS AND THEIR TEACHERS

This book contains two broad goals for you, the writer: first, to develop through practice the strategies of effective composition, from the creation of elegant sentences to the shaping of coherent and unified paragraphs that form the well-written expository essay; second, to use consistently strategies that produce insightful, perceptive content for essays, content that possesses a voice that does more than merely summarize the plot or describe the obvious.

Chapter one will introduce you to basic strategies for developing an Analytical Voice, a voice that closely examines the details, words, and images contained in works of fiction, poetry, and nonfiction, a voice ultimately producing an interpretive perspective found in your thesis statement for each essay and the topic sentences that support it. To understand the process of developing an Analytical Voice, you will be guided through an analysis of a short fiction and nonfiction excerpt. Afterwards, you can work through some of the sample exercises included here and online, exercises designed to help you understand the distinction between merely summarizing the details of a text and saying something meaningful about those details. Included within the discussion of developing such a voice will be an introduction to key aspects of classical rhetoric, concepts that will provide additional ways of observing and commenting upon what you read or see.

Chapter two introduces the concept of WRITING TO SHOW, a technique that hones the powers of observation, a skill critical in developing your Analytical Voice and a skill necessary in crafting your own concrete detail with precise language. In this chapter, you learn to recognize that words can be placed along a continuum, those at one end being vague and general and those at the opposite end, concrete and singular. The choices you as the writer make along this continuum, then, have consequences: if you choose words predominately vague and abstract, your composition will likely be hollow and inconsequential, but when you learn to show the concrete and particular visualization of your ideas, your writing becomes lively, substantial, and meaningful to the reader. When you as the writer employ precise diction, the reader recognizes a more distinctive voice, one able to anchor ideas within the details and images of situations in literary works.

These WRITING TO SHOW techniques become useful when entering chapters three and four; in both chapters the WRITING TO SHOW skills are applied to paragraphing strategies (chapter three), specifically focusing on the issues of unity, coherence, and style. Chapter four concentrates on the crafting of the expository essay, a composition whose thesis statement requires the writing of multiple body paragraphs.

Chapter five is all about the sentence, how you construct and shape it through strategies conducive to developing a style. In this chapter you learn to manipulate the phrases and clauses of the English language, to form sentences with parallel components, and to imitate a variety of syntactical patterns. That this chapter begins with a review of the major grammatical structures in English is purposeful: a young writer like yourself can and ought to understand how the language you seek to master works, insight that over time contributes to the writing of more sophisticated structures within sentences. INSTRUCTION FROM CHAPTER FIVE MUST BE INCORPORATED WITH ALL INSTRUCTION IN THE WRITING PROCESS.

Chapter six contains the editing symbols that provide explanations and illustrations of the key universal writing strategies and concepts that inform this book. These editing symbols are to be used throughout the school year by both your teacher and yourself as you communicate with one another regarding the crafting of effective composition. Below is a list defining the qualities of effective composition this book illustrates. In other words, below is the language you, your peers, and your teacher will use to evaluate, discuss, and produce sophisticated writing of your own.

SOME KEY UNIVERSAL WRITING STRATEGIES AND CONCEPTS

I. WRITING TO SHOW demonstrates distinct characteristics (ch.2).
   A. The writer's language contains words that are concrete and often singular in number rather than vague, abstract, or general.
   B. The writer chooses vivid verbs that are predominantly active in voice.
   C. The writer extensively elaborates with specific details that are neither redundant nor wordy.
   D. The writer crafts concise, clear sentences.
   E. The writer displays skill with a variety of sentence structures so that the prose is neither choppy nor monotonous.

II. Paragraphing concepts emphasize unity, coherence, and style (ch.3).
   A. Unity
      1. The topic sentence usually appears as the first sentence of a body paragraph and indicates clearly the focus of the paragraph.
      2. Concrete textual examples in the remainder of the paragraph—either direct quotations or situations re-created in the writer's vivid diction—provide a clear illustration of the idea in the topic sentence.
   B. Coherence
      1. A method of organizing the material in the paragraph is clear to the reader, the details being arranged by time, place, or idea.
      2. The writer employs word glue and logic glue that indicates his organizational choice[s].
      3. The writer provides a transitional sentence or phrase that follows the topic sentence, a transition that offers the reader an understanding of how the writer organizes EVIDENCE—the diction, imagery, and details found in the direct quotations or the situations from the text re-created in the writer's own words.
      4. Word glue and logic glue link each sentence, assisting the reader in his comprehension of the writer's argument.
      5. The writer stays on topic consistently (the topic string), avoiding unnecessary shifts. The writer continually uses word glue and logic glue to connect sentences back to the topic sentence idea and in his elaboration explains clearly to the reader why the evidence supports the topic sentence. The writer, then, does not merely list evidence without commentary.

C. Style
1. The writer crafts a variety of sentence types and syntactical patterns.
2. The diction emphasizes concrete words and makes appropriate and effective associations.
3. Sentences are concise and clear.

III. The multi-paragraph essay makes a solid, well-written argument (ch.4).
   A. The essay begins with an effective showing-telling introduction that transitions smoothly to a thesis statement.
   B. The thesis statement in the introductory paragraph contains a topic that asserts the writer's opinion—or CLAIM—regarding that topic, an opinion or claim that must be argued as true or demonstrated as logically viable in the essay's body paragraphs.
   C. The topic sentences for each body paragraph employ word and logic glue to assist the reader in understanding the topic sentence's relationship to the thesis statement.
   D. Each body paragraph exemplifies the qualities of unity, coherence, and style discussed in II above.
   E. The writer constructs a concluding paragraph that goes beyond mere restatement of key points, effectively tying the central ideas back to the initial thesis.

1

CLOSE READING STRATEGIES THAT DEVELOP AN ANALYTICAL VOICE

The student has to have tools to understand a story or a novel,
and these are tools proper to the structure of the work,
tools proper to the craft.
They are tools that operate inside the work and not outside it;
they are concerned with how this story is made
and with what makes it work as a story.
"The Teaching of Literature," Flannery O'Connor

WHAT IS THE WRITER'S ANALYTICAL VOICE?

Flannery O'Connor, one of America's finest writers of fiction in the twentieth century, asserts an essential task of the teacher of English, a task that is the focus of this chapter: providing the student with "tools to understand a story or a novel." These tools ultimately become woven into **the voice of the student as writer, a writer's voice that contains a particular interpretive point of view, a writer's voice that explains how ideas emerge from the language and details** in the chapter of a novel, the verses of a poem, or the paragraphs of an essay.

To develop such a voice can be a challenge for the young writer. This voice does more than merely re-create or summarize the details in a work of literature the student-writer has observed; it requires the ability to analyze.

An ability to analyze a work of literature is a learned behavior. It entails a way of "seeing" what you are reading, and that way of "seeing" is primarily a method, or strategy, of thinking about it as you read. Such a strategy of thinking allows you to "see" beyond the mere details of the plot or poem and, instead, guides you toward a discoverable claim or argument about the text you have been reading.

The process of thinking about the literature being read is demonstrated in the following ANALYTICAL VOICE chart. The literary work under consideration can be a poem, a novel, a short story, an essay, a play, a speech—for any aesthetic form, the process, or way of "seeing," is the same.

DEVELOPING AN ANALYTICAL VOICE

LEVEL ONE
Identify the EVIDENCE observed by you, the reader.

DICTION: What types of words are used or repeated?
IMAGERY: How is the image created? What are its parts? What senses are provoked?
DETAILS: What's the setting? Who are the characters? What is the situation?

LEVEL TWO
Identify the CONCEPTUAL ASSOCIATIONS [ideas, qualities, conditions]
that emerge from the diction, imagery, and details of the literary work you are reading.

Examples of concepts that might be associated with diction, imagery, and details
include, but are certainly not limited to, the following:

Fear. Excitement. Joy. Love. Disdain.
Violence. Chaos. Control. Order. Arrogance.
Submission. Humility. Confidence. Authority. Wisdom.
Confinement. Freedom. Tyranny. Benevolence. Refinement.
Skepticism. Faith. Greed. Penury. Parsimony.

LEVEL THREE
Identify the RELATIONSHIPS among diction, imagery, and details, as well as
the concepts associated with them, to the rest of the text.

REPETITION
similarity, analogy, recurrence, echo, parallelism

CONTRAST
incongruity, antithesis, opposition, tension

JUXTAPOSITION
contiguity, adjacency, proximity

SHIFT
turn, transformation, alteration

The RELATIONSHIPS you discover in your analysis
should lead you to a CLAIM about one or more
of the following with regard to the passage under consideration:

Tone. Attitude. Voice. Atmosphere.
Character. Archetype. Theme. Purpose.

To demonstrate this process, I will first provide a discussion of each level of the ANALYTICAL VOICE chart; afterwards, I will examine two passages—one fiction and one nonfiction. As I discuss each passage, I will consider separately each level of thinking so that you understand the concept of each stage. After your skills increase, you will notice yourself simultaneously blending two or more of the levels as you read. Once you begin to write about the passages you have read, WHAT YOU WRITE WILL CONTAIN ALL THREE LEVELS SIMULTANEOUSLY. Now let's examine the ANALYTICAL VOICE chart and its components.

LEVEL ONE

Level One of the ANALYTICAL VOICE chart directs you, as the reader, to observe carefully the passage's details and language (diction and imagery), the EVIDENCE that will later become part of a WRITTEN ARGUMENT. What often distinguishes effective arguments from mediocre ones is the writer's ability to point out details another reader may not have noticed.

Diction

DICTION refers to the words used by the author, words that come in a variety of types, which the careful reader observes: Are these words *concrete, abstract, colloquial, formal, informal, jargon, figurative, foreign*? Do any of the words belong to a specific category (words related to religion, to education, to finance, to sports, to medicine, to the law, to marriage, to war, etc.)?

Imagery

The careful reader will also want to notice how collections of words form mental pictures, IMAGERY that allows the reader to see more clearly a setting, a character, an action or situation. How is the image formed? What components or parts of the image seem prominent or significant? For example, many images of a broken-down car can be created by an author: one image may focus on a mangled hubcap dangling off the rim by one rusty screw; another image may center on the three-inch diameter dent in the driver's side door, the flakes of burgundy paint falling to the dirt.

Details

Finally, what are the DETAILS—or facts—contained in the text? What is the setting: the city? the countryside? the schoolyard? Who are the characters: a parent and child? a teacher and student? two friends? two enemies? What is the situation: a Christmas dinner? an interrogation? a carriage ride to the country? a fist fight? All of these observations will influence what you ultimately say—your interpretative perspective—about the specific work of literature you are reading.

LEVEL TWO

The next level of thinking, Level Two of the ANALYTICAL VOICE chart, involves attaching associations to the details and language we isolated above.

Conceptual associations

So what are associations? While you read, whenever you interact with details, images, and words, your mind makes CONCEPTUAL ASSOCIATIONS. The image of an *infant's foot* may cause you to think of abstract concepts such as *innocence* or *vulnerability*. The repeated use of the word *red* may cause you to associate its use with the idea of *death* or *destruction*. The specific details involving a major character's living arrangements—that the character lives in a mansion with fifty rooms and drives a different sports car for each day of the week—will likely produce the associations related to *wealth*, *power*, and *extravagance*.
Well-crafted speeches are often rich with conceptual associations. Patrick Henry, in his famous speech to the Virginia Convention in March 1775, spoke of the "insidious smile" of the British monarch in response to the colonists' pleas for a respectful resolution of their claims. "Trust it not, sir; it will prove a snare to your feet. Suffer not yourselves to be betrayed with a kiss." Certainly, the word *snare* evokes ideas of *treachery*, *entrapment*, and *deception*, as does the phrase *betrayed with a kiss*, a phrase that reminds those hearing—or reading—Henry's speech of *the betrayal of Christ by Judas*.

Conceptual associations for the student-writer

When you write about any work of literature, you want to move beyond plot summary—the mere re-telling of what happens in the story, poem, play, essay, or speech. You do that by explaining what concepts, or ideas, are anchored in— associated with—the details and language of the text, the details and language providing the EVIDENCE for the written argument you are making about the work of literature.

Not all conceptual associations are equal in value as not all such associations will make logical sense in the context of the work of literature you are reading and about which you are thinking. That's why the student writing about a work of literature must make decisions, must, in other words, SELECT ASSOCIATIONS TO ATTACH TO THE EVIDENCE IN THE TEXT. Once you begin the process of selecting certain associations rather than others, you then begin to develop your ANALYTICAL VOICE, your way of seeing the details and language, your own perspective about the work of literature under consideration.

You cannot attach an associative concept to an image that doesn't make logical sense. That image of an infant's foot is not associated with the concept of evil or violence simply because you say it is or because you may recall another text where some evil act was committed against a child. While there are many ways to talk about a text, and many possible associative words a writer can use, these assertions must be grounded within the logical associations of its language and details. Attaching conceptual associations to textual evidence is not a random or arbitrary activity.

Writing about conceptual associations

As a student-writer, you want to consider the precision of your associative word choices when you write your compositions analyzing a work of literature. Just as an author chooses specific words to form distinct images and to elaborate individual details, you too want to use appropriate diction to explain any of these images or details in the passage under consideration. For example, Lady Macbeth's conversations with her husband, Macbeth, about pursuing the throne of Scotland by murdering the king may be considered "bad," "cruel," "heartless," or "ugly"; but more precise language on your part would find her conversation "shrewd," "manipulative," or "conniving," just as her "crazy" arguments attempting to persuade her husband might be described more aptly as "hyperbolic" and "fallacious." Your task as a writer, then, will also be to broaden your traditional vocabulary.

Selecting conceptual associations

Let's discuss an additional aspect of generating associations: Whenever you begin attaching various associations to parts of the text, some may later be discarded while others may be used to formulate the larger structure of your argument—a thesis statement or its topic sentences.

What associations would you disregard and why? Imagine an image of a stone wall. You may consider multiple and contradictory associations with such an image—on the one hand, walls may be associated with positive ideas such as security, stability, order, protection; on the other hand, they may be associated with negative attributes such as entrapment, concealment, restriction, imprisonment.

Which associations are more reasonable? The answer is to examine the other details contained in the text. Are more pieces of evidence positive or negative? Perhaps white light shines on the wall, whose stone is intricately and beautifully designed. Within the area encompassed by the wall sits a gentleman comfortably relaxing in a chair, his face reflective and at ease, gazing upon a child who is playing in the grass, smiling and gleeful. These additional details direct the TONE of the wall's description and surroundings toward our positive list, particularly if no other details or images are negative. As a reader, you realize that those negative associations regarding a stone wall can be discarded, that the text you are reading contains positive conceptual associative elements.

The general reading principal here directs you to examine all other pieces of evidence in the text: THE ENTIRE COLLECTION OF IMAGES AND DETAILS SHOULD GUIDE A CONSISTENT AND PLAUSIBLE READING. In this case, since no details of the text point to a negative tone, you can disregard those associations that are negative.

Elaborate direct quotations with conceptual associations

These conceptual associations will be used to elaborate on the directly quoted material you cite inside the body paragraphs of your analysis. Many beginning writers often wonder *What do I say next?* after having used a direct quotation from the literary work being analyzed. The answer is that *you discuss those associative ideas that are linked to the evidence you directly quote.* You can, as just one example of what to discuss, **comment on the significance of a single word, image, or phrase within that direct quotation,** *showing how the idea associated with that word, image, or phrase relates to other aspects of the literary work* (how the idea connects to the protagonist's character traits, for instance, or how it underscores a general theme of the work, or how it establishes a specific contrast or similarity with another character or situation in that same work.) Many direct quotations will, of course, have more than one such word, image, or phrase whose conceptual associations call for thoughtful elaboration.

LEVEL THREE

So far you have moved through Level One and Level Two of the ANALYTICAL VOICE chart. We've recognized important associative ideas and have certainly moved beyond merely summarizing the passage. But the analytical voice facilitates even more commentary regarding how the passage works to produce its ideas.

The language of relationship in Level Three will help you further discuss how the passage has been constructed to communicate a variety of ideas; in other words, we're adding more "tools," as Flannery O'Connor says, for you to employ as you "operate inside the work" of literature. At this level you, as a reader, observe the relationships among words and images and details—for these relationships are what form associative ideas into SPECIFIC CLAIMS ABOUT THE WORK OF LITERATURE being examined.

Four general relationships (and their synonyms) appear on the ANALYTICAL VOICE chart—REPETITION, CONTRAST, JUXTAPOSITION, and SHIFT. Under each of these categories in the chart, I have placed various synonyms that, as a writer, you may use to avoid the potential monotony of repeating the same words. We'll explore what these relationships mean in order.

Repetition

similarity, analogy, recurrence, echo, parallelism

The most important relationship in a text is REPETITION, which signals to the reader the key ideas of the passage and the entire work, ideas pertaining to theme, character, setting, and point of view. As the attentive reader becomes aware of repetition in a literary work, patterns emerge. Student-writers make a stronger written argument about a literary work whenever they identify various repetitions and, therefore, convincingly demonstrate that any such patterns exist.

When we notice repetition, we notice not simply *that **exact** words or images* are repeated (though this does sometimes occur), but *that SIMILAR ASSOCIATIONS attached to **different** words or images or details* continue to surface throughout the passage.

An example of such similar associations attached to different details and language is found in this short nonfiction excerpt from Virginia Woolf's essay, "A Room of One's Own." Here, Woolf describes her meal at one of the male colleges at Oxford. She writes that

...the college cook had spread a counterpane of the whitest cream,..... After that came the partridges, but if this suggests a couple of bald, brown birds on a plate you are mistaken. The partridges, many and various, came with all their retinue of sauces and salads, the sharp and the sweet, each in its order; their potatoes, thin as coins but not so hard; their sprouts, foliated as rosebuds but more succulent.... Meanwhile the wineglasses had flushed yellow and flushed crimson; had been emptied; had been filled. (10-11)

The details and language of the situation repeat the associative ideas of *plenty and abundance*: "the partridges, many and various," the "retinue of sauces and salads," the wine glasses "flushed" and "emptied" and "filled." The idea of *consummate beauty* recurs as well: "the whitest cream," the sprouts "foliated as rosebuds." All these different words and images, used collectively in this passage, reinforce the associative idea of *luxury or opulence*.

Contrast

incongruity, antithesis, opposition, tension

Another important relationship for the careful reader to observe is CONTRAST. Contrast in a literary text sends you, the reader, a signal: it indicates the presence of an essential situation—tension, conflict, opposition, difference—a situation that may add a significant complication, require an eventual resolution, or reflect a serious universal idea.

As readers, we often notice first the concrete presence of contrast: one character barks, "Bah humbug," while another character responds, "Merry Christmas"; one setting is marked by a dilapidated house, windows broken and paint flaking off the siding, while the other setting is marked by a house freshly painted, daisies lining its sidewalk. The contrast observed in each of these examples is both concrete and associative. For instance, the comments of the two aforementioned characters reflect a distinction between a pessimistic, or surly, outlook and one that is optimistic or genial; the characteristics of the two houses reveal a contrast between decay and vibrancy.

As a writer, you'll want to communicate to your reader these associative contrasts anchored in the concrete references to the text. Let's explore a further example. In the opening chapter of Charles Dickens' *Great Expectations,* we read of a convict who has escaped prison. Dickens presents two distinctly contrasting images of the convict. The first image is one of a dangerously violent aggressor, a man furtively grabbing the young eight-year-old Pip, exhorting, "Keep still, you little devil, or I'll cut your throat," a character clearly ominous and threatening to Pip. Near the end of this chapter, however, Dickens provides a quite different image of the convict, one in apparent opposition to his initial belligerence. Here, he is a man slipping away from Pip while mumbling, "I wish I were a frog or an eel," as "he hugged his shuddering body in both his arms—clasping himself, as if to hold himself together—and limped towards the low church wall." Both the sentiment and the visualization turn the formerly combative image into one of vulnerability and weakness.

What then is the function of this contrast, this difference in characterization? Contrast allows the author, in this case Dickens, to create a more complex character, one who is more than the monstrous figure that is Pip's —and the reader's—initial impression. If this contrast were absent in this case, the convict would be a static one-dimensional character, our perception of him likewise limited. In addition, the distinct presence of contrast in the novel's first chapter alerts the reader to ideas that may become more prominent as the story progresses: the differences between appearance and reality, the faulty nature of first impressions, the forces of deception present in the landscape of the work.

Juxtaposition

contiguity, adjacency, proximity

A third term, JUXTAPOSITION, helps to emphasize either a contrast or a repetition by placing two items side-by-side, *their close proximity or alignment producing a new idea* that would **not** otherwise be observed if the elements had been placed further apart from each other.

Let's imagine some simple advertisements. First, visualize an image of four red Toyota Corollas linked together on a bright yellow roller coaster. Though such a depiction seems unrealistic and fantastic, by juxtaposing the Corollas with the roller coaster, Toyota fashions a new idea about the Corolla, one the viewer would not have conjured if the car were, in the context of its advertisement, merely placed in a suburban driveway. This juxtaposition, however, envisions ideas associated with the joys and thrills of an amusement park— smiling twenty-year-olds, multiple hands boldly extended into the sunshine— in an advertisement featuring vibrant primary colors. It communicates to consumers that the Corolla inherently possesses a sense of youthful power and exhilaration. It reinforces the idea that purchasing the Corolla will produce a sensational experience not possible with other automobiles.

In another advertisement, The Coca-Cola Company uses juxtaposition to produce a new idea about Diet Coke. The ad contains a sleek black background; in the center a Diet Coke can floats upside down, the silvery can with its bold red and black logo dappled with beads of moisture. Directly above the can are the words "yoga class." In the proximity of "yoga class" with such a Diet Coke can, a new idea about this soft drink emerges. The soft drink, the ad suggests, produces benefits similar to those a yoga class delivers—meditative relaxation, self-discipline, flexibility, an overall health linking the mind and body—benefits that heretofore have not customarily been associated with Diet Coke.

Shift

turn, transformation, alteration

The final term, SHIFT, signals a movement away from one idea and a turn toward a different associative idea. In the advertisements regarding Toyota's Corolla and Diet Coke, the purpose is to shift our notion of these products. In the Corolla ad, Toyota shifts the audience's likely impression of a vehicle that is sedate and lackluster by associating it with the positive attributes of energy, zest, and youthfulness. Likewise, the Diet Coke ad alters the idea of a potentially bland-tasting soft drink severely reduced in calorie content by connecting it to physical, mental, and spiritual health.

The shift, or turn, occurs in all forms of texts, our recognition of such a turn often directing us to a central issue or purpose in the text we are reading. In poetry, for example, the concept of the shift, or turn, is usually the source of the poem's intellectual energy.

The structural fulcrum of Shakespeare's sonnets resides in the turn, the altered perspective, as in *Sonnet 29.*

> *When in disgrace with fortune and men's eyes,*
> *I all alone beweep my outcast state*
> *And trouble deaf heaven with my bootless cries*
> *And look upon myself and curse my fate,*
> *Wishing me like to one more rich in hope,*
> *Featured like him, like him with friends possess'd,*
> *Desiring this man's art and that man's scope,*
> *With what I most enjoy contented least;*
> *Yet in these thoughts myself almost despising,*
> *Haply I think on thee, and then my state,*
> *Like to the lark at break of day arising*
> *From sullen earth, sings hymns at heaven's gate;*

For thy sweet love remember'd such wealth brings
That then I scorn to change my state with kings.

In the first two quatrains of the sonnet, the speaker, "in disgrace with fortune and men's eyes," laments his "outcast state" with "bootless cries." Cursing his "fate," he pines to be someone other than himself: "like to one more rich in hope," with different features, surrounded by friends, "desiring this man's art and that man's scope." The speaker appears the epitome of someone in the midst of despair and bottomless self-pity.

Yet there is that "yet," and it is that very word—a conjunction indicating contrast—that initiates the third quatrain and signals the shift in the sonnet, an alteration that is typical in the structure of the Shakespearean sonnet. With this single word, the speaker juxtaposes the previous quatrains' "thoughts myself almost despising" with his new "state," a transformed mental and spiritual condition, one that occurs when "haply I think on thee." This shift from interior self-loathing to an exterior joy, then, occurs when he who was "in disgrace with fortune" fortunately—"haply"—turns his thoughts to another and recalls "thy sweet love," a recollection anchored in the intimacy of a genuine relationship. This sudden remembrance is so fortunate—bringing "such wealth"—that, his emotional state similar to a "lark at break of day arising from sullen earth," the speaker now "scorn(s) to change my state with kings."

The transformation from misery to exultation becomes the central issue of the sonnet, one that causes the reader to ask how and why the change occurs. In the case of Shakespeare's sonnet, a potential thesis statement might suggest that a person's happiness comes not from coveting attributes others possess but from the loving relationships that we nurture.

The careful reader of any work of literature will want to observe language and details suggesting a shift. Any such turn is likely to become a significant part of your analysis of the work.

OVERVIEW OF THE THREE LEVELS

Heretofore, our focus has centered on the specific levels of the ANALYTICAL VOICE chart. *First*, you as the reader monitor the evidence provided in the text, the evidence being the literary work's concrete details and language (diction and imagery). *Second*, you attach conceptual associations to the details and the language. *Third*, you recognize that relationships among pieces of evidence and the ideas associated with them—relationships of repetition, contrast, juxtaposition, and shift—bring about meaning in a literary work, thus allowing you as the writer to provide your interpretative perspective, your claim, about the work in a subsequent essay.

This inductive reading process—the movement from observing the evidence in a literary work to drawing associative conclusions about the evidence—*is a manner of thinking about the literature, a way of "seeing" as you read, that provides the basis for a thoughtful written analysis.*

Implementation

APPLYING THE ANALYTICAL VOICE CHART TO A PASSAGE FROM A NOVEL

Now let's apply this strategy to a short passage from a novel, *A Tale of Two Cities* by Charles Dickens. [For the purposes of this discussion, the passage will be repeated prior to the explication of each level of the ANALYTICAL VOICE chart.]

Level One: observing the evidence

MONSEIGNEUR, ONE OF THE GREAT LORDS IN POWER AT THE COURT, HELD HIS FORTNIGHTLY RECEPTION IN HIS GRAND HOTEL IN PARIS. MONSEIGNEUR WAS IN HIS INNER ROOM, HIS SANCTUARY OF SANCTUARIES, THE HOLIEST OF HOLIESTS TO THE CROWD OF WORSHIPPERS IN THE SUITE OF ROOMS WITHOUT. MONSEIGNEUR WAS ABOUT TO TAKE HIS CHOCOLATE. MONSEIGNEUR COULD SWALLOW A GREAT MANY THINGS WITH EASE, AND WAS BY SOME FEW SULLEN MINDS SUPPOSED TO BE RATHER RAPIDLY SWALLOWING FRANCE; BUT, HIS MORNING'S CHOCOLATE COULD NOT SO MUCH AS GET INTO THE THROAT OF MONSEIGNEUR, WITHOUT THE AID OF FOUR STRONG MEN BESIDES THE COOK.

YES. IT TOOK FOUR MEN, ALL FOUR ABLAZE WITH GORGEOUS DECORATION, AND THE CHIEF OF THEM UNABLE TO EXIST WITH FEWER THAN TWO GOLD WATCHES IN HIS POCKET, EMULATIVE OF THE NOBLE AND CHASTE FASHION SET BY MONSEIGNEUR, TO CONDUCT THE HAPPY CHOCOLATE TO MONSEIGNEUR'S LIPS. ONE LACQUEY CARRIED THE CHOCOLATE-POT INTO THE SACRED PRESENCE; A SECOND, MILLED AND FROTHED THE CHOCOLATE WITH THE LITTLE INSTRUMENT HE BORE FOR THAT FUNCTION; A THIRD, PRESENTED THE FAVOURED NAPKIN; A FOURTH (HE OF THE TWO GOLD WATCHES), POURED THE CHOCOLATE OUT. IT WAS IMPOSSIBLE FOR MONSEIGNEUR TO DISPENSE WITH ONE OF THESE ATTENDANTS ON THE CHOCOLATE AND HOLD HIS HIGH PLACE UNDER THE ADMIRING HEAVENS. DEEP WOULD HAVE BEEN THE BLOT UPON HIS ESCUTCHEON IF HIS CHOCO-LATE HAD BEEN IGNOBLY WAITED ON BY ONLY THREE MEN; HE MUST HAVE DIED OF TWO.

Now let us explore LEVEL ONE OBSERVATIONS in the passage above. At this stage, you are honing your reading skills, your powers of observation, the critical foundation of writing persuasively. Moreover, at this stage, we are not yet making any assertions about the ideas communicated within the passage or any conclusions that may eventually be part of a claim or thesis statement. The purpose of the discussion that follows is to simulate the close reading process, to pause and notice details, diction, and images as we read through each paragraph. As you practice reading closely, your ability to notice potential pieces of evidence to use in your essay will improve. (Later, in Chapter Two of *Crafting Expository Argument*, the WRITING TO SHOW exercises will also help develop your powers of observation, both as a writer and as a reader.)

In Dickens' opening paragraph, the first line provides us with details regarding the main character, the Monseigneur, and the situation, a reception in a Paris hotel, held "fortnightly" (every two weeks). Notice the word choices in this first line: "great" and "power" and "grand." The second sentence elaborates the specific plot situation: the Monseigneur is "in his inner room" at the hotel, separated—or isolated—from the "crowd," who are "in the suite of rooms without." The diction that Dickens uses in this sentence—"sanctuary," "Holiest," and "worshippers"—is related to religion or the church. In the briefest sentence of the paragraph, Dickens states the precise event that is taking place: "Monseigneur was about to take his chocolate." This otherwise unremarkable detail provokes Dickens to mention that the Monseigneur usually swallows "a great many things with ease" and, in fact, is thought by "some few sullen minds" to be "rapidly swallowing France," an image clearly not literal but figurative. The eating of chocolate, however, is another matter entirely, for it takes four men—make that four "strong" men "besides the Cook"—to get the chocolate into the throat of the Monseigneur.

Dickens requires a second paragraph to elaborate specific features involving the four men whose duty is to serve the chocolate to the Monseigneur. He immediately repeats a detail mentioned at the end of the preceding paragraph, that "Yes. It took four men" to feed the Monseigneur his chocolate, and that "all four" are "ablaze with gorgeous decoration." More specifically, the "Chief" servant could not execute his responsibilities (note the adjective phrase "unable to exist") without a minimum of "two gold watches in his pocket." Note as well, the words "noble," "chaste fashion," "conduct," and the word "happy" modifying chocolate, personifying this object that is about to be swallowed.

Further elaborating the entire procedure, Dickens delineates the separate roles of the four servants, each function administered not simply to Monseigneur but before his "sacred presence"—one to carry the pot, one to stir the chocolate with a prescribed tool ("the little instrument he bore for that function"), one to open the napkin (note it is "favoured"), and one to pour the chocolate, this last servant, we are told once again, possessing the "two gold watches."

The final two sentences of the paragraph emphasize the significance of the detail that Monseigneur required all four men. It would be "impossible...to dispense with one" and still hold his "high place under the admiring Heavens." If fewer men had been used for this activity, the narrator explains, the "blot upon his escutcheon" (a shield bearing the family coat of arms) would have been "deep": three men serving him would indicate an action "ignobly" done, something shameful, even common; had only two served him, "he must have died."

All of these Level One observations may serve as the evidence you cite in an essay or body paragraph, evidence that will prove your particular interpretive perspective.

Level Two: making conceptual associations from the evidence

Monseigneur, one of the great lords in power at the Court, held his fortnightly reception in his grand hotel in Paris. Monseigneur was in his inner room, his sanctuary of sanctuaries, the Holiest of Holiests to the crowd of worshippers in the suite of rooms without. Monseigneur was about to take his chocolate. Monseigneur could swallow a great many things with ease, and was by some few sullen minds supposed to be rather rapidly swallowing France; but, his morning's chocolate could not so much as get into the throat of Monseigneur, without the aid of four strong men besides the Cook.

Yes. It took four men, all four ablaze with gorgeous decoration, and the Chief of them unable to exist with fewer than two gold watches in his pocket, emulative of the noble and chaste fashion set by Monseigneur, to conduct the happy chocolate to Monseigneur's lips. One lacquey carried the chocolate-pot into the sacred presence; a second, milled and frothed the chocolate with the little instrument he bore for that function; a third, presented the favoured napkin; a fourth (he of the two gold watches), poured the chocolate out. It was impossible for Monseigneur to dispense with one of these attendants on the chocolate and hold his high place under the admiring Heavens. Deep would have been the blot upon his escutcheon if his chocolate had been ignobly waited on by only three men; he must have died of two.

Now let's examine Level Two associations. In the first sentence of the opening paragraph of this passage, an appositive phrase identifies the Monseigneur as "one of the great lords in power at the Court." Here, the words "great," "lords," "power," and "Court," as well as his reception being held in a location that is "grand," convey majesty and prestige. This depiction of the Monseigneur becomes associated with the sacred by the second sentence when "his inner room" is identified as a "sanctuary of sanctuaries," a place, then, where sacred rituals of a church are taking place, rituals orchestrated by various priests in service to "the Holiest of Holiests." Hence, the atmosphere of the first paragraph likens itself to a religious ceremony, one conducted with regularity in a temple of a lord and as a type of sacrament. That the ceremony occurs on hallowed ground—"his inner room"—emphasizes the isolation of the Monseigneur from his "worshippers."

That the Monseigneur is "about to take his chocolate"—a choice of words reminding us of those about to take Communion in church—is promptly elaborated by Dickens' commentary on the essential process by which he "takes his chocolate," the act of swallowing. We are told that the Monseigneur "could swallow many things with ease," suggesting how effortlessly he consumes, and suggesting as well the rapidity with which he devours, or feasts upon, those "many things." This initial characterization of the process of swallowing is immediately followed by a figurative image, the supposition by "some few sullen minds" that the Monseigneur is "rather rapidly swallowing France," an image of unrestrained and disproportionate appetite and power. However, the swallowing of chocolate, a morning ritual for the Monseigneur, stands in marked contrast to his usual smooth manner of consumption. With this apparently trivial matter, he requires assistance, a retinue of servants who wait on him—a detail reflecting his affluence and authority. That four men—and specifically "strong" ones—must assist him in such a menial task underscores the excessive and wasteful nature of the Monseigneur's appetite.

As the second paragraph begins, the narrator focuses on the opulence of the Monseigneur's servants, the details reinforcing the notion of prosperity and extravagance: "gorgeous decoration," "gold watches," and Dickens' choice of the descriptor "ablaze" call attention to the visual spectacle of this situation. These accouterments are "emulative of the noble and chaste fashion" of the Monseigneur. Here the word "chaste"—which means, in one sense, that which is simple and restrained and, in another sense, that which is pure and virtuous—stands out as an example of diction that the careful reader would not normally associate with the Monseigneur.

The four lavishly-outfitted servants are about "to conduct" the chocolate to the Monseigneur's lips, the infinitive *to conduct* indicating the formality of a carefully orchestrated and controlled ceremony. Each servant, now referred to as a "lacquey," one who is excessively servile, has a particular role, akin to altar servers during the Offertory of a Catholic mass, a connection implied by the phrase "sacred presence" and elaborated by the specific items the servers bear and the functions they carry out during the ritual.

The final sentences of this paragraph reinforce more strongly associations previously developed and underscore the disproportionate and profligate nature of the Monseigneur's requirements. The use of "impossible" asserts the indispensability to the Monseigneur's prestige of all four lacqueys, their necessity absolute and categorical so that the Monseigneur maintains his "high place under the admiring Heavens," the adjective "admiring" communicating the apparent approval of God. Furthermore, the exclusion of even one of these servants is purported to be a shameful "blot upon his escutcheon," a blot so "deep" as to ruin his reputation. That "he must have died of two" servants—a mere two—attending to his chocolate concludes the scene with hyperbole, an exaggeration reinforcing the profligate and intemperate character of the Monseigneur.

Level Three: recognizing relationships among pieces of evidence

MONSEIGNEUR, ONE OF THE GREAT LORDS IN POWER AT THE COURT, HELD HIS FORTNIGHTLY RECEPTION IN HIS GRAND HOTEL IN PARIS. MONSEIGNEUR WAS IN HIS INNER ROOM, HIS SANCTUARY OF SANCTUARIES, THE HOLIEST OF HOLIESTS TO THE CROWD OF WORSHIPPERS IN THE SUITE OF ROOMS WITHOUT. MONSEIGNEUR WAS ABOUT TO TAKE HIS CHOCOLATE. MONSEIGNEUR COULD SWALLOW A GREAT MANY THINGS WITH EASE, AND WAS BY SOME FEW SULLEN MINDS SUPPOSED TO BE RATHER RAPIDLY SWALLOWING FRANCE; BUT, HIS MORNING'S CHOCOLATE COULD NOT SO MUCH AS GET INTO THE THROAT OF MONSEIGNEUR, WITHOUT THE AID OF FOUR STRONG MEN BESIDES THE COOK.

YES. IT TOOK FOUR MEN, ALL FOUR ABLAZE WITH GORGEOUS DECORATION, AND THE CHIEF OF THEM UNABLE TO EXIST WITH FEWER THAN TWO GOLD WATCHES IN HIS POCKET, EMULATIVE OF THE NOBLE AND CHASTE FASHION SET BY MONSEIGNEUR, TO CONDUCT THE HAPPY CHOCOLATE TO MONSEIGNEUR'S LIPS. ONE LACQUEY CARRIED THE CHOCOLATE-POT INTO THE SACRED PRESENCE; A SECOND, MILLED AND FROTHED THE CHOCOLATE WITH THE LITTLE INSTRUMENT HE BORE FOR THAT FUNCTION; A THIRD, PRESENTED THE FAVOURED NAPKIN; A FOURTH (HE OF THE TWO GOLD WATCHES), POURED THE CHOCOLATE OUT. IT WAS IMPOSSIBLE FOR MONSEIGNEUR TO DISPENSE WITH ONE OF THESE ATTENDANTS ON THE CHOCOLATE AND HOLD HIS HIGH PLACE UNDER THE ADMIRING HEAVENS. DEEP WOULD HAVE BEEN THE BLOT UPON HIS ESCUTCHEON IF HIS CHOCO-LATE HAD BEEN IGNOBLY WAITED ON BY ONLY THREE MEN; HE MUST HAVE DIED OF TWO.

Now let's examine LEVEL THREE RELATIONSHIPS, noting that several relationships become apparent and hence significant—specifically, the functions of repetition, contrast, and juxtaposition.

The primary structure of these two paragraphs relies on juxtaposing two sets of contrasting details and language—the first, introduced in the initial sentences and repeated throughout the passage, creates a specifically sacred or religious atmosphere; the second magnifies the trivial act of eating chocolate with a comprehensive examination of the ritual itself. The question, then, is what is the result of such a contrast, an incongruity established by describing so reverently an act so inconsequential? It certainly causes the reader to think that this is absurd, that something doesn't fit—reflections that point to irony, a disparity between our expectations and the actual reality. In this case, we expect, because of the serious diction, the Monseigneur to be engaged in an equally serious act, but he is not. Not only is there an incongruity present in the passage, but the contrast itself—which is recurrent throughout the passage—is particularly embellished and exaggerated, which marks the nature of satire and a sarcastic voice, both techniques intended to ridicule or criticize someone or some situation. In this case, the Monseigneur is the object of the ridicule.

Blending the three levels of analysis when crafting a composition

So let's look at a short composition about this passage from *A Tale of Two Cities* that combines all three levels of the ANALYTICAL VOICE chart to make a claim. You'll notice that I have merged several statements I have previously written during our examination of each level of thinking.

Dickens sarcastically ridicules the Monseigneur as an emblem of profligate wealth and power. The author's opening sentences establish an apparently reverent atmosphere, comparing the Monseigneur's hotel room to a "sanctuary of sanctuaries," and the Monseigneur himself as the "Holiest of Holiests," a priestly entity separated from the "crowd of worshippers." Such a sacred setting is then juxtaposed to the trivial detail that "Monseigneur was about to take his chocolate," a detail not simply trivial but also one marked by physical pleasure and personal privilege. This idea of desire and appetite continues as the narrator notes the "ease" with which this noble can consume not merely his chocolate but all of France, the present participle "swallowing" reinforcing the excessive nature of his appetite, that he devours all those around him, an image of comprehensive power.

The narrator's elaboration of the Monseigneur's morning ritual skewers the aristocracy. Such an ordinary task as "taking his chocolate," a daily occurrence, requires "the aid of four strong men beside the cook," the adjective "strong" amplifying the ridiculous nature of the situation. Even the physical descriptions of the attendants contribute to the ostentation of the event, for they are "ablaze with gorgeous decoration," the foremost of the four having not one but "two gold watches in his pocket," as they proceed "to conduct the happy chocolate to the Monseigneur's lips," the infinitive "to conduct" evoking not only a form of guidance or conveyance but also the idea of a performance being staged.

The narrator's repetitive juxtaposition of the religious with the ridiculous sharpens his sarcastic voice. Referring to the accoutrements of the servants as part of the "chaste fashion set by Monseigneur" and to the Monseigneur himself as a "sacred presence," the narrator underscores the ironic absurdity of the nobility. This intertwining occurs in the listing of tasks of the Monseigneur's various "lacqueys," the depiction of each one's role, from the "little instrument he bore" for milling and frothing the chocolate to the presentation of the "favoured napkin," suggesting, on the one hand, a very serious and significant ritual, like altar servers assisting the priest in a Catholic mass, while functioning, on the other hand, as mere toadies carrying out a purely menial chore.

The narrator's sarcasm and the absurd characterization of the Monseigneur grows more hyperbolic in the final two sentences, particularly if one notices the carefully placed word choices. The use of "impossible" establishes the absolute necessity of each servant, a prerequisite to please the "admiring Heavens"; the consequence of "ignobly" sacrificing even one manservant would be "deep" and a "blot" not merely to his personal reputation but to that of his entire family, "his escutcheon" referring to a family's coat of arms or shield. The final detail—the outlandish idea that reducing the number of servants who serve him chocolate by two is the equivalent of a sentence of death—reflects the passage's widest contrast between the act of eating chocolate and the gravity of its treatment, an incongruity that underscores the depravity of the Monseigneur himself.

Implementation

APPLYING THE ANALYTICAL VOICE CHART TO A NONFICTION PASSAGE

Here we will proceed to an application of the *ANALYTICAL VOICE* chart to a literary work of nonfiction, in this case a passage from "Living Like Weasels," the opening essay from Annie Dillard's *Teaching a Stone to Talk.*

Level One: observing the evidence

TWENTY MINUTES FROM MY HOUSE, THROUGH THE WOODS BY THE QUARRY AND ACROSS THE HIGHWAY, IS HOLLINS POND, A REMARKABLE PIECE OF SHALLOWNESS, WHERE I LIKE TO GO AT SUNSET AND SIT ON A TREE TRUNK. HOLLINS POND IS ALSO CALLED MURRAY'S POND; IT COVERS TWO ACRES OF BOTTOMLAND NEAR TINKER CREEK WITH SIX INCHES OF WATER AND SIX THOUSAND LILY PADS. IN WINTER, BROWN-AND-WHITE STEERS STAND IN THE MIDDLE OF IT, MERELY DAMPENING THEIR HOOVES; FROM THE DISTANT SHORE THEY LOOK LIKE MIRACLE ITSELF, COMPLETE WITH MIRACLE'S NONCHALANCE. NOW, IN SUMMER, THE STEERS ARE GONE. THE WATER LILIES HAVE BLOSSOMED AND SPREAD TO A GREEN HORIZONTAL PLANE THAT IS TERRA FIRMA TO PLODDING BLACKBIRDS, AND TREMULOUS CEILING TO BLACK LEECHES, CRAYFISH, AND CARP.

THIS, MIND YOU, SUBURBIA. IT IS A FIVE-MINUTE WALK IN THREE DIRECTIONS TO ROWS OF HOUSES, THOUGH NONE IS VISIBLE HERE. THERE'S A 55 MPH HIGHWAY AT ONE END OF THE POND, AND A NESTING PAIR OF WOOD DUCKS AT THE OTHER. UNDER EVERY BUSH IS A MUSKRAT HOLE OR A BEER CAN. THE FAR END IS AN ALTERNATING SERIES OF FIELDS AND WOODS, FIELDS AND WOODS, THREADED EVERYWHERE WITH MOTORCYCLE TRACKS—IN WHOSE BARE CLAY WILD TURTLES LAY EGGS.

In this Annie Dillard passage, let us follow the same process, OBSERVING THE EVIDENCE as we did with the fictional excerpt by Charles Dickens.

Dillard's opening sentence contains several details regarding the setting of these two paragraphs. She begins with the pond's location from her house, a distance involving "twenty minutes" of walking "through the woods by a quarry and across the highway" to reach her destination, a shallow pond—"Hollins Pond," which is also referred to as "Murray's Pond"—that covers "two acres." She calls this setting—a place she enjoys at "sunset" while sitting on a "tree trunk"—"a remarkable piece of shallowness" as those two acres contain "six inches of water and six thousand lily pads."

Though the landscape may not seem a particularly vast wildlife refuge, it nonetheless provides habitat in winter for steers who "stand in the middle of it, merely dampening their hooves," the sight of which, from a distance, she calls "miracle's nonchalance." By the summer, however, a transformation has occurred: the cattle gone, the pond's "water lilies have blossomed and spread to a green horizontal plane," and what was once a shallow stretch of water is now "terra firma to plodding blackbirds, and tremulous ceiling to black leeches, crayfish, and carp." Note the verbs "blossomed and spread," and the adjectives "plodding" and "tremulous."

The second paragraph begins with an abrupt qualification of the previous paragraph: "This, mind you, suburbia." What the reader may have been thinking during the description in the previous paragraph—that we are in the midst of a rural landscape—is wrong; we are in the midst of suburbia. While Dillard's house is located twenty minutes from the pond, once she is there at the tree trunk, she is "a five-minute walk in three directions to rows of houses." Though none of the houses can be seen from the pond, Dillard focuses throughout the remainder of the paragraph on what is visible to the observant eye: the "highway at one end" and the "nesting pair of wood ducks at the other"; each shrub accompanied by "a muskrat hole or a beer can"; all the fields and the woods "threaded everywhere with motorcycle tracks—in whose bare clay wild turtles lay eggs."

Level Two: making conceptual associations from the evidence

TWENTY MINUTES FROM MY HOUSE, THROUGH THE WOODS BY THE QUARRY AND ACROSS THE HIGHWAY, IS HOLLINS POND, A REMARKABLE PIECE OF SHALLOWNESS, WHERE I LIKE TO GO AT SUNSET AND SIT ON A TREE TRUNK. HOLLINS POND IS ALSO CALLED MURRAY'S POND; IT COVERS TWO ACRES OF BOTTOMLAND NEAR TINKER CREEK WITH SIX INCHES OF WATER AND SIX THOUSAND LILY PADS. IN WINTER, BROWN-AND-WHITE STEERS STAND IN THE MIDDLE OF IT, MERELY DAMPENING THEIR HOOVES; FROM THE DISTANT SHORE THEY LOOK LIKE MIRACLE ITSELF, COMPLETE WITH MIRACLE'S NONCHALANCE. NOW, IN SUMMER, THE STEERS ARE GONE. THE WATER LILIES HAVE BLOSSOMED AND SPREAD TO A GREEN HORIZONTAL PLANE THAT IS TERRA FIRMA TO PLODDING BLACKBIRDS, AND TREMULOUS CEILING TO BLACK LEECHES, CRAYFISH, AND CARP.

THIS, MIND YOU, SUBURBIA. IT IS A FIVE-MINUTE WALK IN THREE DIRECTIONS TO ROWS OF HOUSES, THOUGH NONE IS VISIBLE HERE. THERE'S A 55 MPH HIGHWAY AT ONE END OF THE POND, AND A NESTING PAIR OF WOOD DUCKS AT THE OTHER. UNDER EVERY BUSH IS A MUSKRAT HOLE OR A BEER CAN. THE FAR END IS AN ALTERNATING SERIES OF FIELDS AND WOODS, FIELDS AND WOODS, THREADED EVERYWHERE WITH MOTORCYCLE TRACKS—IN WHOSE BARE CLAY WILD TURTLES LAY EGGS.

Once we have observed the various details and language in the passage, we can ATTACH CONCEPTUAL ASSOCIATIONS to our observations.

The details regarding the setting initially reveal images of natural beauty, the wonder of the natural world at "sunset"—the "lily pads," the "blackbirds," the "steers." It is a place where, says Dillard, "I like to go," a location desirable and "remarkable," and therefore worthy of her—and our—attention. This remarkable landscape is at one point likened to a "miracle," a word indicating the extraordinary or improbable, that which inspires awe or amazement, and because of the additional word "nonchalance," something effortlessly—naturally—created. These images are soon combined with man-made images that contend with all this beauty: "55 mph highway," "beer can," "motorcycle tracks."

The idea of movement, change, and transformation is indicated in every sentence of the first paragraph. Dillard herself is moving from her house, "through the woods by the quarry and across the highway" to a specific place, "a tree trunk," from which she proceeds to observe the pond. Since "Hollins Pond is also called Murray's Pond," its name is as fluid as the surrounding land-scape that, with the seasons, transforms from a shallow wading pool for steers to a "green horizontal plane" that is both "terra firma" and "tremulous ceiling" for the varieties of summertime wildlife that populate the pond. The cattle themselves "stand," appearing not to move at all, but of course they do: "Now, in summer, they are gone." In the first paragraph's final sentence, that the lilies "have blossomed and spread" accentuates the sense of growth and vibrancy that accompanies the transformations that occur during spring, whereas ideas associated with the slower, less turbulent movements of summer are linked to the adjectives "plodding" and "tremulous."

In the second paragraph, Dillard asserts the uncomfortable encroach-ment—*encroachment* also a type of movement, and a disquieting one—of human civilization on the splendor of nature. What in the preceding paragraph was a twenty-minute walk from one house is, in this paragraph, a five-minute walk to rows of them in three directions. The "55 mph highway at one end of the pond" reminds the reader of cars and their drivers, a detail suggestive of man's perilous proximity to this natural world. A "beer can" suggests not only human presence but also humans' disregard for their surroundings. Even the wildlife mentioned offers the potential for harmful human engagement: musk-rats are prized for their fur; wood ducks are targeted during hunting season. In the final sentence, Dillard delineates among the fields and woods the intrusion "everywhere" of motorcycle tracks "in whose bare clay wild turtles lay eggs." This concluding image, an off-the-road "highway" where no speed signs are posted, impresses upon the careful reader that wildlife waiting to be born is itself threatened.

Level Three: recognizing relationships among pieces of evidence

TWENTY MINUTES FROM MY HOUSE, THROUGH THE WOODS BY THE QUARRY AND ACROSS THE HIGHWAY, IS HOLLINS POND, A REMARKABLE PIECE OF SHALLOWNESS, WHERE I LIKE TO GO AT SUNSET AND SIT ON A TREE TRUNK. HOLLINS POND IS ALSO CALLED MURRAY'S POND; IT COVERS TWO ACRES OF BOTTOMLAND NEAR TINKER CREEK WITH SIX INCHES OF WATER AND SIX THOUSAND LILY PADS. IN WINTER, BROWN-AND-WHITE STEERS STAND IN THE MIDDLE OF IT, MERELY DAMPENING THEIR HOOVES; FROM THE DISTANT SHORE THEY LOOK LIKE MIRACLE ITSELF, COMPLETE WITH MIRACLE'S NONCHALANCE. NOW, IN SUMMER, THE STEERS ARE GONE. THE WATER LILIES HAVE BLOSSOMED AND SPREAD TO A GREEN HORIZONTAL PLANE THAT IS TERRA FIRMA TO PLODDING BLACKBIRDS, AND TREMULOUS CEILING TO BLACK LEECHES, CRAYFISH, AND CARP.

THIS, MIND YOU, SUBURBIA. IT IS A FIVE-MINUTE WALK IN THREE DIRECTIONS TO ROWS OF HOUSES, THOUGH NONE IS VISIBLE HERE. THERE'S A 55 MPH HIGHWAY AT ONE END OF THE POND, AND A NESTING PAIR OF WOOD DUCKS AT THE OTHER. UNDER EVERY BUSH IS A MUSKRAT HOLE OR A BEER CAN. THE FAR END IS AN ALTERNATING SERIES OF FIELDS AND WOODS, FIELDS AND WOODS, THREADED EVERYWHERE WITH MOTORCYCLE TRACKS—IN WHOSE BARE CLAY WILD TURTLES LAY EGGS.

Both the evidence we as readers observe in the Dillard passage and the conceptual associations we are making with that evidence provide a further opportunity for the reader to recognize relationships as they gradually emerge from a literary work.

Clearly, Dillard juxtaposes the proximity of human and nonhuman worlds, but it is especially interesting to observe how she does it. Notice that in the first paragraph, the only human involved in this natural setting is the author herself. The opening phrase "twenty minutes from my house" indicates proximity but one that still suggests the possibility for a distinct, and delicate, separation of the two worlds. Two other words from the first sentence also allude to humans—"quarry," a pit from which stone and other construction materials are extracted, and "highway"—but the woods are "by the quarry" and the pond is "across the highway." It therefore appears, at first glance, that humans may come close to but not actually involve themselves that much in the peaceful world of Hollins Pond. The one person who does enter and stay sits on a tree trunk and remains the passive observer.

Because Dillard, in this first paragraph, takes the reader through the move-ment of seasons—from the stillness of winter through the vibrancy of spring into the steadier rhythms of summer—she creates the initial illusion that she remains the only human participant in the natural landscape. However, after she closes this paragraph with images of summertime tranquility, an abrupt shift occurs at the beginning of the next paragraph, a shift breaking the illusion of nature's detachment from the world of man.

The shift is heralded with the direct address to the reader: "This, mind you, suburbia." Be careful, she seems to say. Remember where you are. It is then she repeats specific ideas first mentioned in the opening sentence of the previous paragraph. Distance is reiterated but with a twist. While the pond is a twenty-minute walk from her house, we now know that residences "creep up to within a five-minute walk in three directions." That houses surround the perimeter of the pond on three sides indicates that in only one direction remains a link to a world more rural, one from which cattle might in winter emerge. The highway is mentioned again, but the previously unmentioned miles per hour allowed by law is much more suggestive of traffic flow, speed, and people and machinery going to and fro. Wildlife reoccurs as well, the first reference being of wood ducks nesting on the other side of the pond from the highway. Since such ducks can be the object of a hunt, the reader is reminded once again that the woods leading to the pond are "by a quarry" and that one definition for quarry is prey.

As the juxtaposition of the human community and nature becomes tighter and more central to the passage as a whole, Dillard, using sentences whose structures are shorter and less complex than most of those in the first paragraph, concludes with a sequence of stark contrasts. The "muskrat hole" or the "beer can" beneath the shrubs. The series of "alternating fields and woods" woven "with motorcycle tracks." The "bare clay," which is "bare" because of man's actions—not because of the forces of nature itself—now the nesting place for "wild turtles." The adjective "bare" in the final sentence is especially evocative. On the one hand, the clay is presently a nest, its modifier "bare" reminding us of its homonym, "bear," as in *to give birth*. On the other hand, the eggs lying perilously on tracks of bare clay, the adjective "bare" also calls to mind *barren*. Dillard is therefore using two words—bare clay—to make contiguous two opposing ideas, fertility and infertility.

Blending the three levels of analysis when crafting a composition

So let's look at a short composition concerning this passage from Dillard that, as with the analysis of the Dickens, fuses all three levels of the ANALYTICAL VOICE chart to make a claim. Again, you'll notice that I have combined several statements I have previously written in our consideration of each level of thinking.

Dillard suggests not only that the human and natural world are intricately intertwined, but also that the natural world's beauty, though it remains viscerally poignant, is in jeopardy amidst the civilizing impulses of man. The image of nature's serene, harmonious grandeur that occupies the first paragraph is shattered in the subsequent paragraph by the imagery of human civilization besieging the natural world.

The reader's first exposure to Hollins Pond reveals the landscape as a sanctuary, or refuge, for the author. Her journey "twenty minutes from my house" leads her into the meditative solitude of the pond, where "I like to go at sunset and sit on a tree trunk." The reader enters the pond as the author does, leaving behind the markers of civilization, traversing "through the woods by the quarry and across the highway." The marvels of nature await the narrator—and the reader—in "a remarkable piece of shallowness" that "covers two acres of bottomland near Tinker Creek with six inches of water and six thousand lily pads." It is here that the reader, along with Dillard, revels in "miracle's nonchalance": the steers that stand passively in the pond during win-

ter, their hooves "merely dampening." The cattle, she tells us, "are gone" now that it is summer. The tranquil silence of winter has been replaced by summer's steady pulse, the water lilies that "have blossomed and spread" reminding the reader of the vibrancy that accompanies spring's transformations. Now the methodical certainties of summer present "a green horizontal plane that is terra firma to plodding blackbirds, and tremulous ceiling to black leeches, crayfish, and carp," all created with the ease and "nonchalance" of miracle. The narrator's movement through the seasons anchors her—and her reader—in a world thoroughly natural.

At this peaceful moment in the reader's encounter with the natural world of Hollins Pond, Dillard shifts abruptly from the wonder of nature to the perilous encroachment of human civilization upon nature's splendor. Directly addressing the reader, the stark voice of the narrator breaks the illusion heretofore created: "This, mind you, suburbia." Even the syntax of Dillard's sentences shift from the balance and poetry of the opening paragraph to sentences that, in the subsequent paragraph, are more barren, merely cataloguing a serious of sharp contrasts. The image of the tranquil pond is replaced by a landscape already trapped on three sides by "rows of houses." Images of nature, previously harmonious, now align with the pernicious elements of man's world: muskrats and wood ducks evoke images of trappers and hunters, and the "55 mph highway at one end of the pond" conjures up the discord of suburban traffic, noise, exhaust, and road kill. Beer cans are as predominant under bushes as muskrat holes, and the series of woods and fields are "threaded everywhere with motorcycle tracks—in whose bare clay wild turtles lay eggs." This final haunting image brings to the fore the imminent danger that threatens all of Hollins Pond, the past participle "threaded" indicating the inescapable entanglement of human beings in the natural world.

The idea of wild turtle eggs splattered by motorcyclists reminds the careful reader of a potential warning residing in Dillard's previous paragraph. There is, in the first paragraph, one sentence that, because of its brevity, stands apart: "Now, in summer, the steers are gone." As the reader contemplates what is happening in Dillard's sanctuary, it is a sentence that is worth a return. Since the steers could only come and go by way of the one side of Hollins Pond that is not bounded by "rows of houses," it seems likely, considering the scale of the human invasion, that this last portal is in danger as suburbia continues its restless expansion. The steers that are gone in summer may, within a few years, be gone for good. Without cattle in winter, a major source of fertilization for the pond and its wildlife will be removed. What Dillard has revealed in two paragraphs is the process of extinction as the human community overwhelms the natural world.

Further information for developing the analytical voice

The situations portrayed in fiction and nonfiction may also be associated with the elements of CLASSICAL RHETORIC. These elements, which can be found in the Appendix of *Crafting Expository Argument*, also provide another strategy for talking about texts, of saying something beyond the plot.

For additional exercises and samples of this process, go online to www. telemachospublishing.com.

2

STRENGTHENING WRITING SKILLS

OBJECTIVES

To enhance universal writing skills by
• elaborating ideas extensively with concrete singular detail;
• emphasizing the use of active voice verbs;
• controlling verb tense;
• incorporating a variety of sentence structures, and
• eliminating redundancy.

To improve critical thinking and reading skills by
• analyzing and observing details closely;
• considering thoughtfully the purpose and power of diction; and
• transferring these skills to readings in other disciplines.

IMPORTANT RECOMMENDATION

IN ORDER TO STRENGTHEN WRITING SKILLS NOW, it is critical to teach a variety of sentence structures in conjunction with the teaching of Chapters 2-4 in *Crafting Expository Argument.* Therefore, Chapter Five, "Crafting the Sentence," is a crucial adjunct to all instruction in the writing process. The WRITING TO SHOW exercises in this chapter provide an appropriate opportunity to begin teaching students how to manipulate skillfully specific phrases and clauses in their writing. After explaining the differences between clauses and phrases (p. 134), I begin with participial phrases (p. 139). As they are mastered and successfully incorporated into an early WRITING TO SHOW composition, I soon add the adverb subordinate clause (p. 135). For further ideas in the incorporation of grammatical sentence structures into the writing process, see Suggested Lesson Plans posted at www.telemachospublishing.com.

WRITING TO SHOW[1]

When authors write, they don't just *tell* the reader something; they *show* the reader what is meant. What are the pictures and images writers see, hear, smell, touch, and taste? Writers might think of themselves as photographers. What images will be shot to convey meaning? WRITING TO SHOW, however, does not mean creating sentences with multiple adjectives that are vague, abstract, or general.

Editing Symbol

SH

For example, the following list of adjectives reflects *the type* sophisticated writers *avoid*: great, immense, huge, scary, dangerous, bad, strong, powerful. The SHOWING sentence relies on active verbs, concrete singular nouns, and concrete adjectives. For example, "His right foot catches a pile of crumpled white shirts on the floor in the doorway, causing him to stumble as he enters the room, the side of his left ankle sliding across the purple burbered carpeting."

The following two paragraphs attempt to describe the same scene. Read them, noticing all the places where the second paragraph shows the reader details that the first paragraph doesn't.

A *telling* paragraph

The athlete gets ready for the race by tying his shoes. Feeling pretty nervous, he examines his shoes. His ankle hurts. He hears the announcer tell the athletes to get ready. After he gets in a position, he hears the gun start the race. All his limbs are moving fast and his feet pound on the concrete.

A *SHOWING* paragraph

by Mauricio Delgado

Items in bold refer to the accompanying commentary in shaded area.

The muscles in his left leg tense up as he shifts the weight of his body to one side while kneeling down to **tie his right shoe. Cross the first with the second, pull. Loop across, bring around, pull, braiding together the frayed gray laces of his Adidas spikes as skillfully as a seamstress weaves with thread.** With the

> Extends elaboration: tying the shoe

pride of even the fleet-footed Achilles, the athlete inspects his sacred wings of land attentively as he quickly brushes off a few blades of grass and dirt collected on the instep of his sneaker. His ankle soon begins to throb with a lack of blood circulation to his foot; in fact, the knot of his shoe is so tightly laced that he can hardly feel his toes suffocating inside his shoe **like sardines packed in a tin can.** "Participants in the 100 meters, report

> Uses a simile

to the starting blocks. Third and final call." The announcement, monotonous and resounding, trumpets over the loudspeaker, abruptly breaking his current thoughts. At once he reaches down and relieves the pressure of the knot and walks briskly towards the crowded starting line. Crouching down on the red asphalt track, he stretches his hamstrings as a final precaution and positions himself on the starting blocks. "Runners on your marks!" His left leg fully extends backwards with the base of his foot resting gently on the shiny metal block. His right leg is bent almost at 90 degrees directly

---

1 Adapted from Caplan, Rebekah, and Catharine Keech. *Showing Writing: A Training Program to Help Students Be Specific.* University of California, Berkeley, 1980.

underneath him, **sweat beginning to drip from his chin to his thigh**. He finally drops his shoulders and lowers his

Absolute phrase

arms to the blistering asphalt, setting his hands directly behind the painted white starting line. "Get set!" Immediately his rear ascends in the air, followed by his back and then his head. He rocks backwards then forwards, his heart racing anxiously, awaiting the crack of the gun. "Pop!" The whip-like crack of the metal hammer against the cartridge puts his muscles and joints in action. He shoots off the blocks with a sudden electrical vigor. His burning calves energize his quadriceps, which thrust the rest of his body forward. Right leg, left arm forward. Left leg, right arm forward. His limbs propel in rhythmic action while his heart pumps blood to the palpitating muscles. Inhale. His chest grows and his lungs expand with oxygen. Exhale. The body repels harmful gasses as the cycle continues. His breathing grows deeper and faster; the finish line grows more imminent and attainable. **Implanting themselves into the loose gravel and cracked asphalt**, the spikes on his cleats tear up the track as his

Present participial phrase

heels pound the ground. Using his peripheral vision, he spots a blurry figure half a step in front of him in the next lane.

Telling vs. SHOWING

Because the **telling paragraph** is very general, relying on abstract and vague diction, it doesn't show the reader pictures and images; any effort that allows the reader to see, hear, taste, and touch concrete objects is weak or nonexistent. The reader does not see the person "tying his shoes" nor does the reader see the actual tying of a shoelace.

The SHOWING **paragraph** is very specific. It is full of details and examples, which are elaborated—and can continue to be elaborated even more—so that we see what is being talked about as though we were viewing a picture. The writer SHOWS the reader an athlete "who shifts the weight of his body to one side while kneeling down to tie his right shoe." The writer, therefore, is like a painter: The pen is his or her brush that is used to make everything come alive.

What allows the SHOWING writer to achieve this visualization is the diction selected and the ability to extend the elaboration of an image. Let's examine these two issues separately with specific reference to our samples.

First, don't falsely assume that WRITING TO SHOW relies on flowery adjectives. Quite the contrary, the SHOWING writer relies on concrete nouns and vivid verbs, and when he chooses an adjective or adverb, he selects one that possesses some visualization. Let's examine the parts of speech more carefully in the previous two samples, examining the first fifty words of each passage. You'll see that the SHOWING writer selects parts of speech that allow the reader to visualize something concrete while the parts of speech the telling writer selects are too vague to create anything concrete in our minds.

In the first sentence of each passage, the verb choice differs—the telling writing employs "gets" while the SHOWING writer chooses "tense up" for the main verb, then opts for "shifts" inside the adverbial subordinate clause, then adds two verbals, the gerund "kneeling down" and the infinitive "to tie."

Obviously, the verb choice "gets" produces no visual image; the reader does not see what that verb might look like. In fact, if you asked someone to demonstrate what "gets" concretely looks like, he would likely be unable to select from the variety of general possibilities. But "tense up" allows for a visual image to pop into our minds, as does "shift," "kneeling down," and "to tie." If you examine the additional verbs selected for both passages, you'll see how the majority of verbs (and verbals: gerunds, participles, and infinitives) chosen by the writer of the SHOWING paragraph assist the reader in creating a picture. Simply compare the verbs and verbals selected in subsequent sentences by the writer of the telling paragraph to those selected by the writer of the SHOWING paragraph, and the difference between abstract verbs and vivid verbs becomes quite clear: telling paragraph—*feeling, examines, hurts, hears, gets, hears, are moving, pound*; SHOWING paragraph—*cross, pull, loop, bring around, pull, braiding, weaves, inspects, brushes off, collected.* While the writer of the telling paragraph seems to have chosen a vivid verb by chance with his selection of "pound," the writer of the SHOWING paragraph makes the selection of bold, picturesque verbs a matter of habit.

The selection of nouns differs as well. Let's look at the nouns used for the subject position: the telling writer has selected the noun *athlete* while the SHOWING writer selects *muscles*; indeed, this writer's complete subject includes the prepositional phrase *in his left leg*, which focuses our attention to a specific area of the body. Soon thereafter in the passage, the SHOWING writer selects the precise noun phrase, *Adidas spikes*, which presents for the reader a much less ambiguous image than does the telling writer's noun selection of *shoes*.

With regard to modifiers, adjectives and adverbs—including the phrases that function as adjectives and adverbs—become effective when they noticeably add to the visualization of a specific noun or verb. The telling writer selects *ready*, an abstract word that doesn't allow us to see anything precise as it does not reveal what getting "ready" looks like. The problem continues throughout the telling paragraph—the reader does not visualize anything substantial and definite by the subsequent modifiers or modifying phrases chosen: *feeling pretty nervous, to get ready, gets in a position, are moving fast.* However, if we list some of the modifying elements in the SHOWING paragraph, we see that they add to the reader's visualization of the noun or verb being modified: *frayed gray laces; pride of even the fleet-footed Achilles; quickly brushes off a few blades of grass and dirt collected on the instep of his sneaker; the announcement, monotonous and resounding, trumpets over the loudspeaker.*

WHEN **WRITING TO SHOW**, SHOW FROM THE FIRST!

When writing the first sentence, the author begins with images that the reader can see, hear, smell, taste, touch. The goal is to grab the reader's attention and never let it go.

Five threads poke out on the bottom left edge of the cap where the stitching has broken loose.

His brown, greasy hair swats his scarred face with each galloping stride. Gripping his Smith & Wesson in his left hand, he plummets through a pants pocket with his right, in futile search of an additional clip that he knows does not exist. Instead, his bony index finger protrudes through a hole to reach a sticky thin layer of blood on his right quadriceps, where a single shotgun shell met its target.

Tom slides his fingers underneath the corners of the rectangular envelope. He gently breaks the seal and can hear the loud ripping sound as the solid white envelope dismantles.

His clenched fist shoots forward like a bullet out of a barrel as it digs its way into the boy's soft flesh just below his right eye, leaving a bright red trail of warm blood. Trickling down the side of his face, the stream of blood slowly drags itself over the smooth curve of the boy's jaw, and then it drips on to the stiff pocket of the freshly starched shirt just above his rapidly beating heart.

EXTENDING ELABORATION

Editing Symbol

E3

When the writer first introduces an image or idea, he or she should not immediately move to a new image after one sentence or phrase. Take time to make additional comments about the image, extending our understanding of it.

by Michael Spurlin

His right foot catches a pile of crumpled white shirts on the floor in the doorway, causing him to stumble as he enters the room, the side of his left ankle sliding across the purple burbered carpeting. As he puts down his left foot he hears the loud snap of the pencil breaking beneath his bare foot. The splintery wood begins to dig into the arch of his foot. As he slowly lifts his left foot, onehalf of the yellow number two pencil sticks to his foot. He shakes his leg and the pencil piece bounces off the wall and falls to the floor.

by Matt Connolly

A jet black tomcat springs out from underneath the debris on the desk, soaring over a vast array of knives, needles, and thumb tacks scattered across the carpet. The cat lands safely on the yellow stained mattress wedged into the far right corner of the room. Oblivious to the rusty springs that have burst through the mattress cover, the cat stretches out on a pile of dusty pillow feathers at the head of the bed. It begins to swat at a fat green caterpillar crawling slowly toward a small hole in the wall. Being denied the opportunity to complete its destination, the caterpillar is hurled onto the floor a few feet in front of me.

by Chris Hampton

A bead of salt-watery sweat slowly drips down the marred and contorted features of his face. He feels the sting of salt as it travels down and through the three-inch gash just above his left eyebrow; down it creeps, over what would have been the bridge of his nose had it not been smashed into tiny fragments of cartilage, pus, blood, and mucus. The bead continues across the face, a tiny mirror of agony, as it follows each and every groove in the man's face: the jagged and irregular "v" in the nose, the size twelve hiker's boot with the three-inch sole and steel toe that cut his right cheek bone to white ribbons with a touch of red, the lipless mouth, long ago empty of tongue and all but a few chipped teeth, once brilliant, now dull and grotesque with fragments of bone, enamel, and vomit caked over his three thousand dollar smile. The sweat finishes its trail of tears where it deems to rest on his chin, the only area of his face left just as it began. Promptly it falls to the floor, making what the man appears to believe is a huge thud. Where an angelically pure bead of saltwater began, a hellish collage of bone, blood, pus, and oozing vomit now ends.

How Writing to Show Connects to Expository Argument

To begin developing writing skills of students by working with WRITING TO SHOW exercises before working with "pure" exposition is to put the horse where it belongs. In my experience with the teaching of writing, one of the major problems is that most exposition by young writers lacks a spark of interest, a touch of creativity that distinguishes the writing and makes a reader—including the teacher—want to read it. Great writing is not a lackluster vanilla exercise, and that includes the expository essay form. The narrative and descriptive aspects of WRITING TO SHOW that allow students to, among other things, hone their elaboration techniques, their manipulation of sentence structures, and their abilities to work with concrete nouns and vivid verbs prepare students for the crafting of lively expository argument.

More precisely, the SHOWING exercises help the writer produce diction that is singular and concrete, namely, to transform vague and abstract words into singular and precise words. This skill must be used in all modes—description, narration, exposition, and persuasion. As you work through the chapters on the paragraph and the essay, you'll notice how those writers employ the SHOWING skills of selecting concrete diction and elaborating on a key point before moving onto another piece of evidence.

· ·

SAMPLE **WRITING TO SHOW** COMPOSITIONS

· ·

Assignment: SHOW a person in the act of doing something ordinary.

by Akos Furton

The freshman's hazel, almond-like eye **squints** at the spiraling doodles plastered on the lower left corner, **littered with circular pencil craters that rip the paper into four congruent triangles.** He twirls his hexagonal prism-shaped mechanical pencil stuffed with .5 pencil lead; his pudgy fingers **trek** upwards as they creep stealthily to the crumbling, pencil-streaked eraser. His plump thumb **slugs** the eraser lounging on the pencil's apex, driving the pink rubber into the metallic green aluminum divider separating the eraser from the graphite brush. The pencil plummeting, the eraser hastily rubs against the metallic gray streak, spewing tiny filaments of eraser dust all over the typed sheet. As his plump, bright crimson limb sweeps the featherlike eraser dust off of the divot, the writing utensil's sharp tip lingers one centimeter above the L-shaped school desk. The pointed tip of the pencil travels rapidly to the right to cross the first answer, **the slashed-through letter A in the Comic Sans typeface. A streak of metallic gray dust trails the slash, just as a plane's exhaust belches a white column of smoke. The right to left slash commences with a faint hook, looping around and gradually fading out on the left edge of the exam sheet.** The pencil's slanted protrusion of graphite circles the B, hurriedly carving a minute B onto the streak left of the first question.

> Note the past participial phrase and the strong verbs.

> Note how the writer expands the image of the pencil slashing the paper.

Assignment: SHOW a scene in nature with precision.

by Christian Beuchel

A thorn bush protrudes through the miniscule gaps in the Birchwood planks of the fence. Two sword-like thorns wedge underneath the white veneer of the paint, peeling off the exterior in thin sheets, dispersing them between the slender blades of the Augustine grass. A long green vine sprawls out, ensnaring itself into the steel latch holding the fence closed. The slender tips thrust themselves into the rusty hinges and through the deadbolt. **Its tip sharp, one thorn, which measures at about three inches, pierces into the porous surface between the latch and the handle.** As the thorn exerts itself further and further, **small splinters chip off of the plywood and fall like miniscule daggers lodging themselves into the soft humus.** Above the thorn bush, a black crow's talons **contract** together, the sharp nails grasping the narrow power line dangling between two industrial transformers. The graceful tightrope walker attempts to distribute its weight evenly; still, the line steadily **wobbles** back and forth like a ticking clock. The vile fowl **squawks and cackles** in the clamor of the twilight as an eerie breeze **drifts** across its feathers. The waft **squeezes** between the left wing, ruffling the feathers and causing them to stand up at the tips. The peaks **fray**, the moonlight **glistens** on the lush sheen of the avian creature. Its bright yellow eyes **illuminate** as the moonlight **reflects** off the glassy surface of the cornea. The pupils **dilate** to the size of saucers. Within the center of the dark canvas, the image of the moon reflects like in a mirror. As the crow **blinks**, tiny crinkles in the feathery skin run across the bridge of its cheek bone, and a cluster of dead feathers **detach** from the skin. The brittle feathers **flutter** slowly downwards, tips spread out reaching for the sky.

> The "one thorn" is first modified by an absolute phrase [its tip sharp], which serves to introduce the sentence while modifying the "one thorn." Afterwards, an adjective subordinate clause [which measures at about three inches] further modifies the "one thorn."

> With an effective simile, the writer transforms "small splinters" into "miniscule daggers." This is but one example wherein the writer uses foreboding imagery. What other examples can you find?

> Verb choices that are both striking and appropriate add to the evocative quality of the piece.

Assignment: SHOW an athlete in action at a specific moment in time.

by Adam Klugiewicz

Strong hands violently massage Johnny's aching back muscles. Ebony fingers, dancing nimbly, dig into the quivering brawn and knead the soft white dough. **Johnny's glassy stare falls upon the shiny blue mat, cool and azure as a gentle mountain lake; rocking his head back slowly upon its rusty hinges, his gaze opens up to the other side of the ring.** There sits his opponent, nearly a thousand miles away, waiting. For an instant their eyes meet: Blue piercing orbs **stab** Johnny, scorching white hot lances **puncture** him for a brief fiery instant, forcing him to look away. A voluptuous walking carnival of sequins, make-up, and softly colored silk scarves parades around the ring bearing a large white board adorned with the number 12. Johnny **glances** down

> A compound sentence, its two independent clauses joined by a semicolon.

> Note the vivid verbs throughout the piece.

into a gray rusted steel bucket into which he **spews** a grisly mixture of spit and blood. It **splashes** and **ripples** into a miniature whirlpool for an instant, then **sinks** into the cool depths of the tiny cesspool. Dozens of hands without faces attend to him. Fingers **strap** a bandage upon the gouge, splitting his left eyebrow, while others **cram** a water bottle into his cracked, parched lips and **squeeze** lukewarm water into his dry burning mouth; still others wipe the sweat from his brow with a velvety white Nike towel. **Floating directly in front of him**, the only face Johnny can see is Coach O'Reilly's. Finally, Johnny tunes into the coach's gravel-filled voice. "Let's go now, kid! Bring this one home." He can barely distinguish the brass bells' high coppery chime from the low iron bells **already ringing in his head**. A final disembodied hand forces the grimy mouthpiece into Johnny's throbbing jaws, **criss-crossed by haphazard stitching** and **lined with shattered teeth**. With hip flexors painfully groaning and knees cracking sharply, he draws himself up upon two shaky rubber planks. Johnny tediously swings the lead pendulums up from his sides and holds his aching hands in front of him in the fighting position. He valiantly marches to meet his opponent in the middle of the ring. The two opponents' eyes meet again. Johnny's opponent glares at him from behind two red walls of padded glove, **his wiry torso swaying back and forth as the cobra prepares to strike**.

> The first of two present participial phrases coming up.

> Two past participial phrases modify "jaws."

> An absolute phrase extends the elaboration further.

Assignment: SHOW someone afraid without telling the reader that the person is afraid.

by Derek Rollins

His brown greasy hair **swats** his scarred face with each galloping stride. Gripping his Smith & Wesson in his left hand, he **plummets** through a pants pocket with his right, in futile search for an additional clip that he knows does not exist. Instead, his bony index finger **protrudes** through a hole to reach a sticky thin layer of blood on his right quadriceps, **where a single shotgun shell has met its target**. His dark blue-stained velvet coat flies in the wind like the cape of Superman; his reputation proves he is far from heroic. Coming to a stop, he covers himself in the blanket of the far-reaching shadow of a garbage container, hitting against its side with a metallic cling. Sitting down to catch his breath, the seat of his hole-ridden pants crunch against a large brown, abhorrent cockroach, ending its menial existence with a repulsive squish. **A multicolored concoction oozes from the roach's intestines, the roach's blood staining the concrete; but the man remains oblivious to all but the crunching sound**. Off in the distance, past the garbage can that affords him minimal but necessary hiding, and beyond the decrepit old bum that on most occasions inhabits it, he hears the sound. The soft but ever-present rhythmic tapping of the hooves and metal horseshoes of the solitary steed,

> Vivid verb choices enhance the concrete detail.

> An adjective subordinate clause

> This compound sentence, its first independent clause containing an absolute phrase, extends the elaboration of the cockroach mentioned in the previous sentence.

drawing with it the infamous brown wooden stagecoach, with a wheel that squeaks loud enough to warn any nearby criminals to flee, beats against the worn cobblestone pavement. Commanding the vehicle is, as always, Chief Quimbey, the stout, sloppy, yet respectable chief of police for the small English county of Westmorland. He stands semi-upright, knees bent, chubby hands clinched to the reins, holding on for dear life. The hot wind rushes by his fat face, leaving a tingling, burning sensation. He rhythmically casts out the black leather strips, crashing onto his engine's flesh. For the first time, after nearly an hour of swift pursuit, he reaches into the tight left jacket pocket, **retrieving his monogrammed off-white silk handkerchief. He swipes the thick lather of his own warm sweat from his hairy wrinkled brow. He returns the handkerchief to the pocket, hitting another pool of sweat under his arm on the way down. His thin, blue cotton shirt shows off many other such pools.** Immediately, his focus returns to the chase. **As the end of the dark alley approaches,** he slows the horse to a quick trot, a relief from the feverish pace that has been steadily maintained. The panting of the beast is quite audible. He turns his head and glares at the vagabond, who points an

An adverb subordinate clause, beginning with "As," introduces the sentence.

unsteady, dirty, drunken finger past his beloved dump site. Quimbey abruptly pulls the reins up toward his chest, his arms slightly shaking. Glancing down the slope of his belly and with a quick, deft hand, the chief returns a single, golden button that has come undone back to its proper place. **Reaching behind him, he grasps the uncomfortable but official standard English police hat, tall and red with a golden lion crest, and he mounts it on his round head. Out of habit, he pulls the thick plastic arc under his unshaven chin.** Dismounting from the great height of the worn-down coach, he sniffs the air, only to meet the stench

The writer's attention to the singular detail of the hat and what its wearer does with it creates a solid concrete image.

of a week-old carcass of a mid-sized rat, which lies adjacent to his left steel-toed boot. The body looks to have been generously ravaged by fellow creatures of the night. Kicking the gut-wrenching body aside, he casually turns the corner to face his longtime evasive foe.

Assignment: Show *a specific object is old without telling the reader that it is old*

by Travis Baggett

A warped label desperately clings to the inside of the collar by mere threads, as though a previous owner had decided to rip it from the shirt and then changed his mind after the job was more than half-done. The tag's faded orange letters read "X-Large," although the actual size of the article to which it clasps has shrunken to more of a "medium" over the years. The front of the shirt bears a monogrammed logo and name in the middle of the chest; the top of the logo, reaching to within an inch of the collar, extends down

The writer begins description of the sweatshirt with a complex sentence containing two adverb subordinate clauses.

approximately seven inches below this peak height. At its widest point, the logo and lettering are eight inches in breadth. The white, monochrome design reeks of age. The once solid-white screen paint has acquired a mosaic quality, **a composition of thousands of tiny, yet discernible, broken tiles trying**

An absolute phrase extends the elaboration further.

desperately to seek freedom but bound by their enduring chemical properties, **which hold them fixed to the fabric.** The areas of white are like the baked floor of a vast drylands: cracked, weathered, beaten, hard, and flat—coarse to the eye and to the touch. The dull blue permeates the cracks between the broken tiles of paint and, for once, begins to assume a certain vitality against the cold contrast of faded white, as though nourishing the cracked, depleted surface. **The monogram's design features a soccer player clad in a light shirt, dark shorts, and knee-high socks; the player's body staggers sharply to the viewer's right, as if he might explode off that side of the shirt at any moment. A light-colored semicircle, with the rounded side facing up, serves as a background for the top half of his figure.** Inside the top left arc of the background, five blue stars are stamped in a single-file manner along the slope of the curvature, just above the player's right shoulder and outstretched right arm.

The writer focuses on details of the monogram's design.

Assignment: SHOW a person or creature in the act of doing something distinctly ordinary

by Brian Costanza

Standing naked in the middle of the master bathroom, Cameron trembles as the Hunter fan violently blows against the water residue left on his body. White goose bumps magnify as he reaches for his white cotton jockey briefs with the fingertips of his left hand. **The fringed, size thirty-three garment moving closer to his body, Cameron lifts his left leg. As the leg rises, the tendons in his toes retract like a hermit crab. Both arms gripping the elastic band, his quadriceps thrust his left appendage through the abyss of the underwear. As his leg drives its way through the warm undergarment, his shin rubs against part of the front side of the aperture. A shadow trails the underwear during its entire expedition up the hairy leg.** Cameron, who begins to air dry, elevates his right leg to a forty-five degree angle. Since he feels engulfed by ice, his right leg subtly shudders as it embarks on its path through the deep hole. When his leg touches the cold white ceramic tile floor, the hairs on his toes rise in shock. Cameron decides that he will take a stronger grip on the elastic band, which reads *Jockey* around its face. As he attempts to raise the underwear up his legs, the back side of the left leg hole catches itself under his left heel. Cameron releases the white cotton with his left index finger. Cameron, **clasping his left hand back on the elastic band,** exerts all of his strength and energy into the elevation of his underwear. **His forehead wrinkles like an aged prune, and his eyebrows move closer and closer until they eventually take the shape of a single brow.** As the undergarment makes its way past the knees, it violently pulls each hair that it encounters during its journey.

The writer extensively elaborates the left leg's encounter with the jockey briefs.

A present participial phrase located after the noun it modifies

A compound-complex sentence, with one of its independent clauses containing an adverb subordinate clause

THE REVISION PROCESS WHEN **WRITING TO SHOW**

The writer should follow these suggestions and respond to these questions:
- read the composition out loud slowly to others and to oneself.
- seek feedback from a variety of sources.
- purposely make both additions and subtractions:
    - —emphasize what the person or creature is physically doing.
    - —allow yourself to "re-envision" what will happen in your paper;
    - —include details you did not consider showing the first time;
    - —eliminate what does not come across well and what is unnecessary because they merely *tell*.
- make sure each sentence maintains the same focus (on a single character or single action or single object or single emotion) in every sentence.
- strive for each detail being extensively elaborated so that any reader may create a clear mental picture of the detail in all of its particulars.
- keep in mind that plurals are difficult to SHOW or elaborate; it is the singular item, the singular event, the singular individual, the singular action that can best be elaborated extensively.
- avoid sentences that contain lists of vague or abstract adjectives; work toward concrete nouns and vivid verbs to build the showing sentence.
- create an opening sentence that truly grabs a reader's attention.
- combine sentences that entail related ideas by
    - —turning one into a participial phrase and attaching it to the other;
    - —turning one into a subordinate clause and attaching it to the other;
    - —joining two sentences together with a semicolon only or with a correctly punctuated conjunctive adverb;
    - —removing unexciting and unnecessarily repeated words from sentences and combining the crucial details that remain into one complete sentence.
- seek out the verb in each clause: Is each verb in *present* tense? Is each *vivid*?
- rework sentences by eliminating "be" verbs and substituting stronger verbs for them.
- correct misspellings, punctuation errors, run-on sentences, and any sentence fragments.

WRITING TO SHOW ASSIGNMENTS AND ACTIVITIES

The following set of SHOWING assignments helps students develop the universal writing skills they will need when crafting any type of essay:
- elaborating ideas extensively,
- using concrete details,
- focusing on the singular,
- choosing active, vivid verbs,
- controlling verb tense,
- manipulating grammatical structures, and
- grabbing the reader's attention.

    Students should avoid the use of the abstract, vague, or general adjective; instead, students should build their sentences with concrete and singular nouns and active verbs, relying only on a few carefully chosen concrete adjectives.

In addition, with each assignment the teacher requires a particular grammatical structure(s) for students to highlight—present or past participial phrases, adjective or adverb subordinate clauses, absolute phrases, compound or compound-complex sentences, etc.—so that these young writers become accustomed to employing in a gradual and conscious manner syntax that increases the sophistication of their sentences. See Chapter Five in this book as well as Suggested Lesson Plans posted at www.telemachospublishing.com.

Finally, students should recognize that these assignments are not ultimately intended to be exercises in writing fiction. These exercises introduce students to one of the most difficult aspects of good writing: *developing the ability to reflect on a topic and to choose words carefully, selecting words that are concrete and specific.* In other words, they develop universal writing skills that teach students to write with language that is precise and singular. When our language laps into the vague and general, our writing becomes less meaningful.

WRITING TO SHOW Assignment #1

Telling Sentence: *He is scared* or *She is scared.*

or select a different telling sentence, p. 51

Task Using a minimum of 15 lines (maximum 30 lines), write a composition that SHOWS a person afraid without the reader being told that the person is afraid.

- Do not use the telling sentence, or any synonyms for it, in the composition. Therefore, *scared, frightened, horrified, terrified, fear, dread,* and the like will not be used by the writer. That would be telling the reader, instead of SHOWING the reader, that the person is afraid.
- When students wonder, "Where do we begin?" or "How do we begin?" the most appropriate response is often *in medias res*; begin somewhere in the middle of the action. This composition's beginning is whatever the writer says it is, and since the emphasis is on SHOWING an action, then the writer might begin with the starting point of an action.
- SHOW all the senses: sight, sound, touch, taste, smell.
- SHOW each specific movement, detailed action, as if you were filming it frame by frame; let the reader see each particular object involved in the action.
- Avoid plurals.
- Use imaginative vocabulary, vivid verbs.
- Vary the beginnings of each sentence.
- Use present tense only. (When we write about literature, we will discuss the action in the literary text in the present tense.)

WRITING TO SHOW Assignment #2

Telling sentence: *The _____ is a mess* or
The _____ is old.

or select a different telling sentence, p. 51

Task Fill in the blank with the name of an object—the object could be a desk, a racket, a poster, a shoe, a shelf, a drawer, a stove, a binder, a gym bag, a baseball glove, a sock, etc.. Your task is to SHOW that the object is a mess or is old (choose one or the other) without telling the reader that it is.

- Follow all directions for WRITING TO SHOW Assignment #1 (as they are important, it is recommended that the student carefully read once again those directions); for this new assignment, also include the following changes or additions:
- Focus on specific minute details of the object. Spend many sentences—not just one sentence—on each detail before going on to the next detail.
- You must use a minimum of two present participial phrases in your composition. Highlight each of those phrases (do not highlight the entire sentence the present participial phrase is in—highlight only the phrase).
- Be sure your participial phrases are correctly punctuated. Place one of the phrases before the noun it modifies; place the other after the noun it modifies.
- Use spatial transitions to take the reader smoothly from one part of the object to another part. (Examples of some transitions: *next to, to the left of, in the right corner, underneath, adjacent to, on top of, along side of,* etc..)
- Give your piece a title.

WRITING TO SHOW Assignment #3

Telling Sentence: *The athlete is exhausted* or *The athlete becomes exhausted.*

or select a different telling sentence, p. 51

Task The writer is to focus on one athlete performing a specific action that would lead to such exhaustion. This action may be one play in a game or one moment in an event. In a composition of 25–30 lines, the writer must thoroughly elaborate this single action from first sentence to last. Students and teacher might brainstorm possible examples of one athlete in such a specific situation. The term "athlete" may involve any activity that produces physical and/or mental exhaustion. A brainstorming list of this kind could include instances such as the following: a batter hitting a home run, a runner preparing to start a race, a swimmer on his or her final lap, a running back during one play of a game, a chess player's single movement against an opponent, a volleyball player's serve for match point.

After selecting the specific action, the writer might *think of the action as though it were happening in slow motion.* Observe exactly what is happening physically and/or mentally. Note the details, especially the subtle details, as they occur second by second.

- Follow all directions for WRITING TO SHOW Assignment #1; include the following changes or additions:
- Raise the minimum number of lines from 15 to 25.
- Continue using present tense; it's important that students maintain control of tense.
- Students are to employ two to five correctly punctuated present participial phrases, highlighting and labeling each one. (If students have studied past participial phrases, the teacher might require a combination of both present and past participial phrases. Some students will wonder *how a past participial phrase can be used when one is writing in present tense*: although the participle in a participial phrase is a verb form, the participle and its phrase are functioning as adjectives—and adjectives modify nouns or pronouns regardless of the verb tense.)

- Highlight two correctly punctuated adverb subordinate clauses.
- Employ vivid vocabulary: vibrant action verbs and precise concrete nouns.
- Give your piece a title.
- Avoid the excessive use of "be" verbs.
    - *—Kiss "is" goodbye.*
    - *—Make "am" into spam.*
    - *—Kick "are" very far.*
    - *—Turn "was" into fuzz.*
    - *—And give your "were" a burr.*

WRITING TO SHOW Assignment #4

Task Closely observe some person or creature in the act of doing something very ordinary. The following are merely or select a different telling sentence, p. 51 some examples: a student in the act of taking a test, a child learning to take his or her first steps, a bird leaving its nest for the first time, a child chasing a butterfly, a teenager learning to drive a car, a mosquito stinging someone, a dog gnawing on a bone, a person eating a bowl of cereal, someone washing dishes, someone washing his or her hands, the act of slicing a turkey, the act of slicing an onion, someone brushing his or her teeth.

- Follow all directions for WRITING TO SHOW Assignment #1; include the following changes or additions:
- The composition is to be 15 to 25 lines, written in present tense only.
- Every line must elaborate the one ordinary action.
- Highlight and label two of each of the following structures that you have studied up to this point. (*Note to teachers: The grammatical structures you have students highlight are dependent, of course, upon which structures you have taught up to that point.*)
    - —present participial phrase
    - —past participial phrase,
    - —adjective subordinate clause,
    - —adverb subordinate clause,
    - —compound sentence with semicolon, and
    - —compound sentence with a conjunctive adverb.
- Don't unnecessarily tell the reader who the person or creature is. Use suitable pronouns ("he," "she," or "it") and allow your SHOWING to reveal to the reader who or what is performing the ordinary action. Let your word pictures reveal all.
- Give your piece a title.

WRITING TO SHOW Assignment #5

Task Select a telling sentence from the "WRITING TO SHOW List of Telling Sentences." SHOW what the sentence can reveal when language that employs concrete nouns and vivid verbs is used.

- Follow the directions outlined for WRITING TO SHOW Assignment #4.

WRITING TO SHOW LIST OF TELLING SENTENCES

She (he) is very old.

It hurts.

It is the most difficult test I've ever taken.

He (she) is nervous.

I am nervous.

The car breaks down.

He (she) slips and falls.

The flower grows.

He (she) thinks he's (she's) cool.

He (she) steals second.

I am embarrassed.

The athlete is exhausted.

The baby is cute.

He got mad.

The jock thinks he's (she's) cool.

He (she) (it) moves quickly.

Lunch period is too short.

The room is vacant.

He (she) has never been so happy as he (she) is now.

She (he) has a good personality.

The party is fun.

He (she) is scared.

The pizza tastes good.

My parents seem angry.

The movie is frightening.

The _____ is a mess.

The _____ is old.

The house is falling down.

The house is haunted.

He is acting crazy.

_____ is strict

_____ is absent-minded.

OTHER WRITING TO SHOW ASSIGNMENTS

Assignment #6: Destroying WRITING TO SHOW

Directions Select one of the WRITING TO SHOW compositions that you have already completed from the exercises on pp. 48–50. Replace the concrete, singular details with plurals, vague words, abstract nouns, and weak verbs. Remove phrases or sentences where you, the writer, have extensively elaborated.

Assignment #7: Practicing extending elaboration (E3)

Directions Extend the elaboration of the following sentences.
1. His bony fingers brush aside the *Time* magazine.
2. Her math textbook rests along the edge of the desk.
3. Mr. McAlfiend's right hand grasps my biology final exam.
4. She reaches into the refrigerator for the gallon of 2% lowfat milk.

Assignment #8: Begin with a SHOWING image! (SH & V)

Directions Improve the following sentences by removing vague details and replacing them with concrete, singular ones; extend the elaboration of each detail by adding additional sentences. SHOW a specific object or action from the original sentence in much more detail.

> Original: A nervous man with a bag walks at night toward his destination.

Revised: A man in black slithers through the shadows along the wall. He caresses the velvet bag filled with gold coins, just to assure himself of its continued existence.

1. As Mark prepares to go home, behind him his classmates make fun of him.
2. The old man is startled.
3. She drops her textbooks and quickly kneels down to gather them up.

Assignment #9: Using vivid verbs ⌒

Directions Remove the following "be" verbs and use vivid verbs in active voice.
1. The face is sweaty now and his mind is screaming.
2. The overwhelming rage she felt 30 seconds ago is now replaced by the vibrations of her lower lip.
3. He has his rifle ready, and there is sweat dripping from his face. (Change "has" as it, too, is a weak verb.)
4. Her behavior was barbaric.
5. The temperature is too hot.

Assignment #10: Removing vague details (V & WC)

Directions The following sentences contain words or phrases that are too general or abstract; work toward singular, concrete, specific detail. Fix, especially, the words or phrases in bold typeface.
1. The roof **has stains** and **has become frail**.
2. The **heavenly aroma** drifts through the kitchen.
3. He **holds** the football **with all his might**.
4. She always **wears a red cap** when she **plays tennis**.
5. Her purse **appears heavy** and **looks like it has seen better days**.

For additional activities and exercises, see www.telemachospublishing.com

3

THE EXPOSITORY PARAGRAPH

DEFINITIONS

The expository paragraph is the building block of an argument, *an argument for a larger paper* or *an argument answering an essay test question*. In a larger paper, each paragraph's function, its connection to the thesis statement, should be clear. Paragraphs can be classified into two general types, according to their function:

• **One-idea paragraph**
In the larger paper, this paragraph begins with a clear topic sentence and elaborates, or develops, a single aspect of the thesis statement. The one-idea paragraph also provides a single unified answer to *an essay test question*.

• **Subordinate paragraph**
This paragraph begins with a topic sentence connected to a preceding paragraph. This paragraph is *an extension of the idea introduced in the previous paragraph* because one plank (or topic) of the thesis statement may need to be demonstrated or proven by more than one paragraph. For example, one may be writing about courageous characters. The initial one-idea body paragraph may define a single characteristic of courage in its topic sentence and then proceed to elaborate that feature of courage by focusing on a single literary character as an example of such courage. The next paragraph, which is the subordinate paragraph, may provide elaboration of a second character, one who also fulfills the specific facet of courage defined in the preceding one-idea paragraph's topic sentence. The subordinate paragraph, therefore, does not introduce a new idea; instead, it introduces a new example to further illustrate the idea in the topic sentence of the initial one-idea paragraph.

ONE-IDEA AND SUBORDINATE PARAGRAPHS: QUALITIES

Paragraphs possess unity, coherence, and style.

UNITY

In a unified paragraph each sentence provides *evidence and analysis* for the idea in the topic sentence. The following editing symbols reflect the strategies that strengthen paragraph unity:

Topic sentence

Editing Symbol

TS

The topic sentence introduces a specific conceptual idea whose focus serves to unify all the sentences that follow it. A writer uses a topic sentence to support an aspect of a thesis statement in a larger paper or to respond to an essay test question. In most cases it is usually the first sentence of a paragraph, which tells the reader the specific topic and any related issues the writer will be discussing in the paragraph. **If the paragraph is part of a larger paper, the topic sentence will include two parts:** *ORGANIZATION METHOD + ASPECT OF THE THESIS STATEMENT.*

In the example below, all the sentences in the paragraph provide support for the main idea in the topic sentence. Keep in mind that this paragraph is simply one body paragraph in a paper whose **thesis statement** is as follows: *In the play Twelve Angry Men, when debating the validity of the old man's testimony, Juror Eight demonstrates the superiority of logos to flawed emotional appeals.*

by Brad Bradshaw

IN *DEFENSE OF THE OLD MAN'S TESTIMONY, THE THIRD JUROR ANGRILY SPEWS SLANDERING EMOTIONAL APPEALS CONTAINING LOGICAL FALLA- CIES.* At first, the third juror accusingly indicts the eighth juror of **trying to "distort" (43) the evidence and calls him "crazy",** (45) an **ad hominem retort angrily attacking** the eighth juror as a person, **instead of explaining** the alleged distortions. **The attacks continue** with derogatory diction, the third juror **slanderously labeling** the eighth juror's demonstration **as "kid stuff"** and **stating hyperbolically that** he has "never seen anything like this in my whole life" (45), emotional words he hopes will make the eighth juror appear ridiculous and silly. Even some of the other jurors fall victim to his opprobrium as **he maligns them as "old ladies"** (47), further ad hominem attacks that provide no logical substance. The third juror moves beyond ad hominem and **ventures into a slippery slope argument.** He **emotionally asserts that "we're letting him [the boy] slip through our fingers here"** (47), implying that they could be releasing a dangerous past murderer into society and that **acquitting the boy will undoubtedly lead to future murders.** This condemning statement, that also **circularly relies on the premise of guilt,** however, fails to prove that the boy is a murderer, but its imagery of **slipping though fingers evokes fear and the fra-**

> The topic sentence focuses on one aspect of the thesis statement, the fallacious "emotional appeals."

> Observe how the highlighted words and phrases in each sentence demonstrate the unity of the paragraph as they provide evidence and analysis for the idea in the topic sentence.

gility of public security, tactics meant to manipulate the jurors into agreement.

For additional examples of unified paragraphs, paragraphs where each sentence supports the idea in the topic sentence by providing evidence and analysis for that idea, see pp. 77 - 87.

[Note: Not all skilled writers place the topic sentence as the first sentence; some place the topic sentence in the middle of the paragraph or near the end; others write paragraphs in which the topic sentence is assumed. These are skills your teacher may address at a later date, or individually, once you master basic foundations of paragraphing. Beginning writers should first practice using the topic sentence as the opening sentence for paragraphs.]

Elaboration

Several methods assist writers in creating sentences that provide *evidence and analysis* for the topic sentence:
- direct quotations from the text *blended with* the writer's analysis of individual words or images that reflect the idea present in the topic sentence,
- paraphrase of details and situations from the text blended with the writer's interpretive perspective,
- additional explanation of an idea, or
- a discussion of a contemporary or literary comparison.

As you proceed through this chapter, you'll come in contact with other strategies for paragraphing, each strategy connected to a symbol. Additional editing symbols that concern how elaboration influences the unity of the paragraph include the following: EV, E1, E2, E3, O1, SH. See Chapter 6.

COHERENCE

A coherent paragraph is one in which the relationship of one sentence to another is apparent to the reader because the writer employs logical and grammatical connections that indicate not only why one sentence follows the next but also how the writer organizes the *evidence and analysis* to support the topic sentence.

The clear presence of such logical ties can be observed in the previous example paragraph from the *Twelve Angry Men* paper. In composing this expository argument, the writer provides language for the reader that binds each sentence together in support of the topic. The opening ten words of the second sentence [*At first, the third juror accusingly indicts the eighth juror*] reveal to the reader that the argument's evidence is being arranged chronologically [*At first*] and that he is elaborating on the third juror's anger—his anger being a central idea in the topic sentence—by stating that the third juror "accusingly indicts" the eighth juror. This language provides the clarity necessary before the writer begins to incorporate textual excerpts from pp.43 and 45 of *Twelve Angry Men*, excerpts the writer incorporates in the remainder of the second sentence.

If the writer had omitted this opening language, those first ten words, and had instead written the following second sentence—*The third juror says that the eighth is trying to "distort"(43) the evidence, and he contends the eighth juror is "crazy"(45).*—the reader would neither understand the organization nor the logic of the writer's thinking. The smooth linkage back to the topic sentence would be missing.

For the purposes of making your argument clear and comprehensible to any reader, it is essential that the writer use specific strategies of coherence—word and logic glue, topic strings, and appropriate transitions—strategies that help the reader follow the evidence and analysis in support of the topic, which in turn helps the reader see the entire expository argument in the way the writer has intended it.

More elaborate discussion of these strategies of coherence will be found on pp. 64 - 71, Drafting Strategies Two, Three, and Four. Additional editing symbols associated with coherence problems include A, B, L, O2, P2, S, T. See Chapter 6.

STYLE

A lucid, compelling writing style is a style that includes variety in sentence structure and syntax as well as diction that is precise and appropriate to the occasion. See Chapter 5 for exercises involving sentence structure and syntax.

COMPARING A FIRST DRAFT TO THE REVISED DRAFT OF A SAMPLE EXPOSITORY BODY PARAGRAPH

The following expository paragraphs—the first an early draft, the latter the revised final draft—are from a paper that makes an argument concerning George Orwell's novel *1984*. They demonstrate a number of choices by the writer regarding sentence structure and syntax. The paragraphs contain sentences that are simple, compound, complex, and compound-complex. Some sentences begin with the subject and verb and others begin with introductory phrases or introductory clauses. Sentences vary in length, anywhere from as few as ten words to as many as fifty words. Quite a few contain parallel components. Throughout the paragraphs a reader will find both present and past participial phrases, adjective and adverb subordinate clauses, as well as repeat-word and analysis modifiers.

The diction reflects an apt combination of word choices that are both concrete (diary, kitchen, telescreen, Proles, glass paperweight, severed hand) and abstract (solitary resistance, rebellion, depraved, psychological).

The original paragraph, once it has been revised to incorporate more concrete evidence, has become two paragraphs, the second paragraph an example of the **subordinate paragraph** that expands upon the topic sentence introduced in a preceding paragraph. In addition, the last section of the original paragraph, which currently appears in brackets, was omitted because it moved outside the original topic sentence, violating the principle of unity.

The revised paragraph is annotated to emphasize its **Unity**, the evidence and analysis in each sentence clearly supporting the idea in the topic sentence.

Original version of body paragraph for *1984* paper   *by Robert Uhl*

Early in the novel, Winston Smith's resistance comes in the form of a private rebellion, both psychological and physical. Winston's isolated rebellion first occurs in his room sitting in a small niche out of sight of the Party's invasive telescreens. His physical placement signals a small act of defiance, one forbidden by the party, for citizens should be visually in sight of Big Brother at all movements. His location, perhaps more importantly, provides the space for his psychological resistance, the writing in a diary, his documentation of treasonous thoughts within his mind, his a wish to be alone, an act forbidden by the Party. There he writes a diary, a psychological portrayal of solitary resistance, a reflection of his condemnatory views on the Party's corruption of individual freedom. His physical choice to write manifests his rebellious thoughts, in fact, makes his psychological reflections explicit, a gesture of individual expression certainly punishable by death or at least an extreme prison sentence. These thoughts underscore gestures the Party hopes to destroy: free thinking, a disregard of the Party's totalitarian rule, repudiation of the Party's words. Winston's inscribed thoughts on paper that all hope for change and rebellion lies in the Proles leads to his physical rebellion. Deciding to again defy the government, he succumbs to his flitting will for a trip to the Prole neighborhood, a trip where the omniscient Party could follow his route to and from work. Already at risk for entering forbidden territory, Winston recognizes that his transgression could lead to an interrogation by a Party expecting compliance with all laws. [Both physical and psychological resistance occur in Winston's last stand as he lies helpless and defeated in the Ministry of Love, alone yet continuing to revolt. As Smith is tortured, he resists a test where O'Brien demands he should see five fingers held up when only four appear. Although in excruciating pain, he firmly maintains his position against the Party that four fingers and not five appear until he becomes so disoriented he physically cannot see the fingers. Finally beaten and unaided, Winston resolves to fight until the point at which he can fight no longer, a characteristic illustrating the extent to which Winston abhors the Party and willingly sacrifices himself to bring about its demise.]

Revised version of body paragraph for *1984* paper   *by Robert Uhl*

Early in the novel, Winston Smith's resistance comes in the form of a private rebellion, both psychological and physical. Winston's isolated rebellion first occurs in his room, sitting in a small niche

> The second and third sentences of the original version have been combined. The beginning of the original's third sentence [His physical placement signals a small act of defiance] has been turned into a three-word analysis modifier [a physical defiance].

out of sight of the Party's invasive telescreens, **a physical defiance,** one forbidden by the party, for citizens should be visually in sight of Big Brother at all movements. **His location,** in the alcove of his kitchen, provides the space for his psychological resistance, the writing in a diary, his documentation of treasonous and forbidden thoughts condemning the Party's tyranny. Physically choosing to make his illicit

> While the new second sentence focuses on Winston's physical rebellion, "sitting...out of sight," the words that begin the third sentence—"His location"—point back to the "physical defiance" mentioned In the previous sentence so as to introduce the reader to "his psychological resistance, the writing in a diary." Since writing is both a physical and a mental activity, the diction incorporates both concepts: to make his thoughts explicit, he has to "physically choose" to write them down, thus his thoughts become "written musings" and "written transgressions."

thoughts explicit, Winston first reflects upon attending a violent movie the previous evening, his memory of the lower class Proles objecting to the macabre film, a reflection leading to his recognition that the Party cares little for the welfare of these citizens. These **written musings** lead him to understand the manipulative function of the Two Minutes Hate, recognizing how the images of Goldstein critiquing Big Brother produces the emotional frenzy of party members, unified in their hatred toward Goldstein and in their commitment to the Party. The result of **his cognitive violation** manifests in more **written transgressions,** Winston's penning multiple times the phrase "Down with Big Brother," **tangible proof of his willful defiance** against the party's restrictions on psychological freedom. And even if Winston destroys this illicit evidence, he recognizes that his crime has already been committed, for the Thought Police need no physical evidence, for they know his inner thoughts, for a bullet will eventually be fired in the back of his head.

Winston's **inscribed thoughts regarding the Proles, that hope resides in their potential uprising, leads to another physical and psychological rebellion.** He decides defiantly to turn away from his bus-stop and drift through the streets of London, committing an act of OWNLIFE, an illegal gesture of individualism and eccentricity. The initial depraved visual images of his walk—decrepit buildings, filthy water, deformed bodies of the elderly, dissonant screams, a severed human hand on the pavement— provide **a tangible reminder** to Winston of the deceptions regarding the alleged higher standards of living achieved by Big Brother as opposed to the iniquities of capitalism. As he continues his illicit journey, **Winston enters a pub,** following an eighty year-old man in hopes of hearing tales of the pre-Revolution days. While his entrance into the pub and subsequent interactions with Proles places Winston at risk for Thought Police interrogation, his probing for the truth about the past, a

In the orginal version, the writer repeats the idea that Winston writes in a diary and states repeatedly that what Winston writes is what he thinks: "a reflection of his condemnatory views," "rebellious thoughts," "psychlogical reflections," "a gesture of individual expression." What the writer has not done in the original version is make concrete what those thoughts are. This weakness the writer rectifies in the revision when he details the reaction of those attending the "violent movie" and the audience's subsequent involvement in the Two Minute Hate. In this revision we see specific words that Winston has written in his diary— "Down with Big Brother"—the lack of which in the original underscores its need for serious revision.

The revision introduces an additional paragraph, a SUBORDINATE PARAGRAPH that continues the topic of psychological and physical resistance. The first sentence of the subordinate paragraph connects the reader back to one of the concrete details from the previous paragraph, the "lower class Proles," who had objected to the violent movie to which they had been subjected. His thoughts about "their potential uprising" inspire him to take a physical journey through the streets where they live, such a journey being both a physical act of rebellion as well as a psychological one, for he is acting as though his life is his own. Observe, too, that this first sentence in the subordinate paragraph does not introduce a new idea (or topic). Instead, it extends the idea stated in the topic sentence of the previous paragraph. Where the act of writing in the previous paragraph is fully elaborated to show how it is both a physical and mental act of revolt, in the subordinate paragraph, the journey also becomes "another physical and psychological rebellion."

past knowledge intended to expose the contradiction of the Party's revised history texts is more blatantly transgressive, particularly his explicit questioning of the elderly man, asking him whether he is more free under Big Brother than under capitalism. Though Winston's interrogation proves futile, he persists in asserting a forbidden freedom, continually risking an interaction with the Thought Police at each turn. **His pursuit of history continues at the junk-shop where he bought his diary.** There he feloniously chooses to make another purchase, a glass paperweight, an object of beauty from the days prior to Big Brother. His psychological risk intensifies as he entertains additional crimes, pondering the possibility of renting Mr. Charrington's upstairs room, a space free of a telescreen, a space harkening to a world free of Big Brother, a world of personal freedom, marked by books, an inviting fireplace, a warm bed—distinct pleasures outlawed by the Party. Winston's decisions at the junk shop reflect both his physical and psychological willingness to violate the Party's admonitions against freedom.

> The writer's sentences regarding this journey combine the physical trip with the mental activity his observations generate. What he sees becomes a "tangible reminder," diction that relates to both the physical and the psychological. His wanderings take him to various physical locations—a pub, a junk-shop—the physical act of entering these locations and engaging in conversations there engendering psychological acts of rebellion.

Additional editing symbols connected to style include the following—B, C, G, V, W, WC, X, []. See Chapter 6.

· ·
THE WRITING PROCESS: THE BODY PARAGRAPH
· ·

STEPS IN CONSTRUCTING THE PARAGRAPH

Step One: Create the topic sentence.

Write the topic sentence in response to a test question or in support of a thesis.

Step Two: Gather evidence supporting the topic sentence.

Gather evidence that includes specific details (concrete showing details in the literary text) the writer may include in the paragraph. Make sure the evidence proves, or supports, the topic sentence. After evidence-gathering, the topic sentence may need revision.

Consider the following questions, *among others*, when searching for evidence:
- Where does the evidence occur in the plot or poem?
- What actions of a character support the topic? When do these actions occur? Why do they occur?
- What words or images reflect and are associated with the concept in the topic sentence?

- What does a character say that supports the topic? When does the character say it? Why is it said?
- What is revealed by the narrator that provides supporting evidence?
- What words or images reflect, or are associated with, the concept in the topic sentence?

Then, write out key passages that relate to your topic sentence.

Step Three: Apply four strategies for drafting paragraph.

DRAFTING STRATEGY ONE: ORGANIZE THE EVIDENCE.

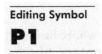

When writers gather concrete details to support a topic sentence, they must decide how to arrange the evidence. Clearly arranging the evidence assists the reader in understanding the writer's argument. What follows are *three* common ways of organizing evidence.

Once a writer chooses an organizational strategy, he then selects words associated with that strategy.

Organizing Method One: TIME

Organize according to *chronology*—the order of the narrative's plot, for instance, or of major details in the poem. When organizing by **Time**, the writer may include a variety of transitional words that assist the reader in following the sequence of events. Such words include FIRST, SECOND, NEXT, LATER, AFTER, AFTERWARD, AT FIRST, AS, BEFORE, FINALLY, IMMEDIATELY, NOW, PREVIOUSLY, SOON, THEN.

Topic: The Sonnet Form and the Mind   *by Frank McEachern*

The sonnet form allows the poet to express man's ability to change. Limited to only fourteen lines, the poem's brevity lends itself to expressing the quickness with which man moves in his thoughts. In "On His Being Arrived to the Age of Twenty-three," the author demonstrates the narrator's quick turnaround. **At first,** the man feels cheated by time: "Stolen on his wing my three and twentieth year" (2), **while** "no bud or blossom show'th"(4). Also, individual words like "thief" and "stolen" are utilized to further demonstrate the narrator's despondency with his life. **Then,** the **last six lines** show the narrator's change as he overcomes his despondency. **Here**, he realizes that the world is a fair one in which time "shall be still in strictest measure" (10). **Next,** he analyzes his limited accomplishments, realizing that his success, "however mean or high" (11), is part of a larger plan and that he should be grateful for what he has, "so that I have the grace to use it so"(13). Therefore, as the man's thoughts change in limited time, the form is an effective tool in demonstrating the rapid change of thought in man.

Organizing Method Two: PLACE

When a writer organizes by **Place**, the writer uses diction indicating location or setting. Additionally, the writer may employ transitional words that assist the reader: ABOVE, AHEAD, AMONG, BEYOND, DOWN, ELSEWHERE, FARTHER, HERE, IN FRONT OF, IN THE BACKGROUND, NEAR, NEARBY, NEXT TO, THERE.

Topic: Joe Gargery as Active Servant of Community in *Great Expectations*

Pip's surrogate father, Joe, frequently safeguards Pip when he is in desperate need, demonstrating throughout the story that a servant must be an active participant in restoring community. In the opening **kitchen** scene, for example, "gentle" Joe guards a young Pip "with his great leg" (14; ch. 2) from an enraged Mrs. Joe and her tickler. Here he actively attempts to shield Pip from being raised "by hand." In fact, Joe tells Pip he "wish there warn't no" (43; ch. 7) beatings for him. Later, at the **Christmas dinner,** Joe again alleviates the attacks on Pip from the holiday guests, who torment him and compare him to "swine." With each insult, Joe gives Pip "more gravy," demonstrating that small gestures can help ease the grief of individuals and move the community closer toward love. Finally, **in London,** Joe helps Pip convalesce after his illness. Joe has chosen to leave the forge, his means of employment, to serve Pip, who eventually recognizes the pain he has caused both Joe and Biddy. Moreover, Pip sees Joe as the true "gentle man," the servant who has helped him become a more loving member of the community.

Organizing Method Three: IDEA DIVIDED INTO ITS SPECIFIC COMPONENTS

Organize according to the **Idea** introduced in the topic sentence, an idea subdivided in the topic sentence into its various parts. The idea may feature a definition, an analogy, a comparison/contrast, a classification, or a cause and effect that the writer will apply to the text.

Cause and Effect

Topic: Madame Defarge's Hunger for Revenge   *by Zachary Kettler*

As one who refuses to be "recalled to life," Madame Defarge allows her desire for revenge to consume her memories of the past, her present life, and her future aspirations. Her brother killed by a member of the Evremonde family, Madame Defarge **dedicates her life to the eradication** of every member of the Evremonde family, including Darnay; in fact, "It [is] nothing to her, that an innocent man [is] to die for the sins of his forefathers. She [sees], not him, but them" (281; ch.14). Seeking her revenge with **anger ascending all boundaries of moral justice,** Madame Defarge tells her husband that he can "tell the Wind and Fire where to stop...but don't tell [her]" (264; ch.12). In the end, **her desire for ultimate revenge results in her own death**—killed ironically by her own pistol. In the same manner as her brother, who is killed in the pursuit of retribution, Madame Defarge dies in **her pursuit of the extermination of Darnay's family,** her obsessive revenge paling in the presence of Miss Pross's love. Killed by Miss Pross and the "vigorous tenacity of love, always so much stronger than hate" (286; ch.14), Madame Defarge forfeits her recall to life because of her odious pursuit of retribution, a pursuit of retribution by iniquitous means leading only to a nefarious end.

Definition

Topic: The Knight's Qualities in *The Canterbury Tales*

Chaucer depicts the knight as a virtuous pilgrim, a person who fights for the

Church, rejects extravagance in exchange for humility, and treats those around him with respect. **Respecting others** means refraining from insults, a habit many others indulge. The Knight, however, "never yet a boorish thing had said / In all his life to any, come what might" (68–69). It is **this courtesy** that people from other countries recognize and revere: "He often sat at table in the chair / Of honour, above all nations, when in Prussia" (50–51). The Knight's respect is juxtaposed with **his humility,** his lack of desire to flaunt wealth extravagantly: "He possessed / Fine horses, but he was not gaily dressed" (71). In fact, not only does he avoid "fine" clothes, but he does not care about trivial aspects of his appearance, arriving at the pilgrimage "with smudges where his armour had left marks" (73). This pilgrimage ranks higher than any worldly concern. For the Knight is most concerned with his **spiritual commitment,** his obligation to the Church. He takes this duty seriously, having "done nobly in his sovereign's war / And ridden into battle" (45–46). Chaucer tells us how often the Knight has **battled successfully:** "In fifteen mortal battles he had been / And jousted for our faith at Tramissene" (60–61). Indeed, these battles, as well as his appearance and behavior toward others, earn the knight Chaucer's praise as "a most distinguished man" (70).

Analogy

Topic: Characters and the Imagery of Birds in *Romeo and Juliet*   by Ryan Wallis

Shakespeare's ingenious utilization of bird imagery creates lucid pictures of man's physical and emotional qualities. The importance of **physical appearance** quickly becomes apparent as we observe people being judged based upon their beauty or their lack of it. Soon after we learn that the maiden Rosaline will not reciprocate Romeo's love, we witness Benvolio, Romeo's companion, encouraging him to attend a party held by the Capulets, enemies of Romeo's family. Benvolio assures Romeo that **Rosaline will resemble a crow instead of a swan** when compared to "all the admired beauties of Verona" (1.2.86). Shakespeare's clever choice of a **repulsive crow** invents a vision of ugliness that contrasts with the **pulchritude of a swan.** Romeo, however, denies that he could ever see Rosaline as anything but the most **beautiful maiden.** Having heard Romeo's declaration of undying love, we find it surprising and a bit amusing when a fickle **Romeo views Juliet at the party and claims she is "a snowy dove trooping with crows"** (1.5.49). Selecting a **snowy dove** to portray Juliet elicits notions of pure and elegant beauty; we can just imagine her niveous complexion. Since Rosaline is now **among the maidens whom Romeo considers crows,** his adamantine vow to forever declare her lovely is broken. Indeed, he now thinks of her as **an unsightly, vexatious bird.** Later, when Friar Lawrence learns of Romeo's new love, he scolds Romeo and other young men for having love that "lies not truly in their hearts, but in their eyes" (2.3.67–68). Friar Lawrence, having lived long and learned much, considers Romeo weak since his change of heart seems to be based on Juliet's **outward appearance** rather than her inner beauty. Likewise, even in today's world, it is true that many people esteem physical attractiveness above strength of character. In addition to the artistic use of the dove and the crow to contrast the beauty and the ugliness of women, Shakespeare employs bird imagery to describe the physical attractiveness of men. Characterized by Juliet's nurse as "a lovely gentleman"

(3.5.220) and having **greener, quicker, and fairer eyes than an eagle, Paris** is chosen by Lord Capulet, Juliet's father, to marry his daughter. Selecting an eagle to demonstrate the physical attributes of Paris proves successful. Undoubtedly, his eyes attract the attention of women because of their **stunning appeal.** The **eagle,** having keen sight above all birds, is a symbol of powerful beauty; Paris, having eyes more astounding than an eagle, portrays an even more exquisite image.

Classification

Topic: The Infernal Marriage in *Great Expectations*   *by Max Rosenblum*

When the story opens, the reader encounters the first marriage, Joe and Mrs. Joe, a disconsolate marriage symbolizing the infernal level of comedy where truth and innocence are preyed upon. In this case, the **cruel Mrs. Joe,** who "takes [Joe] by the two whiskers, [and][knocks[s] his head for a little while against the wall behind him" (9; ch.2), **constantly dispenses blows, both physical and verbal,** to the **honest and innocent Joe,** "a mild, good-natured, sweet-tempered, easy going, foolish, dear fellow" (6; ch.2), belittling him when she complains of being "a blacksmith's wife, and (what's the same thing), a slave with her apron never off" (19; ch.3). **Mrs. Joe exhibits the selfishness** frequently found in the infernal comedy, declaring to Joe and Pip what "a precious pair [they'd] make without [her]," a statement that clearly displays her feelings of self-importance. In an extreme display of selfishness, she dresses Pip up to go off to Miss Havisham's, reminding that "he better go play there…or [she'll] make him work" (46; ch.7) and how beneficial this opportunity will be not for Pip, but "for us" (47; ch.7)— **not** exactly words of a **selfless,** nurturing mother. Even Pip shows confusion regarding Mrs. Joe's motives because he does not know "why on earth [he] was going to play at Miss Havisham's or what on earth [he] was expected to play at" (48; ch.7). Finally, **Mrs. Joe demonstrates hypocrisy,** the last mark of infernal comedy, when she hosts the Christmas party for all of her pseudo higher class acquaintances. Pip points out this quality of insincerity when he describes his sister as "unusually lively on the present occasion, and indeed…generally more gracious in the society of Mrs. Hubble than in other company" (22; ch.3).

Comparison / Contrast

Topic: Mr. Stryver vs. Sydney Carton in *A Tale of Two Cities*   *by Jeff Erfe*

The reader first meets Stryver and Carton at the first trial of Charles Darnay in the Old Bailey, an encounter in which Dickens juxtaposes both characters, revealing their true natures and opening them up for comparison. Dickens initially introduces the man with no first name, a man known simply in the business context as **Mr. Stryver, the greedy opportunist** who constantly strives to edge out the competition and climb the ladder of capitalistic success. Simultaneously funny yet disturbing, Dickens notes how Stryver has "a pushing way of shouldering himself (morally and physically) into companies and conversa-tions" (60; bk. 2, ch. 4), and the reader witnesses this firsthand as **Stryver "shoulders" poor Mr. Lorry out of the group so he can boast** his success at acquitting Darnay. When the bloated Stryver finally leaves, in skulks Sydney

Carton, and the reader is presented with glaring **contrasts** that highlight **Carton's pitiable desperation** and Stryver's worldly "success." As in his own business ventures, Carton does not "shoulder" out others from the group, but instead coolly leans "against the wall" (61; bk. 2, ch. 4) **outside the circle** "where its shadow [is] darkest" (61; bk. 2, ch. 4). Obviously, Carton represents Stryver's polar opposite: whereas Stryver jumps at the opportunity to praise himself and receive adulation, Carton **sits in the corner** and no one makes "any acknowledgement of [his] part in the day's proceedings" (60; bk. 2, ch. 4). Furthermore, he **contrasts** Stryver's previous bombastic assertions by admitting that he has "no business" (60; bk. 2, ch. 4), at least not in comparison with the great Mr. Lorry. By the end of the chapter, he has established himself as a **drunk, self-deprecating loser** for whom "no man cares" (63; bk. 2, ch. 4), the perfect **antithesis** for the haughty and unscrupulous Stryver.

DRAFTING STRATEGY TWO: ADD NECESSARY TRANSITIONS.

A1 = A transition is needed to clarify the direction of paragraph.

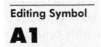

Editing Symbol

A1

After the initial topic sentence, further clarify and identify the path the paragraph intends to take, that is, the organization of material: time, place, idea.

Original
Through examples in gesture and conversation, Dickens depicts Scrooge as miserly, stubborn, and pessimistic. For example, he keeps his door "open so that he might keep an eye upon his clerk" (13; ch. 1).

Revision with transitional sentence added
Through examples in gesture and conversation, Dickens depicts Scrooge as miserly, stubborn, and pessimistic. **Scrooge displays his miserliness in his treatment of his employee.** For example, he keeps his door "open so that he might keep an eye upon his clerk," (13; ch. 1) an eye always alert to anyone, including his clerk freezing by the dying embers of the fire, who might be tempted to replenish the fire with an extra log or two.

Original
Dickens reveals Scrooge's rudeness and anger. For instance, approached by his nephew who wishes him "A Merry Christmas, Uncle," Scrooge rudely sputters out "Bah! Humbug!"—his temper numbing the seasonal joy.

Revision with transitional phrases and clauses added
Dickens reveals Scrooge's rudeness and anger **towards the people around him, particularly his nephew and employee, Bob Cratchit. Such an attitude is reflected in his words and actions.** For instance, approached by his nephew who wishes him "A Merry Christmas, Uncle," Scrooge rudely sputters out "Bah! Humbug!"—his temper numbing the seasonal joy.

A2 = A transition is needed to further define the general idea in the topic sentence.

Editing Symbol

A2

Add a phrase or clause to the end of the topic sentence to further define a general word appearing in the topic sentence. Then apply definition to the text.

Original

The Christmas dinner scene at Bob Cratchit's that Scrooge observes depicts the ideal family. Mrs. Cratchit is dressed in "ribbons, which are cheap and make a goodly show for sixpence" (77; ch.1).

Revision with transitional phrases and clauses added

The Christmas dinner scene at Bob Cratchit's that Scrooge observes depicts the ideal family, **a family that celebrates despite ill fortune, that encourages all its members to share in responsibility, that practices acts of selflessness.** For example, **despite their poverty,** Mrs. Cratchit is dressed in "ribbons, which are cheap and make a goodly show for sixpence" (77; ch.1), **for she is able to express joy and celebration within their economic means.**

Original

Donne uses metaphors to remind us of man's communal nature. He compares the church to one body. He needs the church, "whereof [he is] a member" (10), as a form of support, just as the head, "ingrafted into that body" (10), needs the help of the body, the larger group or structure that provides life. He compares man to a book, demonstrating that they are both "of one author" and that man naturally belongs to a community as a book belongs to a "volume."

Revision with transitional phrases and words added

Donne uses metaphors to remind us of man's communal nature, **metaphors that reveal man's need to belong to a larger group. First,** the poet compares the church to one body. He needs the church, "whereof [he is] a member" (10), as a form of support, just as the head, "ingrafted into that body" (10), needs the help of the body, the larger group or structure that provides life. **Next,** Donne compares man to a book, demonstrating that they are both "of one author" and that man naturally belongs to a community as a book belongs to a "volume."

A3 = Add a phrase to the beginning of the sentence after the topic sentence that indicates how you plan to organize the evidence.

Editing Symbol

A3

The way you begin the sentence immediately following the topic sentence ought to indicate to the reader how you are organizing this paragraph.

Original

Early in the novel, Winston Smith's resistance comes in the form of a private rebellion, both psychological and physical. Winston begins writing in his diary, recording his disdain for Big Brother.

Revised

Early in the novel, Winston Smith's resistance comes in the form of a private rebellion, both psychological and physical. **Winston's physical, isolated rebellion first occurs** when he finds himself in his room sitting in a small niche out of sight from the party's watchful telescreens.

Original

Poe's "To Helen" treats Helen with warm adoration. Poe uses the iambic tetrameter throughout the poem.

Revised

Poe's "To Helen" treats Helen with warm adoration. **This ardor manifests itself in the poem's very first stanza**, wherein Poe's speaker adopts the iambic tetrameter used throughtout the poem.

Exercise: *Adding Necessary Transitions*

Directions Create and insert a separate transitional sentence between the topic sentence and the sentence that currently follows it, or add a transitional clause or phrase to the beginning of the sentence that follows the topic sentence, or add a transitional clause or phrase to the end of the topic sentence.

1. Mark is an ideal father. Last night, his eyes often drooping, he stayed up past midnight working with his daughter on a science project.

2. The public library contains reading material for every interest. A copy of *Sports Illustrated* rests on the cushioned chairs next to the magazine racks.

3. My mother demanded that I organize the mess on my desk. A petrified slice of half-eaten pizza lay atop the essay for English class I never turned in.

DRAFTING STRATEGY THREE: *Maintain the topic string.*

Within a paragraph, a writer's sentences must stay focused on the topic—the central idea—that appears in the paragraph's topic sentence. When the writer crafts a sentence that does not flow from the paragraph's stated or implied topic, such a change—or shift in topic—is likely to confuse the reader. *To prevent this shift in topic*, craft the paragraph's supporting sentences so that whatever appears at the beginning of each supporting sentence maintains the reader's focus on the paragraph's central idea. Regardless of the type of sentence opening, the focus of that part of each sentence *ought to act as a tie, or connection, to the paragraph's topic, such connections being known as the* TOPIC STRING.

To create a strong topic string, the writer uses a number of methods. Sometimes the KEY WORD OR WORDS FROM THE TOPIC ARE REPEATED. Other connecting possibilities includes SYNONYMS AND PRONOUNS FOR THE TOPIC'S KEY WORDS. Since serious writers of expository prose vary the beginnings of their sentences, they strive to avoid monotony. These writers understand that sentences do not have to start with the subject, that quite often their sentences will open with an INTRODUCTORY PHRASE OR AN INTRODUCTORY SUBORDINATE CLAUSE.

Original: The topic string breaks because the writer shifts topic focus.

In _Lord of the Flies_, **Jack's proud nature** leads to the destruction of order and authority on the island. **The conflagration, representing the boys' only hope** to leave the island, burns out due to his lack of supervision, a careless decision that commences the power struggle with Ralph. **Ralph is the elected chief** on the island and he complains about Jack hunting, even though Jack says that "we needed meat" (65; ch. 4), an action defying Ralph's authority and showing that Jack believes he knows what is best for the boys. **Later at that night's assembly, the boys** are disorderly and Ralph attempts to gain control. **He even shouts at Jack,** "You're breaking the rules!" (84; ch. 5) to which Jack responds, "Who cares?" (84; ch. 5) clearly showing his apathy towards Ralph's power and his arrogance believing that he made the right decision.

Revision that maintains the topic string

In _Lord of the Flies_, **Jack's proud nature** leads to the destruction of order and authority on the island. **Jack's pride** first manifests itself when the conflagration, representing the boys' only hope to leave the island, burns out due to his lack of supervision, a careless decision that commences the power struggle with Ralph. **In explaining his course of action, Jack** tells Ralph that "we needed meat" (65; ch. 5), an action defying Ralph's authority and showing that Jack believes he knows what is best for the boys. In response to **Jack's continued rebellion,** Ralph, at a nightly assembly, shouts at Jack, "You're breaking the rules!" (84; ch. 5) to which Jack responds, "Who cares?" (84; ch. 5) clearly showing his apathy towards Ralph's power and **his arrogance** as he believes that he made the right decision.

Exercise: Maintaining the Topic String

Directions In the following paragraph, what begins each supporting sentence shifts the focus away from the topic as stated in the topic sentence. Rewrite each supporting sentence so that its beginning creates a distinct tie to the topic.

Scrooge is an inexorably bitter and greedy man, bitter in his attitude towards the holiday season, and greedy in his refusal to share any of his wealth with people less fortunate. **In the beginning, his nephew** wishes him a Merry Christmas but Scrooge's only reply is "Bah! Humbug!" Money is more of a concern than responding to the kindness of his nephew. **Dickens further shows** Scrooge's cupidity with the cynical questions he later asks his nephew: "What right do you have to be merry? What reason do you have to be merry? You are poor enough" (13; ch. 1). **Christmas is a time to be concerned** with others and their needs rather than one's own needs, a point Scrooge completely disregards even though his nephew attempts to explain the holiday "as a good time; a kind, forgiving, charitable, pleasant time" (15; ch. 1).

DRAFTING STRATEGY FOUR: USE WORD GLUE AND LOGIC GLUE FOR COHERENCE.

Editing Symbol

T1

Word glue and logic glue act as transitions necessary to provide coherence for a paragraph. These transitions from one sentence to another help the reader understand how each sentence supports the topic.

• Word Glue

Word glue is the actual wording a writer uses to tie, or blend, two sentences together so that the reader understands the writer's thinking process. Key words—including their synonyms—and pronouns can act as word glue, as can a large number of traditional transitional words and phrases.

Key words Literal and synonymous repetitions of words in one sentence that refer to an idea from a previous sentence

Pronouns Words such as *it, he, she, they, those, these, this, that* used to refer to nouns in previous sentences

Traditional transitional words (see page 71 for a more extensive list)

for example	furthermore	in addition	therefore
to illustrate	moreover	likewise	consequently
next	later	finally	that is
as a result	even though	for this reason	first, second, etc.

• Logic Glue

Logic glue represents the relationship between two sentences. This relationship is IMPLIED, rather than stated with transitional words. When a subsequent sentence, for instance, continues the same idea of the previous sentence by adding new facts to elaborate that idea, then the IMPLIED logical relationship is an "and" relationship. If a subsequent sentences illustrates the effect that is caused by the idea in the previous sentence, then the IMPLIED logical relationship is a "therefore" relationship.

Although these words—or synonyms for them—will not appear between the sentences, the reader recognizes that they represent the implied logical relationship between them. The following is a list of the types of implied logical relationships that occur between sentences.

and..................continues the same idea with new facts
but/yet.............a change in the idea of the previous sentence
or.....................an alternative for what is stated in the earlier sentence
that is..............a definition or restatement of the idea in the earlier sentence
for example.....an illustration of the idea in the earlier sentence
therefore..........a conclusion or effect based on the earlier sentence
for....................a reason or cause for what is stated in the earlier sentence

Sample paragraph examining the function of coherent language

Each sentence of the paragraph is numbered; the two columns to the right refer to the sentences by their numbers.	**Word Glue** Actual words linking sentences	**Logic Glue** Implied relationship linking sentences
1. Many of us in our competitive society, which emphasizes material success, do not take *personal risks*.	1–2 personal risks	1–2 and
2. We often view *personal risks* as taking too much *time*.		
3. *For example*, some of us would find stopping in the middle of the day to discuss a friend's problem too time-consuming.	2–3 time/for example	2–3 for example
4. We feel *these moments* could be spent acquiring additional *assets*, real estate investments, or stocks.	3–4 time/these moments	3–4 and
5. For many of us, acquiring *this wealth* is an impetuous goal, for we do not often view risk-taking as a lucrative *investment*.	4–5 assets/wealth	4–5 and
6. Unfortunately, our "lucrative *investments*" that monopolize motivations will continue to prevent risk-taking and personal growth.	5–6 investment/ investments	5–6 therefore

Exercise: Working with transitional word glue and logic glue

Directions Place in the blanks the word glue and logic glue that binds each set of two sentences together.

Word Glue / Logic Glue

1. Chaucer not only reveals violations of religious vows, but also violations of basic Christian theology.

2. One such character who flagrantly violates both his religious vows as well as Christian theology is the Friar.

    1–2   <u>violations</u> / <u>for example</u>

3. The elitist Friar deems himself "better than lepers, beggars and that crew" (230), and, in fact, refuses to deal with such "scum."

    2–3   _____ / _____

4. His refusal of service openly contradicts the most basic teachings of Jesus—to love thy neighbor as thyself and to love unconditionally.

    3–4   _____ / _____

5. The Friar loves only those who have money to give, for he knows "nothing good can come of commerce / with such slum-and-gutter dwellers" (239–240).

    4–5   _____ / _____

6. In fact, money dominates the life of the beggar Friar, an open violation of his vow of poverty.

    5–6   _____ / _____

7. The Friar, however, is seemingly ignorant of his vows as a clergyman, particularly those of poverty and chastity: "He kept his tippet stuffed with pins for curls, / and pocket-knives, to give to pretty girls" (230–231).

    6–7   _____ / _____

8. Not unlike the Friar, the Monk, too, openly violates his vow of poverty as a direct result of his affinity towards the material world.

    7–8   _____ / _____

More transitional words

- **Time** after, afterward, at first, as, before, finally, immediately, later, next, now, previously, soon, then, while, subsequently, meanwhile, thereafter, hitherto, heretofore, prior to, preceding
- **Place** above, ahead, among, beyond, down, elsewhere, farther, here, in front of, in the background, near, nearby, next to, there, adjacent to, by the side of
- **Idea** first, second, third, similarly, as, in the same way, for instance, likewise, however, one, two, three
- **Extending elaboration by**

comparing	as, at the same time, by comparison, compared with, equally, in the same manner, like, likewise, similarly, the same as, correspondingly
contrasting	although, and yet, as, as if, as though, at the same time, but, by (in) contrast, conversely, different from, even so, unlike, even though, however, in spite of, instead of, neither, nevertheless, on the one hand, on the other hand, otherwise, provided that, though, unfortunately, whereas, while, yet
emphasizing/clarifying	especially, for instance, in fact, indeed, that is, in other words, expressly, particularly, primarily
adding another example	moreover, most important, now, so, to repeat, additionally, again, also, too, especially, in addition, in fact, last, again, also, besides, equally important, furthermore, related to this, similarly, in contrast

EXAMPLE PROCESS ONE FOR CONSTRUCTING A PARAGRAPH

RESPONDING TO AN ESSAY QUESTION

Essay Question

What is revealed in the opening dialogue of *A Christmas Carol*?

Step One

Write the topic sentence/ answer the essay question.

> In the opening dialogue of *A Christmas Carol*, Dickens creates Scrooge's shallow personality by the repetition of diction associated with money.

Step Two

Gathering evidence.
- "You're poor enough" (13; ch. 1).
- "What's Christmas time to you but a time for paying bills without money; a time for finding yourself a year older…not an hour richer" (14; ch. 1).
- "at the ominous word 'liberality,' Scrooge frowned, and shook his head" (17; ch. 1).
- "I can't afford to make idle people merry…they cost enough" (19; ch. 1).
- "If I was to stop half-a-crown for it, you'd think yourself ill-used…and yet you don't think me ill-used, when I pay a day's wages for no work" (21; ch. 1).

Step Three

Organization method.
TIME: The writer follows the chronology of events in the story.

Step Four

Write the paragraph.

> In the opening dialogue of *A Christmas Carol*, Dickens creates Scrooge's shallow personality by the repetition of diction associated with money. ***Almost every comment Scrooge makes includes economic diction.*** For example, when Scrooge's nephew **first arrives** to greet him a "Merry Christmas," Scrooge disdainfully comments about his nephew's monetary status: "You're poor enough" (13; ch.1), a statement that shows how Scrooge

> Note the transitional sentence bridging the topic sentence to the first supporting detail.

> evaluates individuals by their monetary value. His nephew ignores Scrooge's remark and urges his uncle to enjoy the season. Scrooge instead sees Christmas in terms of money: "What's Christmas time to you but a time for paying bills without money; a time for finding yourself a year older, and not an hour richer" (14; ch.1). Unable to see the holiday as an opportunity for building relationships, Scrooge even disregards his nephew's new strategy of speaking with the diction of economy, stating that "I have not profited" from Christmas. Moreover, when his nephew exclaims, perhaps because he feels his uncle might be suspicious of possible monetary desire, that "I want nothing from you; I ask nothing of

you" (14; ch.1), Scrooge **ends the conversation abruptly,** indicating that since his nephew has expressed no financial motives, there exists no other reason to hold a conversation with him. This language of economy continues when **a few minutes later** two gentlemen arrive to solicit donations for the poor. Scrooge even reacts physically to the notion of parting with his money; the narrator explains that "at the ominous word 'liberality,' Scrooge frowned, and shook his head" (17; ch.1). **Later in the conversation,** he laments that "I can't afford to make idle people merry... they cost enough" (19; ch.1). Therefore, his contribution is "nothing" (18; ch.1). **Finally, Scrooge's conversation with Bob Cratchit,** his clerk, revolves around money. Scrooge moans that Bob will "want all day tomorrow, I suppose?" (21; ch.1) He continues to explain how Christmas has created an economic problem for him: "If I was to stop half-a-crown for it, you'd think yourself ill used...and yet you don't think me ill-used, when I pay a day's wages for no work" (21; ch.1). Here Scrooge demonstrates that he cannot even perceive Cratchit as a human being but as an economic possession, swindling him unfairly.

EXAMPLE PROCESS TWO FOR CONSTRUCTING A PARAGRAPH

RESPONDING TO A THESIS STATEMENT

Thesis Statement

Simon possesses characteristics of a Christ-like figure in *Lord of the Flies*.

Step One

Write the topic sentence.
> First, Simon often helps those in need, paralleling Christ in his selflessness.

Step Two

Gathering evidence.
- "finding for them the fruit that they could not reach, pulling off the choicest from up in the foliage" (56; ch. 3).
- "littluns cry out unintelligibly" (56; ch. 3).
- "shoving his piece of meat over the rocks to Piggy" (73; ch. 4).

Step Three

Organization method.
PLACE: Where/In which places does Simon show he is selfless and helps others in need?

Step Four

Write the paragraph.
> First, Simon often helps those in need, paralleling Christ in his selflessness. This concern for others occurs with both the smaller children and the older ones. For example, **in the jungle** struggling to

find food to preserve his own life, Simon assists the littluns by "finding for them the fruit that they could not reach, pulling off the choicest from up in the foliage, and passing them back down to the endless, outstretched hands" (56; ch.3). Because Simon supplies nourishment for the littluns in a time of need, they "cry out unintelligibly" (56; ch.3) for him to become their provider, just as Jesus' followers intuitively sought his assistance in times of distress. In addition, **at a campfire** Simon demonstrates his willingness to put aside his own needs in order to provide for others by graciously sharing with Piggy. For instance, while Jack denies Piggy a piece of meat "as an assertion of power" (73; ch.3), Simon provides for him by "shoving his piece of meat over the rocks to Piggy" (73; ch.3). Here Simon shows his ability to put aside his needs for someone outcast, much like Christ did, serving and dining with the poor and ostracized.

EXAMPLE PROCESS THREE FOR CONSTRUCTING A PARAGRAPH

RESPONDING TO AN ESSAY QUESTION

Essay Question

What is important about the escape scene in *Huckleberry Finn*?

Step One

*Write the topic sentence/*answer the essay question.
      Huck's escape reveals several characteristics about his personality.

Step Two

Gathering evidence.
- "I had tried to get out of the cabin many a time, but I couldn't find no way. There warn't a window to it big enough for a dog to get through" (52; ch. 7).
- "saw a section of the big bottom log out—big enough to let me through" (54; ch. 7).
- "rid of the signs of my work and drop the blanket and hide my saw" (58; ch. 7).

Step Three

Organization method.
IDEA: DEFINE Huck's personality traits as they appear during his escape.

Step Four

Write the paragraph.
      Huck's escape reveals several charcateristics about his personality. Aware that he's in a dangerous situation, Huck is **determined** to escape: "I had tried to get out of the cabin many a time, but I couldn't find no way. There warn't a window to it big enough for a dog to get through" (52; ch.7). This temporary setback doesn't stop him, and he **perseveres** even after hunting "the place over as much as a hundred times" (52; ch.7). Finally, Huck finds "an old rusty wood saw without any handle"

(58; ch.7); he **cleverly** discovers that "under the table" he can raise the blanket and "saw a section of the big bottom log out—big enough to let me through" (54; ch.7). Not only does he devise this sagacious escape route, but also he knows he must get "rid of the signs of my work and drop the blanket and hide my saw" (58; ch.7). This clever thinking, however, is not enough; he needs his **imagination**: "I says to myself, I can fix it now so nobody won't think of following me" (58; ch. 7). What he fixes is a feigned murder, taking "the gun and [going] up a piece into the woods" where he sees "a wild pig; so I shot this fellow and took him into camp" (58; ch. 7). Its blood spilling on the cabin floor, Huck prepares a **creative** death scene, pulling "out some of my hair, and [bloodying] the ax good,... [sticking] it on the back side, and [slinging] the ax in the corner" (58; ch. 7). When finished, his mind **still thinking**, he takes "a dipper and a tin cup, and my old saw and two blankets, and the skillet and the coffee pot" (58; ch. 7), provisions he knows he'll need later on his journey, a journey apart from the violent danger of Pap.

REVISION PROCESS: QUESTIONS TO ASK ABOUT PARAGRAPHS

Unity

- Does the topic sentence appear as the first sentence of a body paragraph and indicate clearly the focus of the paragraph? [**TS** editing symbol]
- Is the topic sentence too broad or too narrow?
- Do the concrete textual examples in the remainder of the paragraph—either direct quotations or situations re-created in the writer's own SHOWING language—provide a clear illustration of the idea in the topic sentence?
- Is more evidence needed?

Coherence

- Is the method of organizing the material in the paragraph clear to the reader: organization by time, place, or idea? [**P1** editing symbol] And does the writer employ diction that indicates his organizational choice[s]?
- Does the writer provide a transitional sentence or phrase that follows the topic sentence, a transition that offers the reader an understanding of how the writer organizes evidence, the direct quotations or situations re-created in the writer's own words? [**A** editing symbols]
- Do word glue and logic glue appear between each sentence, assisting the reader in the comprehension of the writer's argument? [**T1, T2** editing symbols]
- Does the writer stay on topic consistently (the topic string), avoiding unnecessary shifts? [**T3** editing symbol]
- Does the writer continually uses word glue to connect sentences back to the topic sentence idea ?
- In elaborating does the writer clearly explain to the reader why the evidence supports the topic sentence? Is more elaboration necessary? [**E3** editing symbol]
- Is the writer merely listing evidence without identifying key associative ideas? [**L, S** editing symbols]?
- Does the writer blend the quoted material syntactically within his own

sentences? Or are some quotations awkwardly blended? Does the writer wrap the evidence cited, including direct quotations, with conceptual associations? [**B** editing symbols]

Style

- Does the writer craft a variety of sentence types and syntactical patterns?
- Does the diction emphasize concrete words and appropriately effective associations?
- Are sentences concise and clear?
- Do some sentences need to be combined, using an absolute phrase, a participial phrase, analysis modifier, repeat word modifier, subordinate clause, infinitive phrase, gerund phrase, semicolon, conjunctive adverb?
- Do wordy structures need revising?

The following paragraphs have gone through various stages of the revision process. The teacher may use these examples for general class discussion. As these passages contain annotations pointing out the skills discussed throughout this text, the teacher may find that some paragraphs may be used for imitation or modeling exercises, or as a means for students to identify the qualities of effective writing.

Note: ALL OF THESE PARAGRAPHS ARE EITHER BODY PARAGRAPHS FROM LARGER PAPERS OR SINGLE PARAGRAPHS IN ANSWER TO A SPECIFIC ESSAY-TYPE QUESTION. WHERE ANY OF THE FOLLOWING PARAGRAPHS HAVE BEEN WRITTEN BY AN INDIVIDUAL STUDENT, THAT STUDENT'S NAME IS LISTED ABOVE THE PARAGRAPH. THIS METHOD OF ACKNOWLEDGEMENT IS THE CASE THROUGHOUT *CRAFTING EXPOSITORY ARGUMENT*.

Topic: The Core Heroic Value in **The Iliad**   *by Paul Rodriguez*

Through numerous character descriptions, Homer utilizes armor to portray the aristeia of a warrior, a core heroic value that displays the superior prowess and skill of the individual. For instance, Homer, implying a sense of royalty and supremacy, describes Hector's armor as "the flashing bronze, the horsehair crest, the great ridge of the helmet nodding, bristling terror" (6.560-561). The magnificence of his gear,

> The writer informs us in the topic sentence that "a core heroic value" will be defined "through numerous character descriptions." Observe how this writer moves from one character to another, easily blending what he has just written about Hector into a sentence that turns our attention to Ajax's aristeia. Later, he weaves his thoughts concerning Ajax into his first sentence regarding Achilles and the "core heroic value."

especially the shining metal and the imperial crest, emphasize Hector's superiority as an heir to the throne worthy of such valuable material. Not only does his armor imply his royalty, but it also strikes fear into his enemies because it provides Hector with seemingly insurmountable power and skill. **Similar to Hector, the physical size of Ajax's armor,** "huge body-shield like a rampart, heavy bronze over seven layers of oxhide," reflects the unimaginable strength of the warrior (7.252-253). The ability to hold up this shield alone gives insight into the individual's unique abilities as a warrior, his unmatched strength; any other man would struggle to lift this massive shield. **Just as Ajax's shield unveils his preeminent strength as a fighter, Achilles' spear emphasizes the technical prowess of his fighting style,** "only Achilles had the skill to wield it well" because Homer depicts the spear as "weighted, heavy, tough" (16.168,170). **His power insurmountable,** Achilles exists as the only qualified fighter in the Aegean

> The absolute phrase [His power insurmountable] effectively modifies Achilles and provides the writer another method for varying the beginnings of his sentences. Locate and analyze other examples where this writer uses an approach beyond the more ordinary sentence-opening of a subject and its verb.

ranks capable of wielding this powerful spear. This superiority in fighting capabilities forces enemies and allies to extol Achilles for his individual prowess.

Topic: *Contrasting images in "The Chimney Sweeper"*   *by Brad Bradshaw*

In Blake's first "Chimney Sweeper," the vacillation between dirty, squalid images and pure, joyous ones parallels God's role of repaying those who labor with a life of bliss only after they have died. **The poem opens with a tone of abandonment as "[the speaker's] mother died" and "[his] father sold [him]."** Having been forsaken by his family, the young narrator lives alone in the poorest of conditions, where "chimneys [he sweeps]" and "in soot [he sleeps]." Having no home, living in poverty, and being forced into hard labor, Blake generalizes the life of a

> The writer blends his own words with actual words from the poem. WHEN IT IS NECESSARY TO SUBSTITUTE A DIRECTLY QUOTED WORD FROM THE POEM IN ORDER TO MAINTAIN THE LOGIC OF THE SENTENCE, the writer places the appropriate substitution in brackets. The poem itself begins with "When my mother died…," so the writer substitutes "the speaker's" for "my," while placing the substitution in the brackets. The next line of the poem begins with "And my father sold me…," and the writer of the paragraph substitutes "his" for "my" and "him" for "me." The use of the brackets is essential in order to indicate to anyone reading the paragraph that the words inside of the brackets are a substitution for the poet's actual words. The substituted words, as you can see, remain inside the double quotation marks.

chimney sweep by switching from speaking in the first person to the third, telling the story of "little Tom Dacre." His tale begins as Tom's head is shaved, removing his beautiful "white hair" so that "soot cannot spoil" it, a parallel to how this role as a chimney sweep removes the potential beauty from these boys' lives. This miserable, grimy tone continues in the third stanza, as the narrator recounts Tom's dream, in which he sees "thousands of sweepers," who are "lock'd up in coffins of black," dead. He gives them humanity by naming them "Dick, Joe, Ned, and Jack," emanating an aura of ethereal sadness. **Then, the tone shifts miraculously. "An Angel" carrying "a bright Key" sets the dead boys free by "open[ing] the coffins."** Not only are they freed from the black boxes, but they also escape their squalorous lives into "a green plain" where, as Blake utilizes lighthearted alliteration, "leaping" and "laughing" they are "washed"

> With "then," the writer moves the reader toward a contrast in tone found in the poem as he elaborates on the "vacillation between the dirty, squalid images and pure, joyous ones," the central idea of the paragraph's topic sentence. The highlighted sentence provides an example of HOW TO SUBSTITUTE A DIRECTLY QUOTED WORD'S SUFFIX. The poem's line begins with "And he opened the coffins…," so the writer, in order to maintain the logical sense of the sentence, substitutes the suffix "ing" for the suffix "ed," placing the substitution in the brackets. Later in this paragraph, the writer will again prepare the reader for another contrast, which is further evidence of "vacillation." What is the transitional word the writer uses to initiate this next change?

and "shine in the Sun." The Angel, representing God, lets the boys be cleansed and become pure in Paradise, living in "joy…upon clouds." This happy, clean, free existence explicitly opposes the chimney sweep's earthly position. However, Blake's tone reverts back to its original dirge. In the final stanza, Tom awakens with a "happy" and "warm" feeling from his dream, only to find himself confronted with the "cold, dark" world, the world in which he is abandoned and abused, the world where he is condemned to hard labor until death. Blake reaches his final conclusion here, a fatalistic Kantian philosophy that God will reward those who "do [their] duty," but only once they have died. This realization poisons the marginal hope that little Tom Dacre feels about his role as a chimney sweep, for the only joy he will ever experience must occur after he has died.

H.D.'s poem speaks of Helen as a figure reviled by the population for her faults, whose pride, beauty, and purity only serve to augment this detestation. From the opening lines, the speaker describes the depth of Greece's feelings of animosity towards Helen for her past transgressions. For example, the first words, "All Greece hates," depict the vastness of the revulsion aimed towards Helen, suggesting that the entirety of the populace carries some resentment or dislike. H.D. follows this statement with the imagery of "still eyes" and "the white face." The **color white usually carries connotations of purity and cleanliness, but in this instance, when juxtaposed with the idea of stillness,** the color demonstrates a certain type of arrogance, suggesting that Helen's beauty does not bring with it forgiveness, but only another reason to inspire hatred. **The repetition of the word "white" in the final line of the first stanza, this time paired with the word "hands,"** once again demonstrates her purity that seems to mock the populace for its suffering at her hands, formulating the hatred so prevalent throughout the poem and emphasizing her beauty as the foundation of this loathing. The second stanza, beginning very similarly to the first with a strong statement of widespread abhorrence, "All Greece reviles," continues to tie this hatred of Helen to her attributes, specifically, her "wan face when she smiles." The continuous use of white imagery, coupled with the juxtaposition of the diction in "hating it deeper still," demonstrates that, though Helen does indeed possess extreme beauty, it has caused unnecessary suffering among the Greeks. Therefore, this beauty does nothing to detract from this hatred; rather, the beauty fuels it. The speaker's hatred reaches its climax in the final stanza, where, once again, Helen's physical features, namely her "cool feet and slenderest knees," embodiments of classical beauty, serve as symbols for her goddess-like perfection. In turn, this perfection symbolizes the Greek's perception of her as egotistical, accounting for her widespread abhorrence. Although Helen is described, in perhaps a sarcastic tone, as "God's daughter, born of love," the speaker suggests that, despite her beauty, she is incapable of drawing feelings of respect and love, an obvious contrast to her description. The speaker shows that the Greeks remain unable to see her as beautiful because of her "past ills": the torment she has inflicted upon them through her instigation of the Trojan War. **Finally, the speaker suggests that the only instance in which she could ever be loved remains through her death. The final line, "white ash amid funeral**

> The writer throughout the paragraph associates Helen's physical attributes to the populace's hostility toward her. Observe, for example, how the writer takes one physical idea [the color white] and "juxtaposes" or "pairs" it with another physical detail [her stillness, her hands] to draw a conclusion that substantiates the central idea in the topic sentence.

> The writer has moved the reader through the poem line by line, stanza by stanza, using transitional language that helps the reader follow along. Here, the writer concludes with a mixture of transitional language [Finally, the final line, one final time, however, therefore] that allows even the reader unfamiliar with the poem to follow the expository argument being made about it. Note as well that these last three sentences are glued together by the repetition of "death" and two affiliated words, "funeral" and "graves," this last a reference to the thousands of Greek fatalities as a result of the Trojan War, a war the writer had mentioned earlier. Look back over the paragraph and find other transitional language, including word glue and logic glue, that helps the reader follow the argument.

cypresses," presents the archetype of white one final time; however, the speaker suggests that this white is truly pure and truly beautiful because this white symbolizes the death of the abhorred Helen. Therefore, the Greeks will only perceive her as pure and beautiful when she is laid with those she has sent to their graves.

Topic: *Biddy as exemplar of Pip's better nature in* Great Expectations *by Tyler Green*

Biddy is an ignoble country girl who represents Pip's loving side that cares about other people. Despite being plain and common, Biddy is a loving and devoted person. She works hard as a servant for Mrs. Joe and also manages to be a loyal friend to Pip. Biddy also teaches him, takes care of his family, and listens to his personal problems. Unlike Estella, "Biddy was never insulting, or capricious, or Biddy today and somebody else tomorrow" (122; ch. 17). She likes Pip for who he is and "only wants [him] to do well, and be comfortable" (120; ch. 17), not minding of his social status. Pip can also be selfless like Biddy, such as when he helps Magwitch both on the marshes and in London. **Obligated by his sense of duty to his benefactor,** Pip puts himself into danger on Magwitch's behalf. **Pip's mind, "wholly set on Provis's safety" (404; ch. 54), forgets the risk involved to his own self and reputation.** PIP also helps his friend Herbert, secretly setting him up with a profitable partnership, using his own money to finance his less fortunate friend. Pip acts like Biddy in these situations by putting the well being of others ahead of his own, **a trait that he had inherently as a boy but needed to learn again as he matured.** BIDDY is the embodiment of this inherent good and is the companion Pip would have had if he stayed and worked at the forge. Her character represents the hard, honest, happy life.

> Introductory past participal phrase adds variety to sentence beginnings.

> Writer effectively blends Dickens' words with his own. Note: Provis is the alias used by Magwitch in the Dickens novel.

> Observe the logic glue (pp. 68-69) binding the sentence preceding the underlined word to the sentence that begins with the underlined word. In the case of the underlined Pip, the relationship between the two sentences is AND. In the case of the underlined Biddy, the relationship between the two sentences is THEREFORE. The word underlined (Pip in the first case and Biddy in the second) indicates the point at which two sentences are related by use of logic glue.

> Analysis modifier [a trait that...] extends elaboration.

Topic: *Feasting as a cultural totem in* Beowulf

Feasting, one of the most recurrent themes in *Beowulf*, helps the reader understand the significant elements of the Anglo-Saxon culture. One significant element is gift-giving, not simply a sign of monetary remuneration but a spiritual symbol of appreciation and fulfillment of the sacred *comitatus* bond that maintains order in the tribe. For example, Hrothgar bestows "on Beowulf a standard worked in gold, a figured battle-banner, breast and head armour" (83). In addition, **Wealhtheow, the queen and Hrothgar's wife, also presents to** Beowulf "two arm-wreaths, with robes and

> Topic sentence identifies a focus for the paragraph and suggests a way to organize.

> Writer explains context before incorporating direct quotation.

rings also, and the richest collar the monk has ever heard of in all the world" (83). <u>These gifts</u> represent Hrothgar and Wealhtheow's gratitude towards Beowulf for killing the notorious, malicious Grendel, cleansing their community of evil. Moreover, a warrior's gifts, their quality and quantity, indicate the degree of his heroism. <u>Feasting provides not only gifts and honor</u>, but entertainment as well, a spirit of festivity. In Heorot, "the hall [fills] with loud amusement;

> Underlined words throughout are key words that GLUE each sentence together. Notice how new information appears at the end of the sentence, old at the beginning.

there [is] the music of the harp," while Hrothgar "[gives] out rings, arm-bands at the banquet," and the "men [drink] their wine" (86), activities that allow the community to forget the conflicts that may plague their lives outside the hall. <u>Finally</u>, the feast provides warnings to heroes, tales of past failures. <u>The story of Heremod</u>, a figure called to "assume the kingdom, the care of his people, the hoard and the stronghold, the Scylding homeland" (87), serves to <u>warn</u> Beowulf about the darker side of man's heart, the evil that had seduced Heremod, who became "a deadly grief to his people and the princes of his land" (89). Instead, Hrothgar <u>cautions</u> Beowulf to "put away arrogance" (90) and to know that he has to act justly and morally throughout his life. <u>By contrast, other stories</u> praise virtuous action. <u>For instance</u>, the scop tells of Sigemund, **"who had slain the dragon" and killed a serpent with the "best of swords" (87),** to compare Beowulf's deeds with past Danish

> Adjective clause extends information about Sigemund.

warriors, Beowulf's *kleos* now secured in the legends of the Danes. <u>Not only does Beowulf</u> leave the feast refreshed and <u>honored</u>, but all members of the court also reap the benefits of this cultural exercise, for these hours contain the energy of *communitas*, **that human phenomenon binding people together for a unified purpose,**

> Absolute phrase that modifies "communitas."

reminding them of their shared values; this provides the stamina needed to return to previous roles and to maintain order in their lives.

Topic: Time as a tool in "To His Coy Mistress" *by Robby Markose*

In Andrew Marvell's "To His Coy Mistress," the speaker utilizes the aspect of time to influence his mistress's decision about having a sexual relationship with him. In the first stanza, the narrator uses the concept of time to comfort his mistress. He begins by stating that, if he "had but world enough and time" (1), he would cherish her even more than he already does. He believes that, if they could control time, he would spend a hundred years "to adore each breast" (13) and

> The writer repeats the word "time" throughout the paragraph to maintain clarity and coherence

maybe even "thirty thousand" (14) more years to adore the rest of her body. By asserting this, the narrator convinces his mistress that time is the reason why he cannot satiate all of her needs; this idea also allows her to believe that the narrator really does love her but consequently faces time as an opponent. In the second and third stanza, the narrator uses time to manipulate his mistress's emotions; he places her in a state of fear and discomfort. Although the narrator tells his mistress that his love for her remains strong, he feels that "time's winged chariot [hurries] near"

> The writer employs adverb subordinate clauses, participial phrases, and semicolons for sentence structure variety.

(20). He reveals this in hope that the image of this chase scene will serve as a catalyst to speed up her decision in shifting their relationship to a physical level. **Trying to discomfort her once more**, the narrator uses a morose image to describe the effects of time as he tells his mistress worms will be the first to pleasure her "long preserved" (26) virginity. The narrator, **using this image**, hopes the mistress will want him, instead, to be the first lover to share this experience. Also in the second and third stanza, he tells his mistress that time will strip away her beauty if she continues to allow her "youthful hue / [to sit on] thy skin like morning glow" (33–34). **Since the morning dew evaporates as the day passes**, the narrator warns his mistress she, too, will grow old and die. In these last two stanzas, the narrator hopes that, by scaring his mistress, she will more easily submit to his request. He tells her that we should "rather at-once our time devour, / than languish in his slow-chapped power" (39–40). He believes they should be in a sexual relationship, immediately, before time becomes the reason that forbids them from doing so.

Topic: *The* Yin *of Joe Gargery in* Great Expectations   *by Juan Salazar*

Throughout *Great Expectations*, Dickens develops Joe's *yin* characteristics, those traditionally associated with the feminine, causing us to rethink our stereotype of the father. Joe Gargery's semblance of "a muscular blacksmith, [with a] broad chest" (6; ch. 2), connotes stereotypical masculine imagery, though Pip later contradicts this imagery. As a mother protects her offspring from danger, Joe, too, assumes this task at the dinner table on Christmas Eve. Hearing Pip being battered by the family, Joe extends his "restoring touch" unto Pip, "aiding and comforting [him]...by giving [Pip] gravy" (23; ch. 4), **a benevolent deed that demonstrates not just his concern for Pip, but his willingness to help and care for him;** in fact, Joe, instead of seeing Pip suffer, would "wish to take it [the Tickler] on himself" (43; ch. 7), showing his legitimate concern for Pip's well-being. Apart from his concern for Pip, Joe also desires the unification of the household, his concern for the *oikos*, an important *yin* characteristic. For example, Joe avoids confrontations with Mrs. Gargery when she "is in a cross temper," and gives Pip "encouraging...pieces of wisdom" (64; ch. 9) that help him alleviate his painful feelings of being "common...and wishing that he was not common." In addition, the conflict between Mrs. Joe and Orlick having been suppressed, Joe demonstrates his desire to maintain tranquility in the household. To Pip, Joe's arm is "an angel's wing" (431; ch. 57), a description that identifies Joe as being more than just the male, but the protector of the household.

> Writer proceeds to show and extend elaboration of Joe's feminine qualities.

> Analysis modifier inside a compound-complex sentence whose independent clauses are joined by the conjunctive adverb "in fact."

> Writer effectively blends direct quotations into sentences.

Topic: *Roger unrestrained in* Lord of the Flies   *by Neal Talreja*

Roger represents the intentionally cruel human being whose evil nature emerges once civilized restraints are stripped away. Throughout the novel, Roger demonstrates his cruelty in several scenes. First, while the littluns play on the beach, Roger gathers "a handful of stones and [begins] to throw them" (62; ch. 4) near the children; however, he does not throw the stones directly at them because his "arm [is] conditioned by a civilization" (62; ch. 4). As a young British boy, Roger has grown up in a civilized society where "parents and school and policemen and the law" (62; ch. 4) have instructed him to be kind to others, to become educated, and to follow the laws; however, stranded on an island, the people who enforce these fetters are not present, **an absence of authority that enables "some source of power to pulse in [his] body" (175; ch. 11), a power, or evil nature, that obliterates common sense as well as care for the rules and customs of society.** Roger's destruction of reason and order enables him to abandon his previous life and, consequently, to succumb to the primitive impulses of hunting and killing. These impelling forces appear later in the forest where the boys kill a sow, **Roger prodding "with his spear whenever pig flesh" appears, finding "a lodgment for his point . . . to push" (135; ch. 8),** *actions that show his ability to harm a living creature.* Moreover, when the boys reenact the hunt after performing this gruesome act, Roger demonstrates the intentional cruelty used to kill the sow when he becomes "the pig, grunting and charging. . . [and mimicking] the terror of the pig"(151; ch. 9). The fact that Roger can kill a living creature, then mimic the terror he inflicts upon it, shows how he is aware of the evil of his actions but does not care. Later, on Castle Rock, his incapacity to care advances him to a more homicidal level of cruelty when he, "with a sense of delirious abandonment, [leans] all his weight on the lever" (180; ch. 11), releasing the giant rock that kills Piggy, **who was merely addressing the savages about the need for reason and order on the island prior to his execution.** The fact that Roger kills a fellow human being, particularly the only human being on the island with reason and intellect, shows how he only cares to do what is cruel as opposed to do what is reasonable. This lack of conscience leads to more barbarous behavior on Castle Rock. For example, when Sam and Eric refuse to join the tribe, he threatens to torture them by advancing "upon them as one wielding a nameless authority" (182; ch. 11), a "nameless authority" that once more shows how he has lost his previous identity as a civilized boy due to the truculent nature within. **The deeds of killing a human being and torturing others accomplished,** he concludes his sadistic rampage when he sharpens "a stick at both ends" (190; ch. 12) and saunters through the jungle, hunting for Ralph. Like the stick whetted at both ends, Roger has no kind and civilized side, for his cruel nature has cast him into a domain of evil.

An analysis modifier followed by a repeat word modifier, both of which extend the elaboration of the writer's idea regarding the abandonment of civilized restraints.

An absolute phrase extends elaboration, as does the analysis modifier (in italics) that ends the sentence.

Writer extends elaboration with an adjective subordinate clause noting the irony involved in the situation leading to Piggy's murder.

Writer employs an absolute phrase to sum up Roger's descent into barbarity as he concludes the paragraph with the image of the stick sharpened at both ends.

Topic: Forming community in Donne's "Meditation 17"   *by Young Cho*

Donne uses **metaphors** to remind us of man's communal nature, **metaphors** that reveal man's need

Repeat word modifier used in topic sentence.

to belong to a larger group. First, Donne compares the church to one body. Donne needs the church "whereof (he is) a member" (10), as a form of support, just as the head, "engrafted into that body" (10), needs the help of the body, the larger group or structure that provides life. Next, Donne compares man to a book, demonstrating they are both "of one author" and that man naturally belongs to a community as a book belongs to a "volume." This community is so important to mankind that even after some process of transformation such as death, where one sheds his physical element, thus gaining a more spiritual character, the one aspect that he does not change is that he is still part of a **community, a community now actually better than the first—the kingdom of heaven.** Likewise, a book, after being "translated into a better language," is still part of that "library where every book shall lie open to one another" (11). Similarly, a piece of land serves as a metaphor to man; however, this metaphor reveals how the community also needs man. **Donne says that no piece of land should be "an island entire to itself" (11), deserted, neglected, its environment void of any other lands, a melancholy situation man should similarly avoid. Instead, this piece of land should be "a piece of a continent, a part of the main" (11), as man needs community, and if this piece of land happens to "be washed away by the sea" (11), its continent becomes "the less," meaning it experiences a loss in size, paralleling a community's disappointment and the loss when one of its members dies.** Donne, through use of his metaphors, visually portrays to the reader the relationship between man and community, demonstrating how man is isolated without community and the community "diminished" without man.

> Repeat word modifier extends elaboration.

> The paragraph regarding an aspect of John Donne's classic poem, "Meditation 17," is worth studying as a model of how to blend direct quotations from a work of literature with the writer's own words when making the expository argument. For example, observe how the writer begins these two sentences with his own words before moving smoothly into the poet's words. Each time he quotes directly from the poem, the writer continues the sentence, elaborating extensively with commentary regarding the words quoted from the poem. In the second sentence here, the writer's expository commentary smoothly incorporates further words directly quoted from the poem.

Topic: *Avarice in* Great Expectations   *by Damian Smith*

Some of the minor characters in *Great Expectations*, **people who devote their lives procuring a higher social status and acquiring material wealth, illustrate the greed and hypocrisy inherent in infernal comedy.** Pumblechook represents the acme of hypocrisy, a fearful imposter who presents himself as a venerable aristocrat. His prodigious lies about his knowledge of Miss Havisham reveal him to be a deceitful person, a man of guile rather than veneration. Furthermore, his nauseating "May I's" to Pip, in order to gain his favor after Pip has acquired money, only cause the reader to disdain him even more. Another character similar to Pumblechook in her snobbish pretensions is Mrs. Belinda Pocket; however, while Pumblechook merely desires to become part of the aristocracy, she already believes that, being the daughter of an alleged knight, she is. As she is to be guarded from the acquisition of plebeian domestic

> Writer will apply this definition to examples.

> Writer extends elaboration of Pumblechook.

knowledge, she knows very little about the care of her own children, consequently allowing one child to nearly kill itself with a nutcracker and spurning another child for trying to prevent it, an act of opprobrium revealing not only her stubborn and impetuous mien, but also the absurdity and imprudence of the people she represents. She is a wife and mother,

Note the concrete detail about Mrs. Pocket.

yet she rejects the virtues of a wife and mother, her role as protector and nurturer of her family. In addition, Compeyson, Miss Havisham's ex-lover, is seen as devoting himself to material self-interest, but he represents a more sinister and vile side. One first views him as a perfect gentleman, a smooth one to talk, with his curly hair, and his black clothes and his white pocket handkerchief, but in reality, his business is swindling, handwriting, forging, and stolen banknote passing. As well, he is a man without a heart, cold as death and with the head of the devil, having pity on nothing and nobody. According to George R. Thomas, Compeyson demonstrates the basic unreality of Magwitch's assumption that being a gentleman is one of the best blessings he can bestow on Pip (34). Magwitch's reaction to finally seeing his creation leads one to ascertain that he has given Pip a gift, yet through Compeyson we learn that being a gentleman is not as fantastic as it seems.

Topic: Sydney Carton as a Christ-figure in A Tale of Two Cities _by Ben Bireley_

Before Dickens places Carton into his Passion Story, he first gives the reader images of Carton's similarities to Christ. Dickens accomplishes this through a comparison of the characters' common traits. The author commences this imagery by describing Carton as "wearing the white riding-coat and top boots, then in vogue, and the light of the fires touching the light surfaces of his face made him look very pale, with long brown hair, all untrimmed, hanging loose about him" (240; bk. 3, ch. 9). In this description, Dickens compares both the physical and metaphysical traits the two have in common. First, Dickens' description of Carton shows the physical features he has in common with Christ. Carton

The writer's expository argument is based on an analogy. Observe how this student-writer first employs a direct quotation from Dickens' story, a quotation that focuses on physical detail concerning Sydney Carton. Details from that quoted passage continue to crop up in the paragraph until the writer blends a central image from it [the light of the fires...] to a quoted passage from John. This Biblical passage then allows the writer to blend its content with a later quotation from the novel, a quotation wherein the image of light plays a central role and ties the analogy being made together.

displays the pale face and long brown hair **depicted in the classic European artwork done of Christ.** Dickens begins his metaphysical comparison through color archetypes. Carton wears a white riding-coat, **associating him with the color white,** a color of purity. By linking Carton with white, Dickens connects him to a trait commonly associated with Christ, purity. **To advance the metaphysical comparison between Carton and Christ as the novel continues,** Dickens uses a second archetype. He gives the reader an image of "the light of the fires touching the light surfaces [of Carton]." The repetition of the word "light" in this image forces the reader to connect Carton with light, **an archetype of life,** which is an association that

Writer employs a variety of structures, including the introductory adverb clause, both the past and present participial phrases, the introductory infinitive phrase, and the appositive phrase.

also takes place in the Bible with Christ. For example, in John's gospel, the Bible tells the reader, "What came to be through him was life, and this light was the light of the human race; the light shines in the darkness, and the darkness has not overcome it" (John 1.5). Dickens extends his comparison between Jesus and Carton through imagery showing how Carton's actions bring about "light that shines in the darkness," just as John informs us that Jesus' actions did in the passage above. Directly after Carton's decision to die for Darnay, Dickens says, "Then, the night, with the moon and the stars, turned pale and died, and for a little while it seemed as if creation were delivered over to Death's dominion. But the glorious sun, rising, seemed to strike those words, that burden of the night, straight and warm to his heart in its long bright rays" (294; bk. 3, ch. 9). Dickens' decision to show this specific change in nature, directly after Carton's decision to die for another, forces the reader to connect Carton's actions with the sun, which brings light. This image clearly shows that Carton's actions bring light, or life, just as Jesus' actions did.

Topic: The merits and drawbacks of Egypt's geography

The geography of Egypt provided both benefits and disadvantages to the Egyptian civilization. **On the one hand, the country prospered** because of its natural "walls" surrounding its borders: the Libyan desert on the west coast, the Mediterranean Sea on the north, the Nubian desert to the south, and the Red Sea to the East—formidable obstacles to potential enemies. **Few countries would attempt** the arduous journey required to invade. **Within this protection, a majority of the Egyptians lived close to the Nile River,** which goes through the main part of the country, a big highway allowing the people to move from city to city. **Moreover, every year, the Nile River would flood** in the spring and summer, producing a rich black silt for crops; the Egyptians then built dams and reservoirs to provide irrigation throughout the year. **On the other hand, this insulated geography** caused political stagnation. **For instance, in an 8000 year span, the Egyptians moved through only three political shifts**—a state based on the pharaoh, a state based on noble-civic leadership, and finally, a state based on military leadership. **Though it appeared the Egyptians progressed through separate political ideologies, the pharaoh remained** a part of each system, indicating once more an inability to advance politically. **While Egpyt maintained their intellectual isolation, other countries improved** agricultural methods and methods of war. **For example, the Hyksos surprised the Egyptians** by using horses and chariots, along with bronze weapons, while they were still using donkeycarts and copper and stone weapons. **In addition, years later to the west,**

> Expository argument can be crafted well in any academic course for any field of study. What students learn in English class should carry with them into other courses. The paragraph here is constructed with a clear topic sentence that is organized by idea—the classification of BENEFITS and DISADVANTAGES.

> Observe the highlighted topic strings. The first four connect to the BENEFITS of Egypt's geography, which relates to the topic sentence. The next seven, also relating to the topic sentence, connect to the DISADVANTAGES of the nation's geography.

> Concrete detail is used by the writer to elaborate each element of both classifications: the country's natural borders, the Nile River, the three types of states, the successful invaders. Cite examples of concrete detail elaborating each element.

the Hittites conquered the Egyptians by using iron weapons while the Egyptians still relied on bronze, a softer and less effective metal. **These examples illustrate that the Egyptians failed** to perceive how the wealth of their geographical position could ironically be their own downfall.

Topic: *The Rhetoric of Juror 8 in* Twelve Angry Men

Juror Eight demonstrates his apt **ability to think logically** and hence to demonstrate his own ethical stature. **Consistently making appeals to logos**, Juror Eight inductively concludes that "it's not possible that [the old man] could have heard" neither a falling body nor the boy's alleged statement, "I'm going to kill you." **This logical argument emerges** from a series of observed details, namely, that the train "takes about ten seconds to pass a given point," "the body fell to floor just as the train passed by," and the "train had been roaring...for a full ten seconds." Moreover, what provides **the structure for this claim** is causality, the careful sequencing of events that descend upon an ultimate effect—the old man merely thought he heard an ominous statement and subsequent fall of a body. Finally, the juror's narrative uses **language unmodified by emotional appeals**—the "body fell," "the body falling," "for a full ten seconds before the body fell" rather than exclaiming "the bloody corpse collapsed" or "the helpless father was ruthlessly stabbed." Here Juror Eight's **language demonstrates restraint** and a desire to **focus solely on facts**. Even the **repetition of "ten seconds" and "split second" evokes a mathematical precision** reflecting the juror's own phronesis, or wisdom.

> In this paragraph you can observe the use of WORD GLUE, wherein the writer repeats key words and their synonyms from sentence to sentence to maintain an argument that is coherent, thus allowing the reader to understand clearly how each part of the expository argument being made ties together.

Topic: *An analogy regarding virtue in* A Tale of Two Cities   By Brendan O'Brien

Dickens mirrors the moral dilemma of John the Apostle with his character Charles Darnay, illustrating the New Testament's theme of virtue. At the particular point in the New Testament while Jesus walks towards his crucifixion amidst a tumultuous mob of angry Jews, his apostles face a difficult moral dilemma: either risk their lives in loyalty to their Lord or safely hide, sheltered from this turbulent mob. Only one, John, fights through this adversity to remain loyal to Jesus, "standing nearby" during His grueling ordeal (John 19: 26). As chaos and hostility engulfed Jerusalem, "the disciple whom He loved" and who unceasingly followed Him, John the Apostle embodies true virtue, both courageously risking his life and naturally exhibiting loyalty (John 19: 26). **Like John the Apostle, Charles Darnay demonstrates this New Testament theme of virtue in his own moral dilemma, his reflection of whether to aid his imperiled servant, Gabelle, and return to France, leaving his wife and child behind.** Darnay courageously recognizes "very well the force of these circumstances" in the French Revolution, yet still bravely faces this "course of confiscation and destruction," transcending this setting of chaos to help one in need (238-239; bk. 2, ch. 24). His valor honorable, Darnay embodies John the

> The organization of this paragraph is an analogy subdivided into its two parts, first that involving John the Apostle, then that involving Darnay. Observe how a simply stated simile, at the beginning of the first highlighted sentence, smoothly connects John's moral dilemma to Darnay's.

Apostle's natural tendency towards loyalty and righteousness, a dedication similar to "the mariner in the old story" whose "winds and streams" push him to action, telling him "he must go." **This loyalty eschews "his latent uneasiness" and causes him to see "hardly any danger,"** **both Darnay and John the Apostle recognizing "that glorious vision of doing good…[that] arose before him" (240; bk. 2, ch. 24).** Here, this imagery of virtue in his dreams, clearly seeing "himself in the illusion with some influence to guide this raging Revolution," emphasizes again how natural morality is for the virtuous Darnay, innately part of his subconscious (240; bk. 2, ch. 24).

> The writer weaves the two moral dilemmas together in his concluding sentences. In one of those sentences, highlighted here, the writer blends direct quotations from the novel applicable to Darnay and links them to John the Apostle as well. That one man's dilemma mirrors that of another, as stated in the topic sentence, is thus made explicit.

Assignment 1: Putting a paragraph together

An explanation of this first assignment, which is based on Charles Dickens' *A Christmas Carol,* can be found in "A Suggested Lesson Planning Sequence," which is posted at www.telemachospublishing.com. Many of these activities I use in order to prepare my students for their first expository argument, a paragraph on the literature we are currently studying. Parts of four of the five exercises thereafter also refer to the selection from *A Christmas Carol,* those exercises involving **TS** (topic sentence errors), **E** (elaboration), **B** (blending textual support), **L** (listing plot details), **P** (paragraph errors), **O** (off-topic), and **A** (adding transitions).

A selection from A Christmas Carol

The door of Scrooge's counting-house was open that he might keep his eye upon his clerk, who in a dismal little cell beyond, a sort of tank, was copying letters. Scrooge had a very small fire, but the clerk's fire was so very much smaller that it looked like one coal. But he couldn't replenish it, for Scrooge kept the coal-box in his own room; and so surely as the clerk came in with the shovel, the master predicted that it would be necessary for them to part.

"A merry Christmas, Uncle! God save you!" cried a cheerful voice. It was the voice of Scrooge's nephew.

"Bah!" said Scrooge, "Humbug!"

This nephew of Scrooge's was all in a glow; his face was ruddy and handsome; his eyes sparkled, and his breath smoked again.

"Christmas a humbug, Uncle! You don't mean that, I am sure?"

"I do," said Scrooge. "Merry Christmas! What right have you to be merry? What reason have you to be merry? You're poor enough," grumbled Scrooge.

"What right have you to be dismal? What reason have you to be morose? You're rich enough."

"Humbug."

"Don't be cross, Uncle!" said the nephew.

"What else can I be," returned the uncle, "when I live in such a world of fools as this? Merry Christmas! What's Christmas time to you but a time for paying bills without money; a time for finding yourself a year older, but not an hour richer. If I could work my will," said Scrooge indignantly, "every idiot who goes about with 'Merry Christmas' on his lips, should be boiled with his own pudding, and buried with a stake of holly through his heart. He should!"

"Uncle!" pleaded the nephew.

"Let me leave it alone, then," said Scrooge. "Much good may it do you! Much good it has ever done you!"

"There are many things from which I might have derived good, by which I have not profited. I have always thought of Christmas time, when it has come round—apart from the veneration due to its sacred name and origin—as a good time; a kind, forgiving, charitable, pleasant time: the only time I know of, in the long calendar of the year, when men and women seem by one consent to open their shut-up hearts freely, and to think of people below them as if they really were fellow-passengers to the grave, and not another race of creatures bound on other journeys. And therefore, uncle, though it has never put a scrap of gold or silver in my pocket, I believe that it has done me good, and will do me good; and I say, God bless it!"

"Good afternoon," said Scrooge.

"Don't be angry, Uncle. Come! Dine with us tomorrow. I want nothing from you; I ask nothing of you; why cannot we be friends?"

"Good afternoon," said Scrooge.

"I am sorry, with all my heart, to find you so resolute. We have never had any quarrel, to which I have been a party. But I have made the trial in homage to Christmas, and I'll keep my Christmas humour to the last. So A Merry Christmas, Uncle!"

"Good afternoon," said Scrooge.

"And a Happy New Year!"

"Good afternoon," said Scrooge.

His nephew left the room without an angry word. He stopped to bestow the greetings of the season on the clerk, who, cold as he was, was warmer than Scrooge; for he returned them cordially.

"There's another fellow," muttered Scrooge, "my clerk, with fifteen shillings a week, and a wife and family, talking about a Merry Christmas. I'll retire to Bedlam."

This lunatic, in letting Scrooge's nephew out, had let two other people in.

"Scrooge and Marley's, I believe," said one of the gentlemen, referring to his list. "Have I the pleasure of addressing Mr. Scrooge, or Mr. Marley?"

"Mr. Marley has been dead these seven years," Scrooge replied.

"We have no doubt his liberality is well represented by his surviving partner," said the gentleman. At the ominous word "liberality," Scrooge frowned, and shook his head.

"At this festive season of the year, Mr. Scrooge," said the gentleman, taking up a pen, "it is more than usually desirable that we should make some slight provision for the Poor and Destitute, who suffer greatly at the present time."

"Are there no prisons?" asked Scrooge.

"Plenty of prisons," said the gentleman, laying down the pen again.

"And the Union workhouses? Are they still in operation?"

"They are. Still," returned the gentleman, "I wish I could say they were not."

"Oh! I was afraid, from what you said at first, that something had occurred to stop them in their useful course," said Scrooge.

"Under the impression that they scarcely furnish Christian cheer of mind or body to the multitude, a few of us are endeavoring to raise a fund to buy the Poor some meat. What shall I put you down for?"

"Nothing!" Scrooge replied.

"You wish to be anonymous?"

"I wish to be left alone," said Scrooge. "Since you ask me what I wish, gentlemen, that is my answer. I don't make merry myself at Christmas and I can't afford to make idle people merry. I help to support the establishments I have mentioned—they cost enough; and those who are badly off must go there."

"Many can't go there; and many would rather die."

"It's not my business," Scrooge returned. "It's enough for a man to understand his own business, and not to interfere with other people's. Mine occupies me constantly. Good afternoon, gentlemen!"

Assignment #2: Revising for B (Blending textual support)

Directions Review section on blending text, p. 192; correct passages below.
1. It says in the text that the nephew, "a kind, forgiving, charitable, pleasant time…when men and women seem by one consent to open their shut-up hearts freely."
2. Scrooge doesn't want to make a donation. It says, "Nothing!" after the men say, "What shall I put you down for?"
3. Scrooge threatened his clerk after Bob cheered Scrooge's nephew. "Let me hear another sound from you and you'll keep your Christmas by losing your situation."

Assignment #3: Extending the Elaboration of an Idea E3, E4

Directions Review the explanation and examples for revising E3 or E4, p. 198, and then extend the elaboration of the following sentences.
1. Bob Cratchit is an ideal father. An ideal father values relationships more than material wealth. For example, when Mrs. Cratchit tells Bob that Martha is "not coming," he reacts "with a sudden declension in his high spirits. . . Not coming upon Christmas Day!'"
2. Even when Scrooge's own nephew visits him at work to wish him a merry Christmas, the old man deprecates the nephew's cheerful spirit, insisting that "Christmas is a time for paying bills without money, and a time for finding yourself a year older, but not an hour richer."
3. Scrooge is unable to be generous under any circumstance. For example, the narrator describes the "clerk's fire [as] so very much smaller that it looked like one coal." Here the reader sees that the clerk doesn't have a large fire.

Assignment #4: Adding Transitions A1, A2

Directions After the topic sentence, either attach a transitional clause or phrase, or insert a separate transitional sentence.
1. The opening scene of *A Christmas Carol* presents the conflict between selfishness and selflessness. The narrator explains that Scrooge's "clerk's fire was so very much smaller that it looked like one coal."
2. Dickens depicts Scrooge as the archetypal curmudgeon. Scrooge's only response to his nephew's invitation to dinner is "Good afternoon," a statement repeated four times.

3. Scrooge's nephew represents the spirit of youthful optimism. He questions his uncle, "What reason have you to be morose? You're rich enough."

ASSIGNMENT #5 REVISING FOR O/O2 (OFF-TOPIC) ETC.

Directions Review the explanation and examples for revising O/O2, p. 208, and then revise the following examples of beginnings of paragraphs. Note that the writer may need to address other symbols such as **B3/B4** or **E3** or **T.**

1. Dickens shows Scrooge's loathing of Christmas through his lack of compassion for others. His clerk's fire was "so very much smaller that it looked like one coal." In addition, the clerk couldn't "replenish it [the fire], for Scrooge kept the coal box in his own room."

2. Dickens portrays Scrooge as a greedy selfish man. One reads of how "the door of Scrooge's counting house was open that he might keep his eye upon his clerk," demonstrating his feeling of superiority and seniority over everyone, especially his dedicated worker. Finally, it reads, "Scrooge had a very small fire" but the clerk's fire was "much smaller."

3. Scrooge has no sense of generosity or care for others even though it is the holidays. Although Scrooge shows no holiday cheer, his clerk, Bob Cratchit, returns Scrooge's nephew's greetings of the season cordially. Scrooge ridicules Mr. Cratchit, "My clerk, with fifteen shillings a week, and a wife and family, talking about a Merry Christmas."

ASSIGNMENT #6 DESTROYING A PARAGRAPH

Directions Choose a paragraph from the preceding section of *Complete Expository Paragraphs.* Cross out concrete details; replace with vague diction, weak verbs. Remove places where elaboration has been extended; remove word, logic glue.

FOR ADDITIONAL ACTIVITIES, SEE WWW.TELEMACHOSPUBLISHING.COM

4

CONSTRUCTING THE EXPOSITORY PAPER

DEFINITIONS

• Subject
A subject for an expository paper involving literature may be any broad concept—a play, a character, a novel, a poem, a theme, an archetype, or a pattern—either assigned to the student by the teacher or chosen by the student.

• Topic
A topic is a more specific, more narrow aspect of the subject. This more precise feature of the subject may, *among countless possibilities*, center on a reoccurring image or archetype in a literary work, a specific setting or situation, the language used by the author, or a single character trait.

• Thesis Statement
A thesis statement presents the writer's approach toward, or insight concerning, the topic. Such a statement sets forth the writer's distinct viewpoint. In any expository argument, the thesis statement, consequently, expresses what is an opinion concerning the topic, an opinion that is open to dispute and must, therefore, be argued with evidence logically constructed from the literary text.

THESIS STATEMENT FORMULA = TOPIC + DEBATABLE OPINION

• Topic Sentence
The body pargraphs of an expository paper are the subdivisions of the thesis statement's argument. The topic sentence of a body paragraph states a key idea of the thesis, each idea (or topic sentence) expressing not only an aspect of the thesis statement but also the organizational method chosen for the paragraph.

HOW DOES THE WRITER GENERATE A TOPIC FOR A THESIS STATEMENT?

Option One: Ask and Answer Questions About the Literature

Writers may generate a topic by asking and answering a series of questions about the work of literature they are studying. The answer to a question—or the answers to various questions—may produce a topic and, ultimately, lead to the formulation of a thesis statement.

• Theme
Does the story depict an abstract idea, a moral or psychological struggle, an aspect of human life? Does the story's narrative suggest an analogy?

• Character
Does a character change—if so, why and how? What are a character's prominent qualities? What is the function of a character in the narrative—is he or she the hero, the servant, the sage, the antagonist, a Christ figure, a tempter, a trickster? Is a character similar to another, perhaps a double? Is a character an exact contrast of another, or perhaps a foil? Does the character react in the same manner when confronted by different characters or settings?

• Plot
Is the work a comedy, a tragedy, an epic, a bildungsroman, a fable, an allegory? What are the primary conflicts or problems in the text? What are significant complications in the plot? What plot devices does the author employ?

• Setting
What is important about the setting? Are there multiple settings? How are they different? What does the landscape or dwelling suggest about theme or character?

• Style
How does the writer use imagery, diction, language, syntax to express tone or mood? What is the tone? Is there a motif; what is significant about it?

• Symbol
What does a symbol mean? What is its role in the story? Does its function change?

• Allusions
Does the plot of the story or a specific character remind the reader of an event or figure from history, from the Bible, or from mythology?

• Point of view
What is the function of the narration? How does first person, third person omniscient, objective, or third person limited narration affect the story?

• Exact words
What does any character in a story, play, or epic SAY that stands out and provokes an idea concerning a topic for a thesis statement? What lines in a character's speech or words in a character's dialogue suggest a potential topic?

Option Two: Use Aristotle's topics

ARISTOTLE'S TOPICS provide a way for a writer to generate a topic for the paper as well as to create an actual thesis statement. Aristotle suggests these topics align with the natural way we think and argue any subject.

For our purposes in *Crafting Expository Argument,* ARISTOTLE'S TOPICS are limited to the following four categories: Argument by Definition, Argument by Classification, Argument by Comparison (comparison of similarities, comparison of differences, or comparison by degrees), and Argument by Relationship (the relationship of contraries as well as the relationship of cause and effect).

With each explanation of one of the categories of ARISTOTLE'S TOPICS, at least two examples have been provided. Each example consists of a possible thesis statement as well as the topic sentences for only two of the potential body paragraphs supporting each thesis statement. *Clearly, to be conscientiously argued, many of these thesis statements would require additional body paragraphs based on other topic sentences .*

Because the strategies for making an expository argument based upon a work of literature apply as well to other courses and fields of study, which also require expository writing by students, some of the following examples using categories of ARISTOTLE'S TOPICS have been applied to thesis statements not drawn from literary works.

Definition

WHEN WRITERS ARGUE BY DEFINITION, they assert that the details of the text, or the details of a contemporary or historical situation, provide examples for the definition of a concept (such concepts may, for instance, be justice, fatherhood, decision-making, evil, or friendship). Each concept contains multiple aspects, each aspect, then, serving as the central idea for each body paragraph's topic sentence.

DEFINITION ARGUMENTS FROM A LITERARY WORK

Thesis: In Nathaniel Hawthorne's *The Scarlet Letter,* Roger Chillingworth mirrors various characteristics of evil.
> [The writer will use each topic sentence to define a single quality of evil.]
> TS: Chillingworth practices deception, the attribute of evil that conceals its identity.
> [The writer will show multiple examples of how Chillingworth deceives by concealing his identity.]
> TS: Chillingworth, like evil, manipulates the most vulnerable human characteristic—the heart.
> [The writer will show multiple examples of how Chillingworth manipulates the emotions of others.]

Thesis: In the poem "Mending Wall," the poet Robert Frost creates a specific situation that reveals the paradoxical nature of barriers in human relationships: what separates human beings physically is what allows us to live together amicably. [Here, the writer will be defining the paradox of "the wall" in the poem by examining its apparently contradictory aspects.]

    TS: The poem's speaker is a "mischief"-maker, one who asserts the notion that the wall is an unnatural obstruction, a viewpoint likely shared at first by the reader.

    TS: The actions of both characters in the poem, the speaker and his "neighbor," demonstrate that, though the wall is man-made, it is in fact the natural, indeed instinctive, requirement of forming community.

DEFINITION ARGUMENTS NOT BASED ON A LITERARY WORK

Thesis: True friends respond selflessly, considering the needs of other human beings more paramount than their own.

    [Here the writer defines friendship as selfless concern for the needs of others.]

    TS: Authentic friends sacrifice their own time to help respond to someone else's need.

    [Here, the writer elaborates with examples showing how one or more friends have acted selflessly with their time.]

    TS: Genuine friends offer the moral guidance needed to navigate successfully the difficulties of life.

    [Here, the writer explores one or more specific examples of a friend providing such guidance.]

Thesis: Effective decision-making requires the ability to think logically, to seek wise counsel, and to recognize the limits of one's knowledge.

    TS: Reacting rationally to situations that arise, rather than reacting emotionally, is more likely to result in beneficial decisions.

    TS: Consulting others who have experienced similar situations—so long as time allows it—can lead to more advantageous conclusions.

Classification

WHEN MAKING AN ARGUMENT BY CLASSIFICATION, writers recognize that several examples—or pieces of evidence—within a text have like characteristics and, therefore, these examples belong to a distinct category. Like items in one category, then, are grouped into a body paragraph whose topic sentence identifies the unifying category. Like items in another category are grouped into a separate body paragraph whose topic sentence identifies that unifying category.

CLASSIFICATION ARGUMENTS FROM A LITERARY WORK

Thesis: The government in the novel *1984* employs several methods for controlling its citizenry.

    [The writer will explore and name in the topic sentence each of the "methods."]

    TS: Totalitarian governments often manipulate public information, both the details of history and the facts of the present.

    [The method identified here deals with information control and all the examples from the novel elaborated in this paragraph will demonstrate such manipulation.]

    TS: Totalitarian governments impose physical restrictions upon its citizens.

Thesis: Harry Potter demonstrates that the hero must overcome a variety of personal obstacles regardless of the physical powers of evil.

[In the following topic sentences, the writer will classify the types of challenges, other than physical, Potter confronts.]

TS: One of Harry Potter's challenges involves controlling his fear when confronting dangerous situations.

TS: Harry's own psychology must contend with memories of a painful past, which frequently prevent him from taking immediate action.

[Both paragraphs explore emotional challenges. Subsequent paragraphs might explore challenges that require the use of logic and quick rational thinking.]

CLASSIFICATION ARGUMENTS NOT FROM A LITERARY WORK

Thesis: Deception, or the deliberate concealment of the truth, can be justified when it protects the general well being of an individual or of society as a whole.

TS: When difficult situations arise involving one's child, deception shields innocence from the terror and cruelty of the outside world.

TS: During times of war, the government conceals certain details to protect its troops in battle.

Thesis: Friends fulfill a variety of needs, those which improve the body, the mind, and the soul.

TS: Friends on athletic teams urge their teammates to achieve physically that which others believe cannot be done.

TS: Friends, particularly those more gifted academically, help to teach us intellectual skills.

Comparison: Similarity or Difference or Degree

WHEN MAKING AN ARGUMENT BY COMPARISON, writers place two items side by side (characters, images, symbols, situations, setting, etc.). This side-by-side placement may yield any of three possibilities: that the two items are similar, that the two items reveal differences, or that the two items indicate a distinction of degree.

SIMILARITY

This comparison argument that focuses on similarity identifies the common features of two distinct items under discussion; in other words, the writer believes the two items placed next to each other are *analogous*. When crafting literary arguments, writers often explore this ANALOGY, which serves as a lengthy comparison, involving the resemblances discovered detail by detail between two items normally seen as distinctly different.

SIMILARITY ARGUMENTS FROM A LITERARY WORK

Thesis: The imagery Coleridge creates in "Kubla Khan" corresponds with his philosophy concerning how poetry is conceived and written.

TS: Coleridge uses archetypal images in "Kubla Khan" to portray the fertility of the imagination.

[The writer identifies the initial step in the writing process, the presence of a mind filled with ideas.]

TS: Coleridge's visual imagery in the poem demonstrates the selection

and elaboration of an idea as it pertains to poetic composition.
[The writer focuses on one aspect of the writing process—selecting and elaborating upon an idea.]

Thesis: The characterization in Mary Shelley's novel *Frankenstein* mirrors several qualities found in the characters created by John Milton in his epic poem *Paradise Lost*.
[The writer will define in each topic sentence a single quality that both Frankenstein and one of Milton's characters share.]
TS: Victor, like Satan, challenges God's omnipotent role as master of creation.
TS: Shelley borrows from Milton's Satan as she molds the character of the monster.

SIMILARITY ARGUMENTS NOT FROM A LITERARY WORK

Thesis: Musicians such as The Rolling Stones illustrate the salient characteristics normally associated with archeologists.
TS: As archeologists excavate the soil in search of revelatory artifacts, the Rolling Stones have spent years unearthing blues and country music composed long before anyone in the group could play an instrument.
TS: The instruments the Rollings Stones use to reveal musical relics have much in common with the tools the archeologist painstakingly employs.

Thesis: Fruits and vegetables both contain ingredients that help prevent cancer.
TS: Several green vegetables contain important antioxidants.
TS: A diet rich in berries can provide antioxidant protection against cancer.

DIFFERENCE

The comparison argument that explores differences examines the contrasts between two items within the same class or grouping—between two athletes, two friends, two birthday gifts, two literary heroes, two sonnets.

DIFFERENCE ARGUMENTS FROM A LITERARY WORK

Thesis: Biddy and Estella in Dickens' *Great Expectations* influence Pip's maturation in contrasting ways.
TS: Biddy models for Pip the virtue of humble selflessness.
TS: Estella reinforces the idea that the value of individuals is based upon their social and economic class.

Thesis: Harry Potter and Hermione Granger reflect distinct sets of wizardry skills.
TS: Hermione possesses the ability to learn from situations in the past.
TS: Potter relies on his internal instincts when responding to danger.

DIFFERENCE ARGUMENTS NOT FROM A LITERARY WORK

Thesis: While small colleges and major universities provide a core educational foundation, small colleges emphasize excellence in teaching while universities stress the significance of research.

> TS: Larger universities have gradually transformed their educational mission to emphasize the research its faculty conducts.
>
> TS: The small college campus encourages its faculty to excel at classroom instruction.

Thesis: An examination of medical reponses to influenza epidemics in the twentieth century illustrates the stark contrast between the early part of the century and its latter half, underscoring remarkable advances in medicine.

> TS: The panic created in the early twentieth century highlighted doctors' limited understanding of viruses
>
> TS: While flu continued to cause illness in the late twentieth century, medical advances in prevention and a clearer understanding of virus mutation has thwarted widespread death.

DEGREE

Sometimes writers examine two items in juxtaposition not to demonstrate they are completely different but that they differ by degree. One, for example, may be better than the other or worse than the other, one more effective than another, one more beneficial for the greater good than another, etc.

DEGREE ARGUMENTS FROM A LITERARY WORK

Thesis: Although both are leaders, Odysseus more accurately exemplifies the ideal Greek hero than Agamemnon, the commander-in-chief of the armies.

> [The writer will select for each topic sentence one quality of the ideal Greek hero to unify each paragraph.]
>
> TS: The Greek hero must demonstrate prowess not only on the battlefield but also in the arena of language.
>
> [The initial part of this paragraph will focus on Odysseus then shift to Agamemnon, whose use of language is less effective.]
>
> TS: The ideal Greek hero ought maintain control over his emotions when in a position of leadership.
>
> [Here, Agamemnon's confrontation with Achilles will be compared to Odysseus' with the suitors.]

Thesis: Hermione Granger demonstrates more potential as a young wizard than does Ron Weasely during their first year at Hogwarts.

> [Each topic sentence will explore a singular trait where Hermione is more successful than Ron.]
>
> TS: Hermione, unlike Ron, understands the importance of studying a variety of spells and potions.
>
> [This paragraph might first explore Hermione's study habits, then contrast them with those of Ron.]
>
> TS: Hermione's ability to think quickly in dangerous situations surpasses Ron's ability to react to threats.

DEGREE ARGUMENTS NOT FROM A LITERARY WORK

Thesis: Fiddlers and violinists make music using the same instrument but the music they make reveals differing levels of artistry in the talents they possess.

> TS: The type of music performed by violinists requires a longer period of

time to master prior to performance than does that performed by fiddlers. TS: While violinists must often integrate their instrument into the entirety of an orchestra, fiddlers work within a much smaller grouping of musicians.

Relationship: Contraries and Cause-Effect

WHEN WRITERS CONSTRUCT ARGUMENTS BY RELATIONSHIP, they argue the presence of a clear connection or correlation between the items—situations, events, characters, settings, etc.—under consideration. For the purposes of this book, the two types of arguments by relationship emphasized herein are the CONTRARY relationship and the CAUSE-EFFECT relationship.

CONTRARIES

WHEN WRITERS ARGUE A CONTRARY RELATIONSHIP, they identify polar opposites of items within a category. Just as in the category of temperatures, where hot is the opposite of cold, and in the category of landscapes, where the desert is the opposite of the rain forest, when a writer constructs an argument based on a contrary relationship, he examines two ideas, two characters, two choices, two values that are incompatible.

CONTRARY ARGUMENTS FROM A LITERARY WORK

Thesis: In the play *Twelve Angry Men,* Juror Three and Juror Four spotlight the clash between the ethical and unethical conduct of Jurors in the justice system.
> [The thesis statement focuses on two opposing types of jurors—the ideal juror, who views matters logically, and the distinctly undesirable juror, whose response is largely an emotional one.]

TS: Juror Three recognizes that the ethical approach to jury duty requires the ability to rely on reason rather than emotion when evaluating evidence.
> [This paragraph will walk the reader through a series of examples, arranged chronologically, that highlight the use of reason by this juror.]

TS: Juror Four responds to the details of the case with emotional responses, frequently demonstrating a series of fallacies in reasoning.

Thesis: Madame Defarge and Lucy Manette epitomize the struggle between the anarchic impulse and the desire for order.
> TS: Madame Defarge seeks further destruction within her community.
> TS: Lucy heals those within her community who are wounded.

CONTRARY ARGUMENTS NOT FROM A LITERARY WORK

Thesis: John Locke and Karl Marx are philosophers who represent two contrary political visions regarding the role of government.
> TS: Locke and Marx differ regarding the role government plays in the lives of the governed.
> TS: Both philosophers hold distinctly incompatible views on the nature of the individual and private property.

CAUSE-EFFECT

WHEN WRITERS CONSTRUCT ARGUMENTS BY CAUSE-EFFECT RELATIONSHIP, they argue the presence of a clear correlation between two or more events under consideration, *a connection so essential* as to suggest that one event would have been unlikely to occur without the prior or simultaneous existence of the other event.

To fashion an appropriate argument based upon a cause-effect relationship, the skillful writer nurtures an ability to observe patterns emerging in the literature being read, the history being studied, the issues of the day being debated. The reader of any literary work, for example, discerns the repetition of similar or contrasting situations that establish such a pattern. Perhaps a certain type of outcome is preceded by a pattern of similar events on more than one occasion. Perhaps every time a character acts in X manner or makes X choices, Y results.

Writers then reflect upon these multiple examples in a specific work—examples of effects or causes—and, after due consideration, associate a specific idea with the pattern of examples. Conceivably, all the examples connected to a specific cause can, for instance, be associated with the desire for power; and the examples connected to effect might be associated with the idea of chaos. Once writers have completed identifying the nature of the cause and the effect, they are ready to write a thesis statement that might read like this: THE UNTRAMMELED DESIRE FOR POWER ULTIMATELY LEADS TO CHAOS WITHIN THE COMMUNITY.

One error that young writers sometimes make is to isolate one example of a cause-effect relationship in the text and use that single incident for their thesis. For example, in Homer's *Iliad*, Agamemnon refuses to return Chryses' daughter, a refusal that leads the god Apollo to inflict a plague upon the Greek armies. Here, we clearly see causality, but this example reflects one of several similar instances in the poem where a similar type of causality takes place. So a thesis that states, "If a leader refuses to return the daughter of Apollo's priest, Apollo will destroy his army," merely calls attention to one example of a cause-effect relationship without articulating exactly what the universal cause-effect relationship is.

The writer needs to locate other similar examples in the poem that follow this same pattern. For instance, later on in this opening book of Homer's epic, Agamemnon refuses to allow Achilles to keep his prize, Briseis, which causes Achilles to withdraw from war, leaving the Greeks vulnerable to the Trojans. At this point, as the writer begins to locate additional examples, he will need to assert an associative category for both the causes of several similar examples and the effects. He will then be prepared to craft a thesis statement. In this case, a writer examining the leadership of Agamemnon in *The Iliad* might formulate this thesis: A LEADER WHOSE DECISIONS ARE ANCHORED IN SELF-CENTERED EMOTION IMPERILS THE EXISTENCE OF THE COMMUNITY HE LEADS.

For the purposes of *Crafting Expository Argument*, cause-effect arguments can be constructed by the writer in two primary ways.

1. A cause producing an effect or effects.

The writer can first begin with the cause, formulating a thesis that contends Event A is (was or will be) the cause of Event B happening, that is, the reason why Event B occurs (occurred or will occur). Of course, in many cases, more than one effect can be attributed to a single cause.

A writer may be constructing a paper that examines an historical event such as the Great Depression. His research on the subject may lead him to argue that the Great Depression caused the rise of dictatorship in Europe, scant attention being paid to military defense in democratic countries, and national borders increasingly vulnerable to attack by enemy nations.

A writer may decide to write a paper after reading a literary work such as Leo Tolstoy's *Anna Karenina*. Her study of the novel may lead her to argue that uncontrolled passions inevitably lead to tragedy and to explicate her thesis by examining the title character's descent once she becomes thoroughly enamored of Count Vronsky.

A third example of a cause producing an effect, or effects, can be observed when a writer constructs an essay in support of a specific position concerning a topical issue of the day. Let us say, for example, that Congress is considering legislation that would grant amnesty to any immigrants who have arrived in this country illegally. Passage of that legislation, according to this writer's thesis, would be the cause producing a variety of negative effects, each effect being elaborated in the essay's body paragraph. As with any contemporary issue, another writer's thesis might contend that passage of such legislation would be the cause leading to a number of positive effects.

2. An effect resulting from one or more causes.

A second method of constructing the cause-effect argument is for the writer to begin with the effect, and thus to argue back from the effect to the cause of that effect. Using this approach, the writer develops a thesis proposing that Event D happens (happened, or will happen) because of the prior or simultaneous existence of Event C. Of course, more than one cause (which might be labeled Event C2 and Event C3) can be ascribed to a single effect.

If a writer, for example, is working on an essay that examines what precipitated the French Revolution in 1789 [Event D], her research may lead her to argue a number of causes. Such causal factors [Events C1, C2, and C3] might involve the following: the philosophical ideas concerning political freedom and equality that had saturated much of the populace; the high taxation to support an aristocracy that was no longer respected by the citizenry being taxed; and the French troops' prior involvement in supporting the American colonists in their revolution against the British, such involvement a decade earlier serving as a model for revolution.

Were a writer to analyze a work of literature such as Shakespeare's King Lear, he might argue that King Lear's tragic fall was caused by his disproportionate pride.

In the following examples, some thesis statements will focus on exploring the causes of a particular effect and other thesis statements will focus on exploring the effects generated by a cause. As in previous examples of thesis statements followed by topic sentences, that there are two topic sentences listed does not preclude other topic sentences. The fact is every thesis statement in this section is likely to necessitate more than two body paragraphs to prove and, therefore, more than two topic sentences. These examples merely serve as a guide for how such thesis statements and their topic sentences might be constructed.

CAUSE-EFFECT ARGUMENTS FROM A LITERARY WORK

Thesis: Thomas Hardy argues in his poem "Convergence of the Twain" that human pride resulted in the destruction of the *Titanic,* a ship emblematic of man's arrogance. [CAUSE PRODUCES EFFECT: This paper argues that Hardy's poem demonstrates a singular cause producing a decisive effect.]

> TS: The initial section of the poem explores images of wealth and beauty now decayed, the effect of human pride.

> TS: The second half of the poem introduces the primary symbol of human pride, the *Titanic,* inevitably destined for tragedy.

Thesis: Shakespeare's *Macbeth* serves as a study in the effects of unbridled political ambition. [CAUSE PRODUCES EFFECTS: The writer of this essay posits a singular cause for a number of effects observed in Shakespeare's play.]

> TS: When Macbeth's closest confidant, his wife, nurtures his ambition, the restraints that shield his moral compass gradually loosen.

> TS: Once he becomes king, Macbeth abdicates all moral principles as he seeks to maintain his ill-gotten power.

Thesis: King Lear's tragic fall is precipitated by an unrestrained vanity that adversely affects his judgment. [EFFECT RESULTING FROM A CAUSE: The writer of this paper indicates that each topic sentence will elaborate evidence of such vanity clouding his ability to make wise decisions.]

> TS: Lear's insistence that each of his daughters must declare how much she loves him makes him unable to distinguish genuine familial love from the feigned.

> TS: Because his arrogance brooks no dissent, Lear banishes his most perceptive adviser.

CAUSE-EFFECT ARGUMENTS NOT FROM A LITERARY WORK

Thesis: Aspects of our culture have led to an increase in overweight Americans. [SINGLE EFFECT RESULTING FROM CAUSES: Here the writer focuses on the single effect of obesity and will explore in each paragraph one of a number of causes.]

> TS: The proliferation of fast food has enticed people with its speed of preparation but not with its nutritional value.

> TS: Limited time given to physcal activity, starting at a young age, has produced a generation of sedentary Americans

Thesis: Americans who smoke face a variety of medical and social problems. [CAUSE PRODUCES EFFECTS: Here the writer introduces a single cause—smoking—and proceeds to explore a variety of effects, one effect per paragraph.]

> TS: Americans who smoke increase their risk for stroke and heart attack.

> TS: Smoking decreases the immune system's ability to combat illness.

Thesis: Recessions are caused by multiple variables at work in an economy. [SINGLE EFFECT RESULTING FROM CAUSES: Here the writer focuses on a single effect and will explore in each paragraph one of a number of causes.]

> TS: Regulating monetary policy by the Federal Reserve Bank can often produce volatility.

> TS: Speculation in the real estate market, one of the largest sectors of the US economy, can produce recession.

OBTAIN EVIDENCE THAT SUPPORTS THE THESIS STATEMENT

• Find and Evaluate Evidence

Search for, list, and evaluate possible evidence in the literary text—*evidence* being the details as well as the diction and imagery—related to the topic. Include in your list-making any key passages from the text—*key passages* having words you directly quote from the narrator of the story, or the speaker of the poem, or from one or more characters—that clearly relate to your topic.

As you peruse the evidence and passages, evaluate the following:
1. How does each piece of evidence apply to the topic I have selected?
2. Where and when do specific situations from the evidence occur in the text?
3. How do the details, imagery, and diction relate to each other? What associative ideas are connected to this evidence?
4. In key passages, when directly quoting the narrator, the speaker, or any characters, what is the tone—the attitude toward the subject—conveyed?

• Reflect on the evidence, looking for patterns

While reflecting on this evidence, writers strive to *discover a pattern*. In order to write a thesis statement based upon the evidence relating to your topic—an assertion that goes beyond stating mere plot detail—a writer considers how pieces of evidence relate to one another. In locating these connections, patterns emerge.

To attempt to write a thesis statement without reflecting on the evidence gathered—including re-reading sections of the literary text—is to invite frustration and writer's block. Only after careful reflection on possible textual evidence can an intelligent thesis emerge.

HOW DOES THE WRITER FORMULATE A THESIS STATEMENT?

Broad Subject:...................... A Christmas Carol
Specific Topic: .... Bob Cratchit
Question about the topic: ... Why is he important to the story?
Pattern in the evidence....... Cratchit repeatedly oriented toward his family.
Thesis:................................... Bob Cratchit represents the ideal father.

Check the thesis statement formula: topic + debatable opinion

1. Can the writer identify the topic of the thesis statement? The topic might be a symbol, a character, a motif, an archetype—or any aspect of the ANALYTICAL VOICE Chart from Chapter 1, especially Level Three, the writer examining the *relationships* among diction, imagery, and details, and the *conceptual associations* linked to such evidence.
2. Can the writer identify the debatable opinion—the CLAIM—in the thesis statement? Or does the statement merely identify a detail or fact from the text?
3. Does the thesis statement merely summarize the evidence from the text?
4. Does the diction in the thesis statement include vague or abstract words that contain too many possible meanings, thus preventing a clear focus?

Examples of thesis statements without a debatable opinion
- Ebenezer Scrooge is forced to remember events of the past.
- Huck and Jim experience several conflicts during their travel down the river.
- There are many symbols in the book.
- Dickens repeats images of "hands" throughout the novel.
- Matthew Arnold uses a metaphor involving the sea in his poem.

Examples of thesis statements with a debatable opinion
- Scrooge's encounters with ghosts depict memory's transformative power.
- Huck and Jim's path toward friendship moves through three stages: the meeting, the challenge to survive, and love.
- The archetype of clothing mirrors Huck's desire for individuality.
- In *Great Expectations* the hands motif indicates Pip's location in the journey toward maturity.
- The sea metaphor allows Matthew Arnold to develop a political commentary on the Victorian Age, a time in which man is isolated and void of religious conviction, a situation that can only be rectified by human love.
- The diction and imagery Twain uses in relaying Huck's story reveals his personal struggle with freedom and civilization.

AFTER WRITING THE THESIS STATEMENT, WHAT NEXT?

• Organize the evidence

After looking at the list of textual passages, consider the best way to organize the evidence (the diction, the imagery, and the details). Look for patterns. In some cases, the evidence may best be grouped chronologically, according to sections of the text. *However, in many cases, you will want to organize the evidence according to how you have generated the topic for your thesis statement, your thesis statement being your argument.*

If you have generated the topic for your thesis statement according to one of ARISTOTLE'S TOPICS, you know that each body paragraph will be designed to develop the debatable opinion your paper argues. For example, if your argument involves a definition, each body paragraph will likely examine a specific feature of that definition, the evidence being organized according to how it supports each feature. If your argument involves a comparison that emphasizes similarities, each body paragraph will elaborate a specific similarity, the evidence being organized according to how it supports that similarity. If your argument involves a cause that produces a number of effects, each body paragraph will analyze a distinct effect, the evidence being organized according to its support of that effect.

Of course, you will want to review the ORGANIZATION CHOICES previously discussed in Chapter Three (pp. 60-63): time, place, idea. Beware: Some young writers attempt to organize their papers and write topic sentences for body paragraphs without first examining the evidence. This is an error. *Once you have created your thesis statement, organize the evidence so that it clearly supports all the key aspects of the argument (the thesis) you are making.*

AFTER ORGANIZING EVIDENCE, WHAT DOES THE WRITER DO?

- **Create topic sentences.**

Write topic sentences that will support the thesis statement. Topic sentences show the reader how the writer is organizing the evidence. **Bold-faced phrases** *in the sample topic sentences that follow demonstrate the writer's organization choice; the* underlined words *act as glue tying the topic sentence to the thesis statement.*

Topic Sentence (TS) = Organizing Element + Aspect of Thesis

Organization Choices

1. TIME: Organize chronologically, moving through the events in the novel or poem. (Note that I have only given examples of two topic sentences; these thesis statements often will require more.)

Thesis	The conch in *Lord of the Flies* represents the decay of order and civilization.
TS1	In **chapter one,** the conch is discovered and revered for its power to organize the community of children.
TS2	In **chapter three,** the conch shows signs of losing its civilizing power.

> **TS ≠ PLOT DETAIL ONLY**
> A topic sentence that contains only a plot detail does not communicate an organization choice or an aspect of the thesis. For example, "Piggy discovers the conch near the lagoon in chapter one" is a plot detail and not a topic sentence.

2. PLACE: Organize according to locations in the text.

Thesis	The marriages in *Great Expectations* depict the variety of virtues and vices present in this British community.
TS1	Near the story's beginning, the reader encounters the **residence of Joe and Mrs. Joe,** a home where truth and innocence are preyed upon.
TS2	Later, the reader visits **the Pockets' home,** a place of idleness and self-centeredness.

Thesis	In *The Scarlet Letter,* Hester models the emotional strength uncharacteristic of a stereotypical seventeenth century woman.
TS1	Exiting the **prison door,** Hester's demeanor shows the reader her assertiveness.
TS2	At **the governor's house,** Hester forcefully displays her confidence.

3. IDEA: This approach includes papers organized according to ARISTOTLE'S TOPICS: by definition, by classification, by comparison, and by relationship. The topic sentences, then, articulate separate features of the thesis statement. For example, topic sentences might explain aspects of a definition, classify the evidence into categories, identify effects, etc.

Thesis	In *The Tempest* Prospero possesses the qualities of leadership all communities hope to produce.
TS1	Prospero demonstrates an ability **to restrain his emotions.**
TS2	Prospero recognizes that **those who commit crimes must**

receive consequences.

Thesis	In *The Canterbury Tales,* Chaucer uses his characters to explore three moral categories.
TS1	The **lowest level** Chaucer describes is one of complete depravity.
TS2	Chaucer's **second moral plane is defined** by the perpetration of evil acts: sloth, selfishness, and hypocrisy.

Thesis	In *Great Expectations,* Pip finds himself in a situation paralleling the parable of the prodigal son.
TS1	The **Bible's parable begins** with the prodigal son who, dissatisfied with his present situation in life, asks his father for his inheritance.
TS2	After he leaves his home and father, Pip, the prodigal, **squanders his inheritance** on a life of dissipation.

Thesis	In his play *Romeo and Juliet,* Shakespeare examines the dark heart of "fair Verona," a community whose leaders fail to act in an open, decisive, and forthright manner.
TS1	The political leader of Verona, Prince Escalus, **"winks" at the discord** in the community **rather than acting immediately** to resolve the escalating hostilities.
TS2	The spiritual head of Verona, Friar Laurence, concocts a solution to the crisis that requires **deception and secrecy,** two features ensuring disaster.

CHECK THE DICTION OF THE TOPIC SENTENCES

• Word glue
Does the writer use word glue to connect the topic sentences with the thesis statement? The writer may use synonyms or exact words from the thesis statement. The writer or reader should be able to draw circles around common words in the thesis and topic sentences. If the writer can't, the reader might not understand how the writer plans to prove the argument. *As in the previous examples that demonstrate organization choices, pp. 106-107, the underlined words here are the glue tying the topic sentence to the thesis.*

Thesis	In *Great Expectations* the use of the hands motif indicates Pip's location in the **journey toward maturity.**

• Original First topic sentence
Pip lives in a household of violence and poor relationships. *(This is merely a plot detail.)*

Revised
Pip first encounters the impressionable stage of childhood, wherein Pip is not yet able to evaluate situations critically; consequently, Pip surmises an association between hands and acrimonious relationships.

- **Original Second topic sentence**

Pip begins to hate his life at the forge after he visits Miss Havisham and Estella. *(This is merely a fact from the chapter.)*

Revised

Shortly after early childhood, Pip begins to grow into the more contemplative stage of preadolescence, a stage in which he begins to question his surroundings as well as draw conclusions about them.

Thesis   Coleridge's "Rime of the Ancient Mariner" illustrates man's proclivity since the Fall to **sin without cause,** to possess the **opportunity of reconciliation,** and to have the option to **do penance,** all in hopes of receiving forgiveness.

- **Original First topic sentence**

The Mariner's misfortunes begin by abruptly and without cause killing the albatross. *(A plot detail.)*

Revised

Since the Fall, man often discovers himself <u>sinning without cause</u> and sometimes without explanation.

- **Original Third topic sentence**

The narrator learns that the Mariner must now tell his tale. *(A plot detail.)*

Revised

With <u>reconciliation</u> comes <u>penance,</u> another stage on a path to forgiveness.

MORE EXAMPLE THESIS STATEMENTS + TOPIC SENTENCES

Topic   Scout in *To Kill a Mockingbird*

Thesis   *To Kill a Mockingbird* by Harper Lee focuses the attention of the perspicacious reader on Scout's growth as she transforms from a carefree child into a true lady, one who is a lady at heart, not just a lady in appearance.

TS1   As Scout's father, Atticus plays an important role in teaching her important <u>values that a true lady</u> must possess.

TS2   In addition to Atticus' lessons, Miss Maudie Atkinson, Scout's benign neighbor, helps her <u>grow up to be a true lady.</u>

TS3   Contradictory values of character and <u>appearance</u> confront Scout as she becomes <u>a lady of character.</u>

Topic   Nature imagery in *Romeo & Juliet*

Thesis   In *Romeo and Juliet,* William Shakespeare's skillful use of imagery borrowed from the world of nature paints a vivid portrait of the emotional and physical make-up of man.

TS1   Various <u>light images taken from nature</u> reveal Juliet's brilliant <u>beauty</u> and suggest her <u>growing fears.</u>

TS2   Shakespeare's ingenious utilization of <u>bird imagery</u> creates a lucid picture of man's <u>physical qualities.</u>

TS3   Shakespeare also uses <u>bird imagery</u> to create man's <u>emotional characteristics.</u>

TS4   The use of other <u>animal imagery</u> produces a clear model of the <u>complex emotional nature</u> of man.

Topic   Dictatorial power in Homer's *Odyssey*

Thesis   The grip of power of Antinoos and Eurymachos is analogous to the authority of twentieth century dictators.

TS1   The leaders of the suitors and twentieth century dictators are demagogues who <u>appeal to people's fears and emotions to get them</u> to carry out their <u>commands.</u>

TS2   Both the leaders of the suitors and contemporary dictators <u>rule by force</u> rather than by law or respect for their position.

TS3   Despite the <u>facade of power</u> that Antinoos and twentieth century dictators possess, their positions as leaders are not very stable.

TS4   Both groups also <u>blame the problems of their leadership</u> on others.

Topic   New Testament revisited in *A Tale of Two Cities*

Thesis   Through images synonymous with Christ and imagery depicting the events before the Crucifixion, Dickens identifies the death of Sydney Carton with the death of Christ.

TS1   Before Dickens introduces Carton himself into his <u>Passion story,</u> he first gives the reader *images of Carton's similarities to Christ.*

TS2   Having formed a connection between <u>Carton</u> and <u>Christ</u>, Dickens now begins his version of the <u>Passion story.</u>

TS3   Dickens imitates several aspects of the <u>Last Supper of Jesus.</u>

TS4   Dickens also alludes to <u>Pontius Pilate</u> and <u>the trial of Jesus</u> that determines his sentence.

A FINAL WORD ABOUT ORGANIZATION/CONTENT

• How many paragraphs?

A writer must decide how many paragraphs are necessary to prove or illustrate his or her argument. Each aspect of a student's thesis statement may be equivalent to one or more paragraphs. For example, in longer papers over 1,500 words, a writer will likely use a combination of *one-idea* paragraphs and *subordinate paragraphs*. In shorter papers, however, those under 1,500 words, a student will likely use single-idea paragraphs, explaining each aspect of his thesis statement with one paragraph per feature.

THE SHOWING-TELLING INTRODUCTION

Because the goal of the introduction is to grab our attention with a concise concrete narrative WHOSE DETAILS RELATE ANALOGOUSLY TO THE THESIS, the writer's first step is to locate analogous details. Quite often, these details are—as artfully and as briefly as possible—a re-created situation from literature, history, or contemporary life, each detail relevant to the major point of the thesis. Sometimes these details may be found in a brief but pertinent direct quotation. Either way, this short narrative is followed by a transition—a sentence or two commenting upon the narrative details, explaining their analogous link to the thesis—followed thereafter by a clearly-stated thesis.

METHODS FOR SELECTING ANALOGOUS MATERIAL

As the writer begins drafting his introduction, he or she must grab the reader's attention (through briefly elaborated SHOWING) and then clearly state (thus, **telling**) the thesis.

There are several methods of grabbing the reader's attention:
1. Create a very brief, but SHOWING, story that is relevant to the overall thesis of your essay;
2. Paraphrase a scene from the literary text the writer will discuss, such paragraph relating directly to the writer's thesis;
3. Use a brief but pertinent quotation from the literary text that serves as the foundation for the writer's paper, such quotation containing concrete detail applicable to the writer's thesis;
4. Use a brief but pertinent quotation from a different literary text that helps introduce the subject of the writer's paper, such quotation containing concrete detail applicable to the writer's thesis;
5. Paraphrase a different literary text or historical situation, such paraphrase relating directly to the writer's thesis.

In simple terms, the *SHOWING-TELLING INTRODUCTION* contains these parts:
• analogous narrative situation (literary, contemporary, historical) that is similar in detail to the paper's thesis,
• transitional sentences that comment on the associations contained in the details of the analogy, associations found, then, in the writer's thesis, and
• the thesis statement.

Editing the showing-telling introduction for relevancy to the thesis

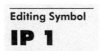

Editing Symbol

IP 1

IP1 = The analogy for the introduction is not effective; too many details of the situation re-created are not applicable to the paper's thesis.

Editing Symbol	
IP 2	**IP2** = Not all of the SHOWING details in the introduction are necessary. Remove those that are not associated with the concepts in the thesis.

Editing Symbol	
IP 3	**IP3** = The writer needs to interpret and comment on the details created in the introduction, highlighting specifically those associations he sees as similar to his thesis.

Sample showing-telling introduction before it is revised

Below is an example of a showing-telling introduction, this introduction following Method 5. It requires more precise editing because of **IP 2** and **IP 3**. The underlined sections point to areas that need revision.

> Shots begin to ring out across the dead forest blanketed with snow. The snow creates large drifts, obstacles to soldiers seeking to fight the enemy. Several soldiers stumble through the snow, creating potential danger as enemy fire ensues. Falling from the hazy gray sky, a mortar lands by a patrol squad and explodes. The particles scatter throughout the air, creating a cloud of smoke. "Medic!" cries a soldier whose buddy now lies on the ground with a bloody hole in his neck. Field medic Eugene Roe, depicted in Stephen Ambrose's *Band of Brothers*, rushes to the downed soldier as bullets and shrapnel fly through the trees. Officers pulling back their men to safer ground, they run back to their foxholes; however, Roe stays with the soldier in an attempt to save his life. Wiglaf, a true soldier, reveals similar characteristics when he battles the dragon with Beowulf. Wiglaf serves to function as both a fearless soldier who contrasts with his comrades and a selfless warrior who aids Beowulf.

Sample showing-telling introduction after it has been revised

The underlined sections can be remedied as follows: Extraneous details— details that do not emphasize the analogy clearly or do not advance the concepts in the thesis—can be removed [**IP 2**]. After the writer finishes re-creating the pertinent details from *Band of Brothers*, commentary on those details—commentary that helps the reader understand the correspondence between the showing details and the thesis—must be made more precise in the transitional sentences prior to the thesis statement [**IP 3**].

> Shots begin to ring out across the dead forest blanketed with snow. Falling from the hazy gray sky, a mortar lands by a patrol squad and explodes. "Medic!" cries a soldier whose buddy now lies on the ground with a bloody hole in his neck. Field medic Eugene Roe, depicted in Stephen Ambrose's *Band of Brothers*, rushes to the downed soldier as bullets and shrapnel fly through the trees. While officers pull back their men to safer ground and run back to their foxholes, Roe stays with the soldier in an attempt to save his life. Dedicated field medics in World War II like Roe have the difficult task of caring for the injured in the heat of battle without regard for their own safety. Just as Roe displays selflessness and bravery in helping others, Wiglaf, in the epic poem *Beowulf*, reveals similar characteristics when he battles the dragon with Beowulf. Wiglaf functions as the archetypal soldier

in *Beowulf*—fearless and selfless, a warrior who stands in stark contrast with his comrades.

Additional questions about the introductory paragraph

- From the first few words, has the writer grabbed the reader's attention?
- Are the verbs active and in the present tense?
- Has the writer re-created a brief but compelling scene that demonstrates a point in his or her essay—a scene or situation from a literary, contemporary, or historical text (the one being discussed or a comparable tale from a different text) or from contemporary life that effectively leads into the thesis?
- Has the writer written a transition sentence or sentences that connect the attention-grabber to the thesis statement?
- Is the writer's thesis statement clearly stating A TOPIC + A DEBATABLE OPINION?
- Has the writer used a variety of sentence structures in the introduction?

SAMPLE SHOWING-TELLING INTRODUCTORY PARAGRAPHS

- In each of the following introductory paragraphs, the **bold-faced sentence** makes the *transition* from the SHOWING introduction to the thesis statement
- The underlined sentence is the *thesis,* or telling, statement.
- The method number refers to "Methods for Selecting Analogous Materials," p. 110.

Methods 4 & 5   *by Aaron Vilfordi*

Gazing upon a shimmering blue sea with the cool wind blowing over a pearly white vessel, Mary Shelley's Victor Frankenstein tells his apprentice, Robert Walton, to "Learn from my miseries, and do not seek to increase your own" (156). The dying Frankenstein admonishes Walton to refrain from the mistake he has made, the mistake of usurping the heavenly task of creating life. With this admonishment, Victor receives some absolution and regains his humanity by compassionately influencing another to think of the consequences before acting on such dreams, although his arrival at this stage is too late. **Charles Dickens' Pip, although a comic hero, emulates Frankenstein in the way he, too, makes bad choices, finally rediscovering his true humanity through his concern and love for his old friend, Joe.** Pip starts out as an innocent boy but is soon corrupted by the dream of becoming a gentleman. Pip struggles with this dream, his life changing for the worse. Finally, Pip realizes what he has done and what he has lost. Unlike Frankenstein, Pip is able to learn from his mistakes and change before his life becomes a tragedy. He receives absolution by restoring his love for Joe. <u>Pip, the main character in Charles Dickens' *Great Expectations,* escapes Victor Frankenstein's tragic life because he completes a journey through four stages that allow him more completely to rediscover his true humanity: innocence, corruption, arrogance, and reconciliation.</u>

Method 1

Mark wipes the blood from his nose on his torn white shirt, grabs his L.L. Bean backpack, and jogs toward home. Behind him he can hear his classmates' derision—"Run, run, look at him run home to Mama"—but he doesn't look back; rather, he begins to imagine his destination, his tree house, built over a year ago with the help of his father. Rounding the corner, most of his tears now dried, he can see the large red oak in his back yard, the rope ladder dangling from the small opening about 15 feet above the ground. He reaches the rope and aims for the wooden planks, rising, swaying back and forth in the air, but moving deliberately upward, closer to safety. His small hands push the square covering and slide it open, pulling himself up on to the floor. He reaches down and pulls up the rope ladder, his breathing still staggered. The rope piled beside him, he closes the door opening and feels safe. **Now he has time; now he can temporarily escape the cruelty of his world. Like Mark's tree house,** the river for Huck, in Mark Twain's *Adventures of Huckleberry Finn*, serves as a symbol of refuge, a world that provides an escape from the cruelties of everyday life.

Method 2 *by Daniel Lawson*

A man in black slithers through the shadows along the wall. He caresses the velvet bag filled with gold coins, just to assure himself of its continued existence. The poor soul he swindled it from this time is a widow with little money. After he had his way with her in bed, he sold her "passage into the Kingdom of Heaven," as he likes to put it. It didn't matter what he called it, as long as he got his money and a little fun on the side, too. He finally reaches the monastery, sneaks through his bedroom window, and falls asleep. **This is not a holy priest. He is a lying criminal who backstabs the helpless for money and, sometimes, sex.** He is the kind of clergyman Chaucer often depicts in *The Canterbury Tales*, one who desires wealth, breaks vows, and exploits the common man.

Method 4 *by Ben Bireley*

As they were going out, they met a man from Cyrene named Simon, and they forced him to carry the cross to a place called Golgotha. There they offered Jesus wine to drink, mixed with gall, but after tasting it, he refused to drink it. When they had crucified him, they divided up his clothes by casting lots. And sitting down, they kept watch over him there. Above his head, they placed the written charge against him: This is Jesus, King of the Jews. Two robbers were crucified with him, one on the right and one on the left. Those who passed by derided him, shaking their heads and saying, "You who would destroy the temple and build it in three days, save yourself! Come down from the cross if you are the Son of God!" (Matthew 27:32–40)

This excerpt from the Bible is part of the Passion story of Christ, one of the most popular stories in Western Civilization. The popularity of the story makes the symbols associated with it easily discernible to any perspicacious reader; therefore, **writers often use imagery and symbolism relating to Jesus' story to convey their thematic ideas. *A Tale of Two Cities*, by Charles Dickens, is one such example.** Through images synonymous with Christ and imagery depicting the events before the Crucifixion, Dickens identifies the death of Sydney Carton with the death of Jesus.

Method 1 *by Joseph McGill*

"Be healed, my brother! Rise up and walk by the healing power of the Holy Spirit!" the minister screams passionately into the microphone. He lays his hands on the young cripple's shoulders, and the boy, on cue, throws down his crutches and embraces the minister. No one in the entire congregation suspects it is a hoax; they sit dumbfounded, amazed by the evangelist's miraculous "healing powers." The minister plays for the rolling cameras, hugging the boy even tighter and squeezing tears out of the corners of his eyes. He can almost hear the telephones ringing non-stop in the back of the "church" with people willing to donate thousands of dollars to "aid his parish." Finally, after the crowd's "Amens!" and "Praise the Lords!" subside, the minister rises again to the microphone and begins his collection speech. "Be generous and give all you can to the good Lord! He looks favorably on those who contribute to his Kingdom and those who spread his message!" He barely contains a greedy grin as the baskets make their way around the church, stuffed with checks and bills. **This sly minister's exploitation of his parishioners resembles the corruption that Chaucer highlights in** *The Canterbury Tales.* Chaucer reveals three main areas of corruption in the Medieval church: a focus on worldly pleasures, a violation of basic Christian theology, and an exploitation of parishioners. These criticisms alert the reader to the human qualities of the clergy; like their parishioners, they too are people who sin and make mistakes.

Method 5   *by Russell Lemmer*

Colonel Sherburn cocks his neck to the left again, proceeds until he feels the second pop, and then returns his eyes to the vast ocean of angry faces that amalgamate to form the bloodthirsty mob. He gingerly spits upon the rooftop, and his eyes once again return to the ocean. "Lynch him! Hang him good!" yells a face, although it cannot be determined exactly which countenance made the entreaty. The ferment is allayed by the silence that succeeds the cry, and the faces begin to turn, left, right, left, right, as if each one were looking for back-up. A clap of thunder, a lightening bolt, the rain pelts harder than before as if aiming to injure. The Colonel still surveying, his lips begin to move and a speech follows. The speech that he delivers is short, yet memorable. It is about how a man will follow a crowd blindly, without purpose and without reason. Though briefly mentioned, the character of Colonel Sherburn plays a significant role in the novel *Huckleberry Finn.* Twain uses this character to get his point across about slavery: People do not even know why they continue it anymore, but they do it because the next man does. **In many novels, minor characters such as the Colonel play a tremendous role in the story. Such is the case with the character of Mr. Pumblechook in Charles Dickens' novel** *Great Expectations.* Pumblechook serves as the stereotypical, middle-class Englishman whose shallow treatment towards others, with respect to their social class, reflects the way society as a whole treats them.

Method 3   *by Jeff Erfe*

It was the best of times, it was the worst of times, it was the age of wisdom, it was the age of foolishness, it was the epoch of belief, it was the epoch of incredulity, it was the season of Light, it was the season of Darkness, it was the spring of hope, it was the winter of despair, we had everything before us, we had nothing before us, we were all going direct to Heaven, we were all going direct the other way—in short, the period was so far like the present period that some of its noisiest authorities insisted on its being received, for good or for evil, in the superlative degree of comparison only. (1; bk. 1, ch. 1)

As early as the opening sentences of *A Tale of Two Cities,* Charles Dickens sets up a recurring theme the reader will encounter throughout the novel: **the restive, combative duality between various opposing forces in the plot. The relationship between Mr. Stryver and Sydney Carton is one such example.** Stryver, although a minor character, plays a significant role as Carton's foil: he epitomizes greedy, inhuman, business-like formality against Carton's selfless and emotional tenderness. <u>In the end, as with all other dualities in the novel, the battle between the human and the inhuman is resolved, with Stryver fleeing as a hypocrite and the unlikely Carton rising as a phoenix from the ashes of desperation to save humanity.</u>

Method 5   *by Anthony Jardina*

After fighting the Trojans for ten years, Odysseus leaves to return to Ithaca; however, his crew has raped one of Athena's priestesses, causing her to impede his homecoming. She sends the crew on perilous journeys across the sea, eventually leaving Odysseus as the only surviving member, imprisoned on the goddess Calypso's island. After Odysseus mourns for many long years, he leaves, Athena's rage assuaged, on a small boat, yet his arduous journey continues, being tossed around by a storm, finally washing ashore naked and badly bruised. The sea has simultaneously expelled him and metaphorically cleansed him of his vices— pride, anger, and intemperance. The water has baptized Odysseus, cleansing him of his iniquities and allowing his new virtues to emerge. **This use of the sea as metaphor occurs as well in Charles Dickens' A Tale of Two Cities**, <u>where the sea functions as a metaphor to amplify events of the French Revolution highlighting its chaotic, engulfing nature.</u>

Method 4   *by Matt Joseph*

"I would die of shame to face the men of Troy/ and the Trojan women trailing their long robes/ if I would shrink from battle now, a coward."
(Homer 6.523-525)

As these words from the *Iliad* illustrate, the concept of duty is an old one. Just as Hector of Troy realized he would have to sacrifice his life in service to his city, so too have countless individuals been forced into a contemplation of what "duty" truly means. **Out of these meditations, several full-fledged philosophical systems have emerged. One such system is deontology, a philosophy regarding the nature of duty, a system which hypothesizes that reason must be foremost in human endeavor.** <u>In *Macbeth*, the selective, self-contradictory deontology of Act 1 Scene 7 contrasts with that of Act 4 Scene 3, a slightly more encompassing, accurate ethic that nonetheless also falls short of Kantian perfection.</u>

THE NON-SUMMARY CONCLUDING PARAGRAPH

1. The writer <u>does not summarize</u> the essay nor merely restate the thesis in a concluding paragraph. A well-written essay needs no summary in its concluding paragraph because the clarity of its organization throughout would make a summary conclusion merely redundant.
2. Instead, the writer connects the thesis to a larger issue—to the community, to the writer himself or herself, to other works of literature.
3. Blend the thesis, or its primary feature, into this larger issue.
4. Where appropriate, the writer might consider finishing the conclusion by "bookending" a significant detail from the SHOWING part of the introductory paragraph, or the writer might even subtly allude to a major detail from the body.

Ask these questions about the concluding paragraph

- Does the conclusion avoid merely summarizing the main points of the paper?
- Does the writer attempt to discuss what is significant about the paper's thesis?
- Does the writer attempt to relate the thesis to our contemporary culture in an elaborately extensive fashion?
- Does the writer attempt to relate the thesis to other works of literature?
- Does the writer attempt to "bookend" with a feature in the SHOWING part of the introductory paragraph?
- Should the writer extend the elaboration of an idea in the conclusion by providing a more concrete example?
- Are there any wordy structures? Are there any vague or confusing statements that could be more precise?
- Do sentences need combining? Are a variety of sentence structures used?

SAMPLE NON-SUMMARY CONCLUDING PARAGRAPHS

Subject: 1984 *by Brendan O'Brien*

Though 1984 has come and passed, O'Brien's exploitive techniques of seizing power over Winston remain a serious problem even in today's society. From Zimbabwe in Africa to Iran in the Middle East to Cuba in the Caribbean, many a nation's leaders continue to oppress and mislead their own people just for the superiority they gain from it. No such example illustrates this better than the tyrant ruling North Korea, Kim Jong Il. Like O'Brien, Kim Jong Il deceives his subjects, proclaiming in state-run media that the world loves him, celebrating his birthday, and even stating that he invented the hamburger, thereby convincing his people that he possesses both unrivaled charisma and innovation. In addition, Kim Jong Il similarly exploits fear to establish power over his subjects, holding vast amounts of nuclear weapons and sending hundreds of thousands of citizens, including children, to labor camps for such "crimes" as hoarding food and other "anti-socialist" activities. In a world full of men like Kim Jong Il who are willing to do anything for power, the character of O'Brien is terrifyingly real, and the power struggle that occurs between Winston and O'Brien could happen to any one of us. Therefore, the oppressing and dehumanizing dystopia that befalls Winston enhances the meaning of the literary work—a warning against allowing individuals or governments to gain power through exploiting our weaknesses with fear and deceit.

Subject: Beowulf
by Michael Ways

In many ways the heroic ideal of *sapienta et fortitudo* occurs in our modern military heroes. While no single warrior may possess the supernatural elements found in *Beowulf*, great soldiers must possess a combined intellect and physical fortitude, successful warfare requiring the blending of both human qualities. Without George Washington's intellect to attack and surprise the British forces, the colonists might not have been victorious in the American Revolution. And George Washington's intellect would have been of no use if his forces did not possess the physical and mental fortitude required to carry out his plans. Our current US military, the most powerful force in the world, achieves this status by combining the intellectual training found in our military academies with the physical demands found on the battlefield. Only through this ancient concept of *sapienta et fortitudo* can a people remain free from the powers of evil.

Subject: Poems on Helen of Troy
by Matt Joseph

Important figures in history have almost always proved polarizing ones as well—any figure that has brought change to the world has inevitably aroused opposition. One notable example is that of the late civil rights leader Malcolm X, who drew tens of thousands of supporters in his work for the black separatist Islam and, later in his life, racial equality, but also made himself many sworn enemies—one of whom eventually killed him. But it is men and women like these that change the world. Though they may draw our anger, may attract our adulation, and may throw our beliefs into question, they often make us better for it.

Subject: Scout in *To Kill a Mockingbird*
by John Tapee

Scout eventually transforms into a true lady of character. This examination of Scout's growth as she matures into a lady reminds the reader of Pip in *Great Expectations*. In that novel, Magwitch believes that money and looks will make Pip a gentleman, but Joe, the true gentleman, teaches Pip to be such a man by teaching him qualities that will help him mature. Through his education and maturity, Pip, like Scout, eventually becomes a true gentleman, comforting Magwitch on his deathbed and, truly penitent, returning to expiate his abandonment of Joe. In today's society as well, the term "lady" can be misunderstood to mean a lady in appearance. While Mother Teresa, one of the most beneficent people of our time, is the true lady, she would not be considered one by someone who believes that the title of "lady" is merited based on appearance. Through this scrutinization of Scout's growth, the reader can clearly see that she matures into a real lady—not a lady like many of the "ladies" of Maycomb, but one who cares about who she is, not what she looks like.

Subject: Loyalty
by Jason Uy

Through Madame Defarge and Miss Pross, Charles Dickens reveals the light and dark sides of loyalty. Such allegiance drives heroes and villains alike. While loyalty can drive heroes to do impossible things to help those around them, it can also drive villains to go too far and hurt those around them. Loyalty is, at its core, nothing more than a tool, wielded by anyone who can dedicate himself or herself to a goal. What makes a character a hero or a villain is not whether one is loyal, but what one is loyal to. A character loyal to improving one's self or helping others is a hero, while a character loyal to hurting others is a villain. One should always be loyal to some cause or purpose and fight for some goal with passion, but one should also remember that loyalty is not a goal in and of itself—it is a tool, a weapon with which to fight for the cause of justice.

Subject: Odysseus
by Andre Valdivia

After taking note of all of Odysseus's shortcomings, people can look to him as an even greater hero than before because we can better relate to him. Usually, people tend to make a hero seem like the epitome of everything desirable and appealing in a person, and in doing so, we make that hero seem superhuman. Then, when we try living up to these superior standards we have created, we hold ourselves in disdain when we fall short because we are not perfect, or we become severely disappointed when we discover our hero is not as great as once thought, which was the case with John F. Kennedy. Odysseus is not perfect; however, despite all the instances where he lacks virtue, he is still extremely revered by Greek society and is considered a hero because he is abundantly more beneficent than malevolent. Odysseus, therefore, can serve as the true paragon of a hero, one to whom mankind can relate. Unlike some superhuman creation, Odysseus is human because he falls into temptation and he makes mistakes, just like everyone else. So rather than comparing oneself to an image of perfection we conjure up only to find ourselves constantly wanting, we can look to Odysseus and see a true human hero.

Subject: *Great Expectations* and the prodigal son
by Patricio Delgado

Because a parallel between *Great Expectations* and the parable of the prodigal son exists, two pieces separated by more than 1,800 years, we may deduce that their basic theme of sinning, repenting, and forgiving is timeless. In other words, every human of every age in some way or another asks for his inheritance, or sins by pursuing his own selfish desires, becomes unhappy and unfulfilled in this pursuit, and re-evaluates his situation, returning to God or remaining in a state of misery. Because this theme includes the option to repent, we discover a permeating feeling of hope surrounding humanity. No matter in what era or place, we shall not be denied forgiveness and salvation if we repent for our sins, if we do as the prodigal son and Pip did and give up our selfish and self-centered pursuits in favor of God and His love. For this reason, *Great Expectations* as a whole is a novel about hope for humanity rather than despair.

Subject: Tragic theory and *Frankenstein*
by Joe McGill

By examining *Frankenstein* as a tragic story, the true richness of the story is revealed, and all characters have a place in the plot. Robert Walton, who appears in the "frame story," does not seem to have much importance in the novel unless looked at from the tragic perspective. From the tragic perspective, however, Walton's place in the novel is not only obvious but crucial. At the end of the story, Walton's decision to return home serves as the pointing towards reconciliation. After listening to Victor's advice, Walton and his crew head home, which symbolizes that the violation of nature has ceased. Also, by examining the story as a tragedy, the reader can understand why Shelley spends so much time describing Victor's family. She gives many detailed descriptions of the family so the reader will know the characters and realize the abject suffering that Victor endures because of their deaths. Shelley's masterpiece of writing can only be fully appreciated if the reader views the story as part of the tragic realm.

Subject: The Canterbury Tales   *by Mauricio Delgado*

In criticizing the Church, Chaucer beckons us to be more like the parson who transcends his own poverty, preferring to give "to poor parishioners both from Church offerings and his property." What Chaucer describes and denounces in the timeless and universal *The Canterbury Tales* not only occurs in the Church but in our own community, our own classroom. We should avoid falling into the greed, hypocrisy, and abuses that plague these members of the clergy, and follow the true teachings of Jesus Christ. Even in the sacred Jesuit community, I see students who degrade others because of their financial situation; I see students who learn about justice in theology class one period, yet ridicule a student the next period. Most importantly, though, I see myself in many of these situations, going against my inherited beliefs and hurting another person. What is clear, though, is that we are human beings who sin and make mistakes. Members of the clergy, though seemingly holy, are also people who can fall into evil.

Subject: The Odyssey   *by Michael O'Hanlon*

The voluminous number of similarities between the leadership of the suitors and twentieth century dictators reveals a pattern of rule that tyrants follow. Intimidation and threats have always been used by despots to control dissension and to subjugate the population at large. Many leaders who rely on these methods consistently blame others, especially dissenters, for problems that they themselves have caused or are unable to solve; in addition, they coerce people to go along with and carry out this persecution. These types of regimes, whether on a small or large scale, usually end with the violent death of the rancorous rulers at the hands of heroic forces fighting for justice, thus offering hope to those suffering from unjust leaders. For these reasons, the *Odyssey* serves as a paradigm of rule by malevolent rulers, a paradigm that traverses time.

Steve Kovatis   Kovatis 1
Mr. Degen
English 3
23 April 1997

Simon and the Tao

A bird sings its sweet song from the trees. The warm sun penetrates the foliage and illuminates intermittently the soft, tender earth below. Walking through
this forest, the simplicity of the truth of the earth begins to appear; the Tao
begins to reveal itself. "When the Tao is taught, / people know where to go and
what to learn / Because they know that they will not be harmed / But will receive
great peace" (Lao 44). This promise of achieving peace and harmony by discov-
ering the Tao, the mysterious, omnipresent, and multifariously defined "way" of
the truth, has echoed throughout Chinese civilization through the teachings of
Lao Tzu. In *Lord of the Flies,* Simon presents us with a modern day example of
the proper search, according to Taoist tradition.

Taoism first stresses the union with nature, becoming one with the Tao, or
path, which our surroundings reveal to us, a path followed by Simon. Nature
provides us with a wholeness, for "One who does not separate his being from the
nature of universal wholeness lives with the universal virtue of wholeness" (Lao
8). Literally, and figuratively through the novel, "Simon turned away...and went
where the just perceptible path led him" (56; ch. 3), demonstrating Simon's
union with nature in three ways. First, the image of Simon turning away from the
group shows a sense of individuality, a rejection of follow-
ing the ideas of the community. Second, the passage glori-
fies nature, indicating that it indeed is a "just" and correct
path to follow; additionally, it implies a "perceptible" path,
discernable to Simon. Third, though diffident, Simon follows that path he sees in nature, and he surrenders himself
to the direction that nature indicates, **a point central to the
Taoist message of following nature.** Similarly, in another
instance, Simon "knelt down and the arrow of the sun fell
on him" (57; ch. 3), giving the image of the sun, **representative of greater nature,**
pointing him in the direction of harmony. In response to this call of the wild,
Simon "cocked a critical ear at the sounds of the island," willing and able to listen
to the directions he has been given. Simon even reunites with nature in death.
According to Taoism, "In the natural flow of energy transformation / Mankind
conforms itself to Earth" (Lao 31). When Simon dies, "Somewhere over the dark-
ened curve of the world, the sun and moon were pulling" (154; ch. 9) at Simon's
body, encouraging him to join the sea. Then, "softly, surrounded by a fringe of
inquisitive bright creatures, itself a silver shape beneath the steadfast constella-
tions, Simon's dead body moved out toward the open sea," joining that which
had guided him since his arrival on the island.

> Steve extends his
> elaboration of the
> quotation from Lao
> by weaving its ideas
> into Simon's situation
> at various points in
> the tale.

Simon also demonstrates the mystical, the "Esoteric," aspect of Taoism. Here, Taoism essentially argues that by "cultivating '**stillness**' a few key individuals in each community could become perfect receptacles for Tao" (Smith 201), which then in turn would "cultivate perfect cleanliness of thought and body" (Smith 201). As previously indicated, Simon "turns away" from the group to cultivate his **stillness,** to become receptive to the Tao. In solitude, Simon consistently retreats to his small clearing in the forest. As he sits there, "**nothing moved** but a pair of gaudy butterflies that danced round each other in the hot air" (57; ch. 3), indicating Simon's willingness **to be still** and let nature move while he observed, always learning.

> In this second body paragraph, Steve develops the topic of Simon as mystic by keeping the reader focused on the idea of stillness as a generator of healing in the story.

According to Taoism, **a still person** would also **"radiate a kind of healing"** for the larger group. For example, Piggy waits for his serving of meat from Jack's first hunt, but Jack "meant to leave him in doubt" (73; ch. 4) and withholds Piggy's portion, as Piggy drools with hunger. Here Simon "shoved a piece of meat over the rocks" (74; ch. 4) to a starving and drooling Piggy, **a clear act,** at least on a small scale, **of healing** or alleviating a small form of suffering.

Lastly, grasping a part of the Tao brings with it a knowledge greater than that of the community, greater than traditional knowledge. "To return to the true self / End[s] the endless search / for segmented, intellectual knowledge" (Lao 23). As the tension mounts during an early assembly concerning what to do about the beast, Simon proposes that "maybe there is a beast…maybe it's only us" (89; ch. 5), taking a clear leap beyond the group as well as beyond the realm of logic. Simon does not see a beast in the traditional sense that the others see it, namely a large, gross monster, but as a disease in the human character. He is the only one in the group to discover the reification of the beast that has poisoned, and will continue to poison, the unity and purity of the tribe. How ironic, then, that this reification by the tribe eventually causes his own demise, as the tribe mistakes him for the imaginary beast and kills him. In this same demonstration of an almost omniscient knowledge, Simon later affirms to Ralph that he "will get back all right" (111; ch. 7) to England, a statement originated from no logical source. Simon then does not elaborate on his statement, for when challenged as to how he knows this, Simon only reiterates his original thesis, which later turns out to be true, **a knowledge from an inexplicable origin, a knowledge above the comprehension of the rest of the tribe.**

> Note the style of the final sentence of this paragraph—it ends in parallel analysis modifiers.

Simon's example depicts the acme of proper Taoist existence. Such an example becomes especially helpful because one of Lao Tzu's teachings is that the "Tao, the path of subtle truth / cannot be conveyed with words / the subtle truth is indescribable" (Lao 1). In absence of words, we must turn to human examples to lead us to the proper search for the Tao; specifically, we must at least evaluate Simon's example. Taoism must be understood and lived by the whole person, beyond the realm where words fall short, and Simon provides us with that silent leadership. Only by truly understanding, beyond the realm of language, can we reap the benefits, and only then can we be in harmony with heaven; in this way, we must follow Simon's footsteps.

Works Cited

Golding, William. *Lord of the Flies*. New York: Putnam, 1954.

Lao Tzu. *Tao The Ching*. Rpt. in *The Complete Works of Lao Tzu*. Trans. Ni Hua Chung. Los Angeles: Shrine of the Eternal Breath of Tao, 1989.

Smith, Huston. *The Religions of Man*. New York: Harper & Row, 1958.

Note: WHEN A WRITER INCORPORATES INFORMATION FROM SOURCES beyond the literary text being examined, a Works Cited page is appropriate. Generally, a student should place the Works Cited entries on a separate page. For some teachers, adding the entries after the concluding paragraph is acceptable. Always consult your teacher if you are unsure.

See the Appendix of *Crafting Expository Argument*, pp. 235-240, for information regarding parenthetical citations for the documentation of direct quotations as well as information about the proper formatting of the works you cite in your paper.

Brian Campbell
Mr. Degen
AP English
22 May 2002

Macbeth, Banquo, and the Initial Revelation of Character

"'Bah! Humbug!'" Scrooge responds to his nephew, who is "all in a glow" about the Christmas season. In this famous opening scene of *A Christmas Carol,* Charles Dickens uses dialogue between Scrooge and his nephew to reveal their opposed personalities. In fact, these two contrasting personalities provide the conflict for the entire novel—greed battles generosity. Perhaps Dickens borrowed this technique from William Shakespeare, who uses short scenes in the openings of his plays to establish the conflict eventually to be resolved. In Shakespeare's *Macbeth,* the dialogue early in the play among Macbeth, Banquo, and the three witches reveals important aspects of the two thanes' characters. Macbeth, the commanding war hero, follows ambition over reason, a choice that actually leads him toward demise rather than power; Banquo, however, depends more on reason and is portrayed as a noble, but cautious, skeptic.

First, Macbeth asserts his power over others. After he hears the witches' "prophetic greeting" (1.3.78), for example, Macbeth, **dissatisfied with their incomplete predictions,** demands of the three, "Stay, you imperfect speakers, tell me more" (1.3.70) and "Speak, I charge you" (1.3.78), **commands that degrade the sisters by implying their servitude toward Macbeth.** Macbeth's use of "imperfect" (1.3.70), for instance, takes on a double meaning, **implying both "incomplete" and "defective,"** which insults the witches as being flawed, possibly in contrast to Macbeth's opinion of his perfect self.

> Among the sentence structures Brian uses in the first body paragraph are a past participial phrase, an analysis modifier, and a present participial phrase.

Macbeth's military might, ironically, is powerless to withstand the witches' guile. Earlier in the play, Macbeth "like valor's minion / carved out his passage" and "unseamed [the merciless Macdonwald] from the nave to the chops" (1.2.16–22). Now this strength becomes futile because Macbeth allows the sisters to control him through his desires, particularly his ambition to become king, a desire that has manifested itself in the thane's "horrible imaginings" (1.3.139) of the king's murder, a murder that would allow Macbeth to seize the throne. As the witches tamper with his ambition to become king, Macbeth's "bold commands" seem to wither and, instead, more closely resemble entreaties to the witches: "Stay. . . tell me more" (1.3.70). The image of Macbeth, chasing after the witches, suggests his supplication to them and actually becomes humorous as the noble warrior, who "fixed Macdonwald's head upon [the] battlements" and fought near Forres like a "[cannon] overcharged with double cracks" (1.2.23,37), now follows after the three weird sisters, practically begging them for information.

> Brian focuses on the ease with which Macbeth changes once he learns of the witches' prophecies concerning him. The dominating military figure shrinks to a beggar.

Banquo, unlike Macbeth, depends upon reason, which he displays through his repeated skepticism. As he addresses the witches, Banquo first wonders: "Live you? Or are you aught / that man may question? (1.3.42–43) ... Are ye fantastical, or that indeed / which outwardly ye show?" (1.3.53–54). Refusing to immediately believe the witches' prophecies as credible, Banquo maintains an objective distance to prevent being misled by a false prophecy, this distance securing himself from harm; in fact, he makes certain not to submit himself to the witches, but instead emphasizes his own power: "Speak then to me, who neither beg nor fear / your favors nor your hate" (1.3.60–61). Banquo understands that if he does not take the initiative to dominate the witches, then

> In the topic sentence of this third body paragraph, the writer contrasts what the opening scene has revealed of Macbeth's pliable character with Banquo's determination not to be manipulated by that which conflicts with his reason.

they may successfully manipulate his ambition for their own gain. In addition, in questioning the existence of the witches—"Were such things here as we do speak about, / or have we eaten on the insane root / that takes the reason prisoner?" (1.3.83–85)—he describes reason as a tool that allows one to perceive reality, his questions demonstrating the reasoning process, considering all logical possibilities to explain the mysterious disappearance of the three weird sisters.

Furthermore, Banquo still remains cautious even after Macbeth becomes the thane of Cawdor. **The prophecy having been fulfilled,** Banquo does not heighten his trust in the witches and believe them now to be honest in their predictions; instead, he warns Macbeth, "Oftentimes, to win us to our harm, / the instruments of darkness tell us truths, / win us with honest trifles, to betray's / in deepest consequence" (1.3.123–126). With the mention of "honest trifles," Banquo acknowledges that, although the witches' predictions have come true, the sisters may be using that anticipated newfound trust to plot evil deeds. Banquo's adamant skepticism illustrates his refusal to yield reason even after the witches are proven to be credible. This skepticism, though it seems unnecessary and rather cold,

> In this sentence beginning with an absolute phrase concerning the fulfillment of one of the prophecies, Brian emphasizes Banquo's skepticism about these "honest trifles" and, in the sentences that follow, explicates his judicious advice to Macbeth.

aids Banquo in preventing outside forces—the witches, for example—from dominating him; otherwise, without his disbelief, Banquo, no matter how powerful he may be, would fall under the control of others, just as Macbeth does.

Shakespeare and, later, Dickens demonstrate to the reader the importance of beginning scenes, how they serve to establish some of the major themes of the play or novel. One recognizes, too, that paying attention to what characters say and how they say it will implicitly reveal a character's strengths and weaknesses. Even in our lives today, we may practice observing seemingly insignificant scenes more carefully, listening to language people use in dialogue with one another, uncovering unarticulated conflict or character strengths and weaknesses. Perhaps, as in the case of Scrooge, recognizing conflict can lead to self improvement.

Works Cited

Dickens, Charles. *A Christmas Carol*. New York: Penguin, 1984.

Shakespeare, William. *Macbeth*. New York: Bantam, 1988.

Dr. Degen
AP English
26 March 2010

Chimney Sweepers

> The marriage-day was shining brightly, and they were ready outside
> the closed door of the Doctor's room, where he was speaking with
> Charles Darnay. (182; bk.2, ch. 28)

As Dr. Manette, in the above excerpt from Dickens' *A Tale of Two Cities*, exits his room with Charles Darnay, his daughter's future husband, the narrator notes how "he was so deadly pale—which had not been the case when they went in together—that no vestige of colour was to be seen in his face" (182; bk.2, ch. 28). What had just transpired was Dr. Manette's act of forgiveness and selfless love for his daughter, who will marry the nephew of Evremonde, the aristocrat who unjustly imprisoned the once young doctor. With his remarkable forgiveness, Doctor Manette chooses life rather than seek retribution for the nefarious crimes committed against him. Madame Defarge, in contrast, a victim of the same Evremonde family's malice, chooses vengeance as she knits names into a register, names of those she and her fellow revolutionaries seek to brutally execute with the guillotine. **These opposing responses to the same crime mirror the contrary reactions of William Blake's** speakers to the sin of child labor in his two companion poems, both entitled "The Chimney Sweeper," one part of *Songs of Innocence*, while the other from *Songs of Experience*. While both speakers expose the evil of child labor, the speaker from *Innocence* employs images of Christian redemption that evoke hope, while the second speaker from *Experience* sarcastically condemns the hypocrisy of the Christian world.

> Kolker's introductory paragraph begins with two contrasting situations involving characters from *A Tale of Two Cities*, the characters—Dr. Manette and Madame Defarge—having experienced similar horrors but each ultimately reacting differently. Observe how Kolker transitions (see highlighted sentence) to the thesis statement, the first part of his transitional sentence focusing on the contrasts from *Two Cities* as they serve to parallel similar contrasting situations in the two poems by Blake, both entitled "The Chimney Sweeper."

The speaker in the poem from *Songs of Innocence* responds to the bleakness of child labor by producing hopeful images of heaven and redemption(3). Opening with a desolate image of a helpless child whose "father sold [him]," the poem establishes the malevolent nature of life as a chimney sweeper, magnified in bleakness by the failure of the father to protect and provide for his child. **This abandoned child destined to the squalid fate of sleeping "in soot,"(5)** the chimney sweeper suffers even in his time of rest, **sleep no longer the archetype of rejuvenation and, as Macbeth says, "the balm of hurt minds."**

> Kolker begins the sentence with an absolute phrase modifying the information about the chimney sweeper in the remainder of the sentence, a sentence which concludes with an analysis modifier that effectively elaborates the suffering of the chimney sweeper.

The most salient image, in stanza three, of desolation —"thousands of sweepers/... were all of them lock'd up in coffins of black"(12-13)—hyperbolically captures the universality of this suffering and identifies the gravity of their misery as death. The word "lock'd" establishes a sense of ensnarement from which the sweepers absolutely lack power to escape. Yet, to show the hope of salvation in store for these miserable children, the speaker immediately contrasts this image with "an Angel who had a bright key,"(14) the word "bright" contrasting with the "coffins of black" and the word "key" suggesting that they will be "all free"(15) from the present enslavement of child labor. Countering the chimney sweepers' misery, the Angel makes a divine promise that the boy could "have God for his father & never want joy,"(21) a promise of newfound perfect happiness in God. This shift to peace, brought about by the angelic vision, which makes the boy feel "happy & warm" even "tho' the morning was cold,"(24) expresses that true Christian joy in the midst of suffering.

In the second poem from *Songs of Experience*, the speaker uses the evil of child labor to sarcastically criticize Christian self-righteousness. This poem opens with an image emphasizing the hypocrisy of adult Christians, who would leave a boy "among the snow"(2) in order to go "up to the church to pray,"(5) **the irony revealing Blake's intention to disparage adult Christians for their belief that they live morally and serve God well despite their harmful actions.** In the second stanza, the child speaker scorns his parents for clothing him "in the clothes of death"(8) because this act contradicts their Christian duty to

> Kolker uses an absolute phrase at the end of the sentence to modify the preceding information as he analyzes the ironic nature of the poem's opening image.

serve those in need. The visceral word "death" emphasizes the despondency of the child's situation, which constantly weighs him down, as suggested by the image of "clothes," items that remain on one's person at all times. Similarly, to show his parents' turpitude, the speaker claims that they "taught [him] to sing the notes of woe,"(9) a comment in which Blake distorts the usually joyful image of singing into the child's "woe," additional irony that underscores the bleak and tragic landscape now typical of childhood. This distorted parental archetype is further underscored by the slant rhythm in this stanza:—"heath / death"—which formalistically reflects the discord of a deleterious relationship.

Moving to the second poem's third stanza, the speaker continues castigating adult Christians. He excoriates his derelict parents, who "think they have done [him] no injury,"(11) revealing through their negligence of this suffering the failure of these Christians to truly imitate Christ. In fact, the speaker repeats their self-righteous

> Kolker creates a SUBORDINATE PARAGRAPH to focus specifically on one stanza of the second "Chimney Sweeper," this paragraph's topic sentence clearly echoing the topic sentence of the previous body paragraph.

and hypocritical devotion, mentioned earlier in stanza one, now to "praise God & his Priest & King,/ Who make up a heaven of our misery," (12-13)specifically the juxtaposition of the words "heaven" and "misery" exposing the Christian belittlement of the chimney sweepers' suffering. The speaker's sarcasm in these final lines calls attention to the moral disorder plaguing this society, one that constructs a false portrait of the Christian God, a conception that allows a blindness to the true "injury" done to His children.

These two poems reflect distinct points of view: *Experience* dwells on the evil at hand, focusing only on the pain, lacking any hope, while *Innocence* transcends this same evil with hope. This dichotomy, which also occurs in Charles Dickens' *A Tale of Two Cities*, illustrates the nature of human freedom, the ability to respond to evil with either malevolence or benevolence, the choice to walk toward a moral darkness or a transcendent light. And this message, frequently grounded in the great poets of the world, remains timeless, challenging readers to reflect upon the effect of each response to the world's imperfections.

Works Cited

Blake, William. "The Chimney Sweeper." *Songs of Experience*. Romanticism: An Anthology. Ed. Duncan Wu. 2nd ed. Malden, Massachusetts: Blackwell, 1998. 75.

Blake, William. "The Chimney Sweeper." *Songs of Innocence*. Romanticism: An An Anthology. Ed. Duncan Wu. 2nd ed. Malden, Massachusetts: Blackwell, 1998. 63-64.

Steve Simion
Dr. Degen
AP English
26 March 2010

William Wordsworth's Appeal to John Milton in "London, 1802"

Ah, Douglass, we have fall'n on evil days,
Such days as thou, not even thou didst know,
When thee, the eyes of that harsh long ago
Saw, salient, at the cross of devious ways,
And all the country heard thee with amaze.
Not ended then, the passionate ebb and flow,
The awful tide that battled to and fro;
We ride amid a tempest of dispraise.
Now, when the waves of swift dissension swarm,
And Honour, the strong pilot, lieth stark,
Oh, for thy voice high-sounding o'er the storm,
For thy strong arm to guide the shivering bark,
The blast-defying power of thy form,
To give us comfort through the lonely dark.
by Paul Laurence Dunbar

In Paul Laurence Dunbar's sonnet, "Douglass," the speaker laments the condition of the United States post-abolition, a country marred by racial prejudice, a country faced with more conflict than freed slave Frederick Douglass "even thou didst know." For Dunbar, the country suffers a storm, an "awful tide that battled to and fro." His solution is to invoke the memory of the moral leadership of Douglass to help guide the country out of the disharmony of racism. **Great moral leadership from the past is frequently invoked when nations face moral discord. The British are no exception, for they, too, find themselves in search of ethical clarity in times of despair.** Using the sonnet form as well, William Wordsworth in "London, 1802" explores how the invocation of virtuous leadership, the leadership of the epic poet John Milton, can restore a nation's glory, repairing a moral depravity.

> The writer examines Wordsworth sonnet, "London, 1802," by offering as an introductory mirror, Paul Dunbar's sonnet, "Douglass." Two sentences serve as a transition to the thesis statement.

In the poem's octave, the speaker outlines the moral despair of England, delineating the salient problem to be addressed. England finds itself in a decaying moral status, as it has become now "a fen/ of stagnant waters," (2-3) imagery that suggests a disgusting landscape of swampy filth, with water, normally an image of purity, now lifeless and "stagnant," the nation's leaders inert and complacent to the country's internal disorder. The decay widespread, it specifically applies to all areas of British culture—the "alter, sword, and pen,"(3) the metonymy referring to the country's crumbling sense of religion, heroism, and art. The English have abandoned these fields of honor, in fact, have "forfeited their ancient English dower/ of inward happiness,"(5-6) **Wordsworth emphasizing with "for-**

> Steve uses an absolute phrase, appearing at the top of the next page [Wordsworth emphasizing...], to elaborate in detail the significance of the specific words quoted ["forfeited their ancient..."] from the sonnet.

feited" how freely the English have given up their historical righteousness and justice and now recognize that their loss of these values results in a lack of contentment, an internal absence of tranquility. Equally troubling is how the English possess no respect for others; they have become "selfish men,"(6) a people deeply in need of "manners, virtue, freedom, power,"(8) a people trapped by their own vice, viscerally in need of liberty from the shackles of egoism. This moral turbulence ironically manifests itself in the poem's sonnet form, whose surface reveals, in the octave, order and balance in its consistent rhyme [abbaab-ba], a fact that contrasts with its disordered "inward" moral content, a situation emphasizing the dissonance of appearance versus reality.

In the poem's sestet, the location of the traditional turn in the sonnet form and the movement toward resolution, the speaker requests the aid of the Christ-like John Milton to repair their fallen souls. **The speaker repeatedly uses language of the divine to delineate Milton's moral goodness, a man whose "soul was like a star," setting him above the earth, uniquely part of the heavens, a man who "dwelt apart," living distinctly, purely, and righteously(9). Milton's supremacy is marked by his "voice whose sound was like the sea: Pure as the naked heavens, majestic and free"(10-11). His voice reflects the freedom found without sin, a voice imbued with the grandeur and power of the archetypal sea, a voice "pure" and "free" from the vices plaguing the British subjects, and a voice ordained by the "heavens," one sanctioned by the authority of God.** These attributes distinguish Milton from the common man, like Christ, who as both God and man provides a model for action, who humbly travels "on life's common way, / In cheerful godliness; and yet [his] heart/ the lowliest duties on herself did lay"(12-13). The speaker's emphasis here underscores Milton's similarity to Christ, acting out of a "godliness" and serving the "lowliest" of humanity, serving with a pure "heart," a generosity of spirit. This sense of humility and commitment—moral "duties"—to those most in need can provide the answer to England's need, a selfless gesture to respond to others less fortunate. Now the form of the poem matches the content, the rhythmic consistency and balance of the end-rhyme [cddece] matches the solution, a focus on humility, a virtuous commitment to something outside the self, a moral equilibrium of generosity.

The moral challenge, negotiating the tension between the self and the needs of man, serves as the proper solution to national disorder, an order reflected in the sonnet form. Both Wordsworth and Dunbar address the influence of virtuous leaders guiding a nation toward righteousness. The leadership of these figures affects not only people's opinions but also, more importantly, their actions. Our own nation has

---

From the second sentence of this paragraph forward, the Steve smoothly BLENDS HIS OWN WORDS WITH THOSE QUOTED from Milton's sonnet. Whenever the writer quotes directly from the sonnet, he continues his personal commentary on the words quoted. The blending is clear to see in the second sentence. The third sentence ends with a direct quotation from the sonnet, a quotation in which Wordsworth focuses on the sound of Milton's "voice." The writer's subsequent sentence begins with commentary about Milton's "voice," commentary that continues throughout the sentence.

The concluding paragraph moves from the central idea of the thesis—"virtuous leadership" invoked from the past in order to heal a wounded nation—to a variety of leaders who might be so invoked in our own country. Note that the writer bookends his final sentence with the final line of the poem quoted in the introductory paragraph.

benefited from the strong forces who have guided and shaped the strength of our country, from the founding fathers of the Constitution to the moral voice of Frederick Douglas during abolition to the strength of Martin Luther King, John F. Kennedy, and Ronald Reagan in our most recent century. A single voice clearly demonstrates the possibility of transformation that will, as Dunbar writes in his sonnet, "give us comfort through the lonely dark."

Works Cited

Dunbar, Paul Laurence. "Douglass." *Glencoe Literature*. Ed. Jeffrey Wilhelm. American Literature ed. Columbus: McGraw-Hill, 2010. 570.

Wordsworth, William. "London, 1802." *The Norton Anthology of English Lit erature*. 8th ed. Vol. D: The Romantic Period. Eds. Stephen Greenblatt, M. H. Abrams, Jack Stillinger, Deidre Shauna Lynch. New York: Norton, 2006. 319.

QUICK ESSAY CHECKLIST

Introductory paragraph (p. 110 +)

1. Does the writer grab the reader's attention from the first sentence?
2. Does this showing-telling introduction provide an appropriate analogy to the thesis statement?
3. Does the writer include a transition sentence that connects the SHOWING part of the introductory paragraph to the thesis statement?
4. Does the thesis statement contain a *topic + debatable opinion*?
5. Is the topic of the thesis statement generated from one of ARISTOTLE'S TOPICS (option two), or does it derive from a series of questions the writer has asked about the literature (option one)?

Body paragraphs (p. 59 +)

1. Is the topic sentence for each body paragraph focused and written with clear diction? *Topic sentence = Organizing Element + Aspect of Thesis.*
2. Does the writer's topic sentence contain language found in the thesis statement?
3. Does the body paragraph organize the evidence according to time, place, or idea?
4. Does the writer provide commentary about the evidence in each body paragraph, explaining why the evidence supports the topic sentence, or does the writer merely list the evidence with little explanation and elaboration?
5. When the writer uses direct quotations, does he smoothly blend this text with his own words? (p. 192 +)
6. Does the writer avoid summarizing plot?

Concluding paragraph (p. 116 +)

1. Does the conclusion go beyond summary or restatement of the thesis statement?
2. Does the conclusion attempt to connect the thesis to one larger issue—to the community, to the writer, to other works of literature?
3. Does the writer finish the conclusion by "bookending" a feature from the SHOWING part of the introductory paragraph or from a major detail in the body?

Additional Suggestion: Read the essay aloud to a friend or family member. Listen carefully to yourself as you read your own words. Not only do you want honest constructive feedback from your listener, but you want to be aware of the argument you are making as you are reading aloud. Search for weaknesses in your argument and ways to make the argument more effective. Listen for grammatical errors too. Make corrections as you read aloud.

FOR ADDITIONAL ACTIVITIES, SEE WWW.TELEMACHOSPUBLISHING.COM

5

CRAFTING THE SENTENCE

This chapter's central concern is the crafting of the sentence. It focuses the student-writer's attention on the two major grammatical structures that lead to the formation of well-written sentences: the phrase and the clause. That students fully understand these two structures—and how to manipulate them with increasing confidence—is the goal of this chapter.

When crafting the sentence, student-writers need to be conscious of syntax. For the purposes of *Crafting Expository Argument,* SYNTAX is the arrangement of words to form coherent sentences, sentences that convey exactly what the writer means to convey. Comprehending the function of specific phrases and clauses in any sentence will amplify the writer's awareness of syntax.

Skilled writers have at their disposal multiple options for crafting sentences as they internalize a variety of syntactical possibilities for putting words together. At the secondary level of education, writing style matures when the writer is given numerous opportunities to practice forming sentences possessing increasing levels of sophistication. To facilitate this process, this chapter provides numerous sentence-combining activities. Mastering the manipulation of phrases and clauses that form syntactically sound sentences, however, can only come when writers are expected to use each structure in their compositions once they have been taught it. As more structures are taught and practiced, students must be expected to include all of them in their essays.

What is the difference between a phrase and a clause?

A PHRASE is a group of words.

A CLAUSE is a group of words with a subject and a verb.

The PHRASE itself will *not* have a subject and a verb; however, within the PHRASE, as we shall see, there may exist a subordinate CLAUSE, which, of course, contains a subject and a verb, but that CLAUSE will be functioning as a noun, adjective, or adverb in that PHRASE.

CLAUSES

Two Categories of Clauses

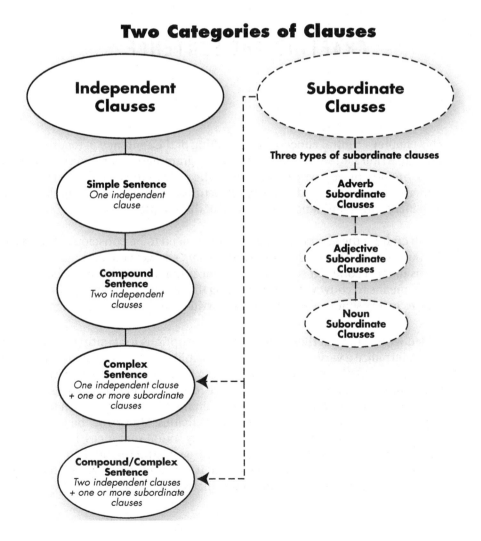

What is the difference between independent and subordinate clauses?

Both categories of clauses contain, by definition, subject-verb combinations; INDEPENDENT CLAUSES, however, can stand on their own as sentences, while SUBORDINATE CLAUSES are always subordinate to (or dependent upon) an independent clause in order to exist in a sentence. SUBORDINATE CLAUSES begin with words that join them to INDEPENDENT CLAUSES; these words are **subordinating conjunctions** and **relative pronouns**.

SUBORDINATE CLAUSES

What words begin subordinate clauses?
Subordinating conjunctions usually begin the ADVERB subordinate clause.

after	as though	once	unless
although	because	provided that	until
as	before	since	when*
as if	even though	so that	whenever
as long as	if*	than	where*
as soon as	in order that	though	while

* *if, when,* and *where* may also begin ADJECTIVE or NOUN subordinate clauses

Relative pronouns often begin ADJECTIVE and NOUN subordinate clauses.

that	who	whichever	whose
how	whom	whoever	whether
what	which	whomever	why

ADVERB SUBORDINATE CLAUSES (ADVSC)   (Exercises, pp. 164, 166–167)

- **Function:** Modify verbs, adjectives, or adverbs.
- **Provide this information:** The **ADVSC** tells *how? when? where? why? to what extent?* or *under what condition?* about the word being modified.
- **Begin** with subordinating conjunctions (see the list above).
- **Location in a sentence:** Anywhere, usually before or after the independent clause.
- **Punctuation rules:**
    1. If the **ADVSC** begins the sentence (or, in other words, is located before the independent clause), *always* place a comma after it.
    2. If the **ADVSC** is located after the independent clause, a comma is *usually not* needed.

    Because I did not study for the test sufficiently, I barely passed.

    Whenever Miranda looks at me, I just want to hide my face *until she goes away.*

    My sister will need to do the dishes *as soon as* she can *so that* she will be ready *when* her friends get here.

    Although we have already purchased our tickets to the concert, I want to arrive *before* the doors open *since* all seats are general admission.

ADJECTIVE SUBORDINATE CLAUSES (ADJSC) (Exercises, pp. 164-167)

- **Function:** Modify nouns or pronouns.
- **Provide this information:** The **ADJSC** tells *what kind?* or *which one?* about the word being modified.
- **Begin** with relative pronouns, plus at times *where* and *when* (see list, p. 135).
- **Location in a sentence:** The **ADJSC** always follows the noun or pronoun being modified.
- **Punctuation rules:**
    1. If the **ADJSC** is ESSENTIAL to the meaning of the sentence, DO NOT SEPARATE IT from the independent clause with commas.
    2. If the **ADJSC** is NOT ESSENTIAL to the meaning of the sentence, SEPARATE IT from the rest of the sentence WITH COMMAS.

> **Teaching and learning punctuation**
> The punctuation rules for a specific structure are best taught and learned at the time the structure itself is taught and learned.

The musicians *whom we enjoyed more than any others* were the members from North Texas University's One O'clock Lab Band.

Jairo Salazar, *who has attended this school for only six months,* has already achieved the highest grade point average in his class.

Shakespeare's sonnets, *which I've read more than once,* are among my favorite poems.

Have you seen the new car *that Kenny is driving?*

The reason *why Margot dislikes her biology class* has nothing to do with her teacher, Mrs. Herredia, *whom she likes,* and everything to do with snakes and fetal pigs, *which the students are dissecting.*

USING WHO, WHOM, THAT, AND WHICH

Use *who* and *whom* to refer to **people**; use *that* and *which* to refer to **things**.

Who and Whom

Use *who* under two circumstances: when the subordinate clause requires a subject or when it requires a predicate nominative (that is, when the subordinate clause's main verb is a linking verb).

Use *whom* when the subordinate clause requires a direct object (because the clause has an action main verb and already has a subject).

- The student *who won the award* is Tanisha.
- Does anyone know *who he is?*
- Joseph Montgomery, *whom I have known for a year,* is my best friend.

That and Which

Use *that* to begin essential adjective subordinate clauses; use *which* to begin nonessential adjective clauses.

- The novel *that I am reading* is terrific.
- Wuthering Heights, *which I began last night,* is a terrific read.

NOUN SUBORDINATE CLAUSES (NSC) (Exercises, pp. 166-167)

- **Function:** The **NSC** can function as any noun can function: as a subject, a predicate nominative, a direct object, an indirect object, an object of the preposition, or an appositive.
- **Provide this information:**
  1. If the **NSC** is a subject (**S**), it tells *who* or *what* the sentence is about.
  2. If it is a predicate nominative (**PN**), it identifies the subject.
  3. If it is a direct object (**DO**), it tells *whom?* or *what?* receives the verb's action.
  4. If it is the indirect object (**IO**), it tells *to whom? to what? for whom?* or *for what?* an action is done.
  5. If it is an object of the preposition (**OP**), it is being connected to another word in the sentence by that preposition.
  6. If it is an appositive (**AP**), it is identifying a noun that comes before it.
- **Begin** with relative pronouns, plus at times *where, when,* and *if* (see p. 135).
- **Location in a sentence:**
  1. If the subject (**S**) , the **NSC** is usually at the beginning of the sentence.
  2. If it is a predicate nominative (**PN**), the **NSC** follows a linking verb.
  3. If it is the direct object (**DO**), the **NSC** follows an action verb.
  4. If it is the indirect object (**IO**), the **NSC** comes between an action verb and a direct object.
  5. If it is an object of the preposition (**OP**), the **NSC** follows a preposition.
  6. If it is an appositive (**AP**), the **NSC** comes right after the noun it identifies.
- **Punctuation rule:** The NSC is ***not separated*** from the rest of the sentence ***by commas unless*** it is functioning as a ***nonessential appositive.***

  How Louis survived four days in a blizzard on Mt. McKinley is the subject of his new book. **NSC = S**

  A solution to the problem is *what I am seeking.* **NSC = PN**

  Achilles believes *that Agamemnon has dishonored him.* **NSC = DO**

  Ms. Jamison will give *whoever needs one* a ticket to the fair. **NSC = IO**

  The meaning of *whatever you just said* is apparently beyond my understanding. **NSC = OP**

  Yesterday's Supreme Court ruling, *that anyone accused of a crime must first be read their Miranda rights,* has been established practice for some time. **NSC = AP** [The commas separate a nonessential appositive.]

  Sometimes the word that begins a noun subordinate clause may be omitted.

  Alfonso's mother said *he must leave at this instant.* [The relative pronoun *that* has been omitted before the **NSC**, which is functioning as a **DO** in this sentence. The relative pronoun *that* is, therefore, understood.]

COMPLEX, COMPOUND, AND COMPOUND-COMPLEX SENTENCES (Exercises, pp. 165-68)

Complex Sentence (CX)
One independent clause + one or more subordinate clauses

- *When Macbeth remembers meeting the witches,* his lust for power increases.
- King Lear, *whose old age did not produce excessive wisdom,* makes a fatal decision *that destroys his family.*
- The autographed baseball, *which John Henry has had on his bookshelf for years,* will bring him thousands of dollars *as soon as the next auction is held.*

Compound Sentence (CP)
Two independent clauses

- Two witnesses noticed the man in question beforehand, but neither of them saw the crime being committed.
- Johnny rode his bicycle to the grocery store; his front tire had a flat along the way.
- Marcella decided to study the Chinese language in college; in fact, she made this decision her junior year of high school.

Compound-Complex Sentence (CPCX)
Two independent clauses + one or more subordinate clauses

- The playwright *whom Roberto enjoyed more than any other* was Shakespeare, and his interest in becoming an actor grew from the moment *when he acted the part of Mercutio in the school play.*
- Mercutio's unpredictable temperament sometimes startled people; however, Romeo, *who was his closest friend,* ignored most of his explosive outbursts.
- *After Tybalt killed Mercutio,* Romeo entered the fray; this decision would change the entire direction of his life.

WHAT ARE THE THREE WAYS TO JOIN TWO INDEPENDENT CLAUSES TOGETHER TO FORM A COMPOUND OR COMPOUND-COMPLEX SENTENCE?

If you closely examine the three sentence examples above for both the compound sentence and the compound-complex sentence, you will observe that all three ways are demonstrated. They are

- with a *comma followed by* a coordinating conjunction ——→ , yet
- with a solo semicolon ——→ ;
- with a conjunctive adverb *preceded by a semicolon* and *followed by a comma* ——→ ; consequently,

See p. 154 for the list of seven coordinating conjunctions and the list of conjunctive adverbs.

THE VERBAL TOOL CHEST

Verbals are forms of verbs that are used as other parts of speech: nouns, adjectives, and adverbs. For a writer, verbals—especially THE PHRASES CONSTRUCTED FROM VERBALS—become one of the primary tools for developing an increasingly mature writing style.

The PARTICIPLE is a verbal that functions as an adjective as does the participial phrase. The GERUND is a verbal that functions as a noun as does the gerund phrase. The INFINITIVE is a verbal that may function as any of three different parts of speech—a noun, an adjective, or an adverb—as does the infinitive phrase. Among the phrases discussed hereafter are the three verbal phrases.

PHRASES

PARTICIPIAL PHRASES AS ADJECTIVES

> **Present Participles =**
> Verb forms ending in **ing** such as walking, hoping, being

> **Past Participles =**
> Verb forms ending in **d, ed,** or an irregular form such as seen, given, brought

Present participial phrases PrPP   (Exercises, pp. 169–173)

Past participial phrases PaPP   (Exercises, pp. 170-171)

- **Function:** Modify nouns or pronouns.
- **Contain** the present or past participle and any complements (such as direct objects or predicate nominatives) or modifiers (adjectives and adverbs, whether they be single words, phrases, or subordinate clauses).
- **Provide this information:** The **PrPP** and **PaPP** tell *what kind?* or *which one?* about the word being modified.
- **Location in a sentence:** The **PrPP** and **PaPP** will appear directly before or after the noun or pronoun it modifies.
- **Punctuation rules:**
   1. When the **PrPP** or **PaPP** begins the sentence (that is, it comes directly before the noun or pronoun it modifies), *always separate* the phrase from the rest of the sentence *with a comma*.
   2. When the **PrPP** or **PaPP** follows the noun or pronoun it modifies, *separate* the phrase from the rest of the sentence with commas *if it is a nonessential* phrase; *if* the **PrPP** or **PaPP** is *essential, no commas* are used.

Essential or nonessential participial phrase?
- The student *running down the hall* slipped on the banana peel. (The **PrPP** is essential, for it identifies which student is being referred to. No commas needed.)
- Carlton, *running down the hall,* slipped on the banana peel. (The **PrPP** is not essential to the meaning of the sentence: The reader knows who slipped on the peel. Use commas.)

- The kite *blown away by the fierce wind* is the only one of ours that remains lost. (The **PaPP** is essential, for it identifies which kite is being referred to. No commas needed.)
- Janelle's kite, *blown away by the fierce wind,* is the only one of ours that remains lost. (The **PaPP** is not essential for identifying the kite. Use commas.)

Verb or adjective?

When is a present or past participle functioning as a **verb**? When it has a helping verb before it: (present) *is* running, *has been* galloping, *might be* recording, *would have been* consuming; (past) *had* given, *will be* finished, *are* written, *were* cooked.

When is a present or past participle acting as an **adjective**? When it has no helping verb in front of it and is, at that time, modifying a noun or pronoun.

- Forrest Gump became a *running* machine at one point in his life.
- Parents of the children brought *baked* goods to the school festival.

Present participial phrases

- *Running for his life,* Forrest eventually escaped from the young men out for a joyride in their pickup.
- Forrest, *running for his life,* eventually escaped from the young men out for a joyride in their pickup.

- *Crouching down on the red asphalt track,* Royce stretches his hamstrings as a final precaution and positions himself on the starting blocks.
- Royce, *crouching down on the red asphalt track,* stretches his hamstrings as a final precaution and positions himself on the starting blocks.

- *Throwing tomatoes at passing cars yesterday,* the boys were severely disciplined by their parents today.
- The boys *throwing tomatoes at passing cars yesterday* were severely disciplined by their parents today.

Past participial phrases

- *Envied by the flat-footed Achilles,* Hector inspects his worn Nikes and quickly brushes off some dirt.
- Hector, *envied by the flat-footed Achilles,* inspects his worn Nikes and quickly brushes off some dirt.
- *Destroyed in the heat of recent battle,* the forlorn village stood silently in the frosty night.
- The forlorn village, *destroyed in the heat of recent battle,* stood silently in the frosty night.
- *Ripped apart in an encounter with a crazed mongrel,* the teddy bear has been mailed to the teddy bear repair factory.
- The teddy bear *ripped apart in an encounter with a crazed mongrel* has been mailed to the teddy bear repair factory.

ABSOLUTE PHRASES

Absolute phrases (AbP)   (Exercises, pp. 174-175)
- **Function:** Modify all or part of the sentence to which it is connected.
- **Contain** a noun that is immediately followed by an adjective, often—but not always—a participle or participial phrase.
- **Location in a sentence:** The **AbP** is frequently found either at the beginning or at the end of a sentence.
- **Punctuation rule:** The **AbP** *is separated* from the rest of the sentence *by a comma*.

> The boy stares into space, *his face being white with fear*.

> *His strength invincible*, Beowulf undertakes the formidable challenge.

> *The act of violence having been committed*, Macbeth shakes with terror.

> "Ronald Reagan appears out of the darkness, *his head bowed in conversation with a vaguely familiar man in business*."
> —*U.S. News*, Jan.'96

GERUND PHRASES AS NOUNS

Gerund phrases (GP)   (Exercises, pp. 172-174)

> **Gerunds =**
> *Verb forms that end in **ing** and that function as nouns*

- **Function:** Act as the subject, predicate nominative, direct object, indirect object, object of a preposition, or appositive of a clause or sentence.
- **Contain** the gerund and any complements (such as direct objects or predicate nominatives) or modifiers (adjectives and adverbs, whether they be single words, phrases, or subordinate clauses).
- **Provide this information:**
    1. If the **GP** is a subject (**S**), it tells *who* or *what* the sentence is about.
    2. If it is a predicate nominative (**PN**), it identifies the subject.
    3. If it is a direct object (**DO**), it tells *whom?* or *what?* receives the verb's action.
    4. If it is the indirect object (**IO**), it tells *to whom? to what? for whom?* or *for what?* an action is done.
    5. If it is an object of the preposition (**OP**), it is being connected to another word in the sentence by that preposition.
    6. If it is an appositive (**AP**), it is identifying a noun that comes before it.
- **Location in a sentence:**
    1. If the subject (**S**) , the **GP** is usually at the beginning of the sentence.
    2. If it is a predicate nominative (**PN**), the **GP** follows a linking verb.
    3. If it is the direct object (**DO**), the **GP** follows an action verb.
    4. If it is the indirect object (**IO**), the **GP** comes between an action verb and a direct object.
    5. If it is an object of the preposition (**OP**), the **GP** follows a preposition.
    6. If it is an appositive (**AP**), the **GP** comes right after the noun it identifies.

- **Punctuation rule:** The **GP** is **not separated** from the rest of the sentence *by commas unless* it is functioning as a *nonessential appositive.*

  > *Keeping one eye on her watch and another at the door* was very difficult for Estellita. **GP = S**
  >
  > Latrell's favorite activity is *playing chess.* **GP = PN**
  >
  > The great challenge, *keeping the peace,* now presents itself. **GP = AP**
  >
  > The legislation proposes *requiring helmets.* **GP = DO**
  >
  > The thought of *reading over five chapters in my physics text tonight* makes me a bit sleepy. **GP = OP**

VERB FORMS ENDING IN *ING*: PARTICPLES OR GERUNDS?

Remember that function is what determines whether *knocking,* for example, is a participle or a gerund. When its function is as an **adjective**, *knocking* is a **participle**.

> The girl *knocking on the door* pleaded for someone to answer.

Here *knocking* is a **participle** because the phrase *knocking on the door* modifies girl.

When the function is that of a **noun**, *knocking* is a **gerund**.

> *Knocking on the door* caused temporary pain.

Here *knocking* is a **gerund** because it [and the words connected with it] acts as the subject of the sentence, which is a noun function.

INFINITIVE PHRASES AS ADVERBS, ADJECTIVES, NOUNS

Adverb infinitive phrases (ADV-IP)   (Exercises, pp. 173-174)

- **Function:** Modify verbs, adjectives, or adverbs.
- **Contain** the infinitive and any complements (such as direct objects or predicate nominatives) or modifiers (adjectives and adverbs, whether they be single words, phrases, or subordinate clauses).
- **Provide this information:** The ADV-IP tells *how? when? where? why? to what extent?* or *under what condition?* about the word being modified.
- **Location in a sentence:** You might find an **ADV-IP** anywhere in the sentence, usually at the beginning of the sentence or somewhere after the verb.
- **Punctuation rule:** If the ADV-IP *begins the sentence*, place *a comma after* it; otherwise, no comma is usually needed.

> **Infinitives =**
> *Verb forms preceded by **to**,*
> *such as to talk, to destroy, to warn, to love*

> The students rose *to cheer the performance.*

> *To annoy his baby sister,* Esteban began calling her "a little cockroach."

> Nikita worked harder than anyone else at track practice *to ensure that she would win a full athletic/academic scholarship to Duke.*

Adjective infinitive phrases (ADJ-IP)

- **Function:** Modify nouns or pronouns.
- **Contain** the infinitive and any complements (such as direct objects or predicate nominatives) or modifiers (adjectives and adverbs, whether they be single words, phrases, or subordinate clauses).
- **Provide this information:** The **ADJ-IP** tells *what kind?* or *which one?* about the word being modified.
- **Location in a sentence:** The **ADJ-IP** always follows the word it modifies.
- **Punctuation rule:** The **ADJ-IP** will *usually never be separated* from the rest of the sentence *by commas*.

> Many writers have a tendency *to use too many commas*.

> The challenge *to bench press three hundred pounds* was successfully met by three of our school's athletes.

> The one *to ask about life in Thailand* is Tiffany.

Noun infinitive phrases (N-IP)

- **Function:** The **N-IP** can function as any noun can function: as a subject, a predicate nominative, a direct object, an indirect object, an object of the preposition, or an appositive.
- **Contain** the infinitive and any complements (such as direct objects or predicate nominatives) or modifiers (adjectives and adverbs, whether they be single words, phrases, or subordinate clauses).
- **Provide this information:**
    1. If the **N-IP** is a subject (**S**), it tells *who* or *what* the sentence is about.
    2. If it is a predicate nominative (**PN**), it identifies the subject.
    3. If it is a direct object (**DO**), it tells *whom?* or *what?* receives the verb's action.
    4. If it is the indirect object (**IO**), it tells *to whom? to what? for whom?* or *for what?* an action is done.
    5. If it is an object of the preposition (**OP**), it is being connected to another word in the sentence by that preposition.
    6. If it is an appositive (**AP**), it is identifying a noun that comes before it.
- **Location in a sentence:**
    1. If the subject (**S**), the **N-IP** is usually at the beginning of the sentence.
    2. If it is a predicate nominative (**PN**), the **N-IP** follows a linking verb.
    3. If it is the direct object (**DO**), the **N-IP** follows an action verb.
    4. If it is the indirect object (**IO**), the **N-IP** comes between an action verb and a direct object.
    5. If it is an object of the preposition (**OP**), the **N-IP** follows a preposition.
    6. If it is an appositive (**AP**), the **N-IP** comes right after the noun it identifies.
- **Punctuation rule:** The **N-IP** is *not separated* from the rest of the sentence *by commas unless* it is functioning as a *nonessential appositive*.

> *To invest with success in stocks* may require a knowledge of economics that you do not possess at this time. **N-IP = S**

Jermaine's goal, *to bicycle across South America from Venezuela to the southernmost tip of Chile,* has been something he has trained for during the past two years. **N-IP = AP**

Consuela plans *to graduate a year early from Harvard Theological Seminary.* **N-IP = DO**

King George's decision was *to deploy British troops to the colonies across the Atlantic.* **N-IP = PN**

APPOSITIVE PHRASES

Appositive phrases (AP)   (Exercises, p. 175-176)
- **Function:** Identify or provide additional information about another noun or pronoun.
- **Contain** the appositive and any words that modify it, be they single words, phrases, or subordinate clauses.
- **Location in a sentence:** An **AP** is usually located directly after the noun or pronoun it is identifying; occasionally, the **AP** will begin the sentence directly before the noun or pronoun it is identifying.
- **Punctuation rule:** *If* the AP is *nonessential, separate* it from the rest of the sentence *with commas*; *if* it is an *essential* AP, *do not* use commas.

> **Appositive =**
> *A noun or pronoun used to **identify** another noun or pronoun*

The startling announcement, *an edict from the king,* trumpets over the loudspeaker.

A strikingly inventive person, Najeera has the admiration of all of her peers.

My friend *Katie McAllister* departs for Cambridge University tomorrow.

Clarence Darrow, *the most famous American defense lawyer at the turn of the previous century,* is the great-grandfather of our algebra teacher.

The Hannah-McCloskey kidnapping and murder, *this city's crime of the century,* was never solved.

NOUN: A WORD, PHRASE, OR CLAUSE NAMING A PERSON, PLACE, THING, OR IDEA

e.g. words as nouns
car, London, toy, hate.

gerund phrases as nouns
Recording a Top Ten hit is this musician's primary ambition. **GP = S**
David received a ticket for *running a red light.* **GP = OP**

infinitive phrases as nouns
Shaniqua wants *to defeat her opponent decisively.* **N-IP = DO**
To serve in the Peace Corps remains Donyelle's intention. **N-IP = S**

noun subordinate clauses
Whoever finishes the test first will probably fail it. **NSC = S**
Clay did not hear *that tomorrow's concert has been cancelled.* **NSC = DO**

THE FUNCTIONS OF THE NOUN IN A CLAUSE OR SENTENCE

Nouns can be the subject (S) of a clause or sentence.

The *town* of Weatherford celebrates its Peach Festival every July.
[The single-word *town* is the **S** of this sentence.]

Listening to her favorite singer puts Alicia in a splendid mood.
[The gerund phrase *listening to her favorite singer* is the **S** of this sentence.]

To speak slowly and distinctly is something that Jackie rarely does.
[The infinitive phrase *to speak slowly and distinctly* is the **S** of the sentence. This sentence contains an adjective subordinate clause, *that Jackie rarely does,* and *Jackie* is the **S** of that clause.]

Which of the hockey teams will win the Stanley Cup is anybody's guess at this point in the series.
[The noun subordinate clause *which of the hockey teams will win the Stanley Cup* is the **S** of the sentence; since *which of the hockey teams will win the Stanley Cup* is a clause, it, too, contains a subject, and that **S** is *which.*]

That he risks injury and even death makes Alberto's job as a stunt man especially uninviting for most people.
[The noun subordinate clause *that he risks injury and even death* is the **S** of this sentence; the pronoun *he* is the **S** of the noun subordinate clause itself.]

> **What is a subject?**
> A subject is *who* or *what* the clause or sentence is about. Any noun can be a subject, which means a single-word noun, a gerund phrase, a noun infinitive phrase, or a noun subordinate clause may be functioning as the subject.

Nouns can be the predicate nominative (PN) of a clause or sentence.

William Faulkner was a *winner* of the Nobel Prize for Literature.
  [The single-word *winner* is the **PN** of this sentence.]

Karen's future goal is *singing for a living.*
  [The gerund phrase *singing for a living* is the **PN** of this sentence.]

Tabitha's favorite line from Shakespeare has always been "*to be or not to be.*"
  [The compound infinitive phrase *to be or not to be* is the **PN** of this sentence.]

Johnny is *who will receive my vote for class president.*
  [The noun subordinate clause *who will receive my vote for class president* is the **PN** of this sentence.]

> **What is a predicate nominative?**
> A predicate nominative is a noun that follows a linking verb and identifies the subject. Any single-word noun, gerund phrase, noun infinitive phrase, or noun subordinate clause can be a predicate nominative.

IS THAT NOUN REALLY FUNCTIONING AS A PREDICATE NOMINATIVE?

First, make sure it follows a linking verb (see p. 150). Keep in mind that, since the predicate nominative identifies the subject, you can interchange the two. Therefore, to test whether a noun that follows a linking verb is actually the predicate nominative, rearrange the parts of the sentence: Make the predicate nominative the subject and the subject the predicate nominative. If you can do that so that the sentence retains its original meaning, you know that you have a predicate nominative. Rearrange the second example above. Change KAREN'S FUTURE GOAL IS SINGING FOR A LIVING to SINGING FOR A LIVING IS KAREN'S FUTURE GOAL. *Goal* is now the predicate nominative; *singing for a living* is now the subject.

Nouns can be the direct object (DO) of a clause or sentence.

Randolph tossed his *cap* into the air at graduation.
  [The single-word noun *cap* is the **DO.**]

Carla Sue's dad enjoys *dancing to the music of the Rolling Stones.*
  [The gerund phrase *dancing to the music of the Rolling Stones* is the **DO.**]

> **What is a direct object?**
> A direct object, when a sentence or clause has one, is a noun that follows action verbs and receives the action of that verb. Direct objects answer the questions **what?** or **whom?** after an action verb. Any single-word noun, gerund phrase, noun infinitive phrase, or noun subordinate clause can function as a direct object.

Judge Holland decided *to dismiss the case for lack of evidence.*
  [The infinitive phrase *to dismiss the case for lack of evidence* is the **DO.**]

Although my sister likes *eating pineapple pizza,* I knew *that she would not even taste any of the pepperoni.*
  [The adverb subordinate clause *although my sister likes eating pineapple pizza* begins the sentence; the gerund phrase *eating pineapple pizza* is the **DO** of that clause. The noun subordinate clause *that she would not even taste any of the pepperoni* is the **DO** in the independent clause.]

Nouns can be the indirect object (IO) of a clause or sentence

Henry handed his best *friend* the secret diary.
[The single-word noun *friend* is the **IO**.]

If Juanita brings the *class* donuts Friday, Andre may bring soft drinks.
[*Class* is the **IO** in the adverb subordinate clause that begins this sentence.]

Kimberly gives *repairing automobiles* her undivided attention.
[The gerund phrase *repairing automobiles* is the **IO**.]

This particular class has shown *whoever teaches them* a masterful approach toward studying.
[The noun subordinate clause *whoever teaches them* is the **IO**.]

> **How can an indirect object be distinguished from a direct object?**
> An indirect object, if there is one, always comes between the action verb (never a linking verb) and the direct object; in addition, the indirect object answers one of these questions after an action verb: *to whom? for whom? to what? for what?* Any single-word noun, gerund phrase, and noun subordinate clause can be an **IO**. It is doubtful that you will discover many infinitive phrases functioning as indirect objects because of the word "to" in the infinitive; however, if one were to write **The literary committee gave To Kill a Mockingbird an award,** then **To Kill a Mockingbird** would be an infinitive phrase as indirect object.

Nouns can be the object of a preposition (OP) in a clause or sentence

Paula listens to *music* around the *clock*.
[In this sentence the single-word noun *music* is the object of the preposition "to" and the single-word noun *clock* is the object of the preposition "around."]

Jaye believes that she lost her hearing from *playing in a heavy metal band.*
[This sentence contains a subordinate clause, *that she lost her hearing from playing in a heavy metal band.* Within the subordinate clause, the gerund phrase *playing in a heavy metal band* is the object of the preposition "from." Within the gerund phrase, there is also a prepositional phrase, *in a heavy metal band,* and *band* is the object of the preposition "in."]

I addressed the letter to *whom it may concern.*
[The noun subordinate clause *whom it may concern* is the object of the preposition "to."]

Nouns can be the appositive (AP) in a clause or sentence

My friend *Erica* sends all of her favorite singers fan mail.
[The single-word noun *Erica* is the **AP** identifying the friend in this sentence.]

Jeffrey's hobby, *building model airplanes*, keeps him busy most every weekend.
[The gerund phrase *building model airplanes* is the **AP** identifying the hobby.]

Only a few of us were amazed by Geraldo's somewhat complicated wish, *to become both a professional football player and a professional ballet star before the age of 25.*
[The noun infinitive phrase *to become both a profes-*

> **What is an appositive?**
> An appositive is a noun that is located next to another noun and identifies it in some way. Any single-word noun (with or without modifiers), gerund phrase, noun infinitive phrase, and noun subordinate clause can be an appositive.

sional football player and a professional ballet star before the age of 25 is the **AP** identifying the wish.]

Dat's belief, *that the sale of handguns should be prohibited,* caused a major debate between him and his friend Stephen, who thought he couldn't be more unwise.

[The noun subordinate clause *that the sale of handguns should be prohibited* is an **AP** identifying the belief; the single-word noun *Stephen* is an **AP** identifying the friend.]

PRONOUN: A WORD USED IN PLACE OF A NOUN

e.g. *I, me, you, he, him, her, it, myself, herself, yourself, each, neither, who, which, somebody, few, most.*

THE FUNCTIONS OF THE PRONOUN IN A CLAUSE OR SENTENCE

Anything a noun can be, a pronoun can be.

A pronoun's antecedent: a word or group of words to which a pronoun refers. e.g. The engineer of the train blew *its* whistle repeatedly. (*Train* is the antecedent of *its*.)

Pronoun-antecedent agreement: A pronoun *must agree with its antecedent in number*; in other words, when the antecedent is singular, the pronoun should be singular. This is especially tricky regarding indefinite pronouns.

Indefinite Pronouns

Singular			Plural	Singular or plural
anybody	everyone	nothing	both	all
anyone	everybody	neither	few	any
anything	everything	somebody	many	most
each	one	someone	others	none
either	no one	something	several	some
	nobody			

Subject-verb agreement
When the subject is a SINGULAR indefinite pronoun, ignore any prepositional phrase that may immediately follow that pronoun. *Each of the boys is ready to play* is grammatically correct. *Each,* not *boys,* is the subject.

Quick Review

Nouns—and pronouns—can function as **subjects, predicate nominatives, direct objects, indirect objects, objects of prepositions,** and **appositives** in a sentence or clause. Since nouns function in this way, that means that **gerund phrases, noun infinitive phrases,** and **noun subordinate clauses** have these same functions.

One other function of any noun—or pronoun— is in **direct address,** as in *Gloria, did you bring your homework?* In this interrogative sentence, *Gloria* is a NOUN OF DIRECT ADDRESS.

The his or her dilemma

To write *Everyone must sit down quietly at <u>his or her</u> desk before receiving <u>his or her</u> test materials* is a grammatically correct sentence construction. After all, *everyone* is always a singular indefinite pronoun (one of those peculiarities of the language that we might as well accept without undue stress) and, if the group in question has both males and females, then it is appropriate that the personal pronouns *his or her* be used in this situation. Admittedly, this is very awkward and when continually using *his or her* in sentences, the writing becomes inelegant, indeed. So **avoid** using **his or her**.

What's a solution?

- Go to the plural. *<u>Students</u> must sit down quietly at <u>their</u> desks before receiving <u>their</u> test materials.*
- Eliminate the need for personal pronouns. *Students must be seated in order to receive test materials.*

In other words, if you don't want to go overboard with *his or her,* which easily happens, take a different approach.

VERBS

Two Categories of Verbs

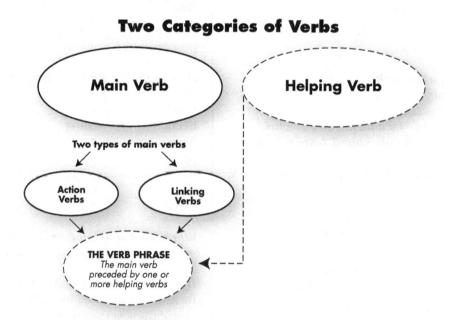

How is a helping verb distinct from a main verb?

Helping, or auxiliary, verbs are *only used* when a sentence or clause contains a VERB PHRASE; in other words, there is no helping verb unless the verb consists of more than one word. Moreover, the helping verb always precedes the main verb, whether that main verb is an action verb or a linking verb. Therefore, the main verb is always the last word in a verb phrase. If the clause or sentence contains only one word as the verb, then that verb is always the main verb.

THE _BE_ VERB CAN BE EITHER A HELPING VERB OR A LINKING MAIN VERB

BE
as a linking main verb

am is are was were be been being

BE
as a helping verb

When the **BE** verb is either the _only verb_ in the clause or sentence, or it is the _last word in a verb phrase,_ then the **be** verb is the **main verb.**

Shelly _is_ the secretary of the homecoming committee.

The twins, Darius and Shawanna, <u>have _been_</u> ill for a week now.

Everyone believes that Joshua <u>will _be_</u> shy like his father.

More about linking verbs
Linking verbs—almost always followed by either PREDICATE NOMINATIVES or PREDICATE ADJECTIVES—include the **be** verb plus SENSORY verbs like **sound, taste, appear, feel, look, smell,** and verbs that express CONDITION like **become, remain, seem, stay, grow.**

The SENSORY and CONDITION verbs can be _either action or linking verbs._ How do you tell if one of these is action or linking?

• If you can substitute a **be** verb and the sentence makes sense, it's _linking._

• See if what follows the verb is a predicate nominative or predicate adjective.

• What are these verbs—_action? linking?_

Tybalt _looked_ surly.

Juliet _looked_ at the stars in the night sky.

The Friar _grows_ a variety of herbs.

Mercutio _grows_ more and more belligerent

When the **BE** verb appears before a main verb, it is always a helping verb in that clause or sentence.

The lady in the lavender blouse <u>has _been_ waiting</u> for you since eight o'clock.

The bass player <u>_was_ jumping</u> backwards at the time that the lead singer fell off the stage.

Both letters <u>_were_ composed</u> on a word processor by Gwendolyn.

How many helping verbs are there? 23

am	is	are
was	were	be
been	being	
have	has	had
do	does	did
may	might	must
shall	should	will
would	can	could

When does a helping verb stop "helping" and become a "main" verb?

If it precedes a main verb, it is always functioning as a helping verb. However, IF any of these verbs are used as either the ONLY VERB in the clause or sentence or the LAST WORD IN A VERB PHRASE, then what is often one of the 23 helping verbs is now functioning as a main verb.

• Tommy _has_ five fingers on his right hand.

• Mikey will _do_ it

Forms of the verb

Present tense	Past tense	Past participle	Present participle
go / goes	went	(has) gone	(is) going
bring / brings	brought	(has) brought	(is) bringing
talk / talks	talked	(has) talked	(is) talking

Other tenses

Present perfect	Past perfect	Future	Future perfect
He has run.	He had run.	He will run.	He will have run.
He has seen.	He had seen.	He will see.	He will have seen.

Voice

Active Voice	vs..	Passive Voice
Quentin *eats* the pizza.		The pizza *is eaten* by Quentin.

An action verb is in ACTIVE VOICE when the subject performs the action of the verb. Unless a specific reason determines a need for passive voice, the skilled writer will concentrate on the prudent use of active voice verbs.

An action verb is in PASSIVE VOICE when the action of the verb is done to or performed on the subject. Passive voice is formed by using a **be** verb (such as *is, are, was,* or *were*) with the past participle form of the verb.

Phrasal verbs

A PHRASAL VERB consists of *the main verb plus* a preposition or adverb. Treat the entire phrasal verb *as a main verb*. Some will have helping verbs. Some will take direct objects, and some won't. Here are two examples of phrasal verbs:

Dr. Godfrey *called on* Peter to answer the question.
The twins *have worked out* at the gym five days a week for the past year.

MODIFIERS: ADJECTIVES, ADVERBS, AND PREPOSITIONAL PHRASES

ADJECTIVE

a word, phrase, or clause that modifies (by describing, specifying, or limiting) a noun or pronoun. An adjective tells *what kind, which one, how many,* or *whose* about the word being modified:

Adjectives
answer the questions
what kind?
which one?
whose?
how many?

> **e.g. words as adjectives**
> a *rotten* apple, the *green* ink
> *several* assignments, *my* computer

> **prepositional phrases as adjectives**
> the house *on the corner*, a teacher *with a strict demeanor*

present participial phrases as adjectives

The student *hurdling down the hallway* fell into the trash can.
Polishing the antique table, Carol suddenly noticed a distinct smell *drifting in from the kitchen.*

past participial phrases as adjectives

Knocked down by an inside fast ball, the batter slowly dusted himself off and prepared for the next pitch.
Sonja Martinez, *disturbed by the raucous behavior of her classmates,* asked the counselor for a transfer.

infinitive phrases as adjectives

The most important team *to beat this time* is the Yankees.
The counselor *to see about college entrance exams* is Mrs. Juarez.

adjective subordinate clauses

Anthony, *who missed two weeks of school because of pneumonia,* asked for tutorial assistance from some of his teachers.
The twenty-two answers *that I missed on the algebra exam* certainly didn't help my grade.

ADVERB

a word, phrase, or clause that modifies (by describing, specifying, or limiting) a verb, adjective, or another adverb. An adverb tells *how, when, where, why, to what extent,* or *under what condition* about the word modified.

Adverbs
answer the questions how? when? where? why? to what extent? under what condition?

e.g. words as adverbs

I *cautiously* approached the fox.
We attended the play *yesterday.*
Jason's laughter sounded *extremely* ridiculous to my ears.
The children ran *outside* to play after the thunderstorm.

prepositional phrases as adverbs

The children ran outside to play *after the thunderstorm.*
Underneath my sister's bed, our tri-color collie slept.

infinitive phrases as adverbs

To irritate his older brother, Tony repeated his every word.
Felicia's mother wrapped the rolls with a towel *to keep them warm.*
The children ran outside *to play after the thunderstorm.*

adverb subordinate clauses

Because I could not locate my tennis shoes, I wore high heels to school.
No one will pass Mr. Hollister's exam *unless you study well.*
As the graduation ceremony ended, everyone stood to sing the school song.

PREPOSITION

a word that connects the noun or pronoun that follows it to some other word in the clause or sentence. A **prepositional phrase** begins with a preposition and ends with a noun or pronoun, the **object of the preposition.**

A list of some prepositions

aboard	at	down	off	in
about	before	during	on	toward
above	behind	for	onto	under
across	below	from	out	underneath
after	beneath	in	outside	until
against	beside	inside	over	up
along	between	into	past	upon
among	but (except)	like	since	with
around	by	near	through	within
as	concerning	of	throughout	without

A list of some compound prepositions

according to	because of	in front of	next to
ahead of	by means of	in spite of	on top of
along with	in addition to	instead of	out of

Functions of prepositional phrases in a clause or sentence

**All prepositional phrases function as
MODIFIERS**

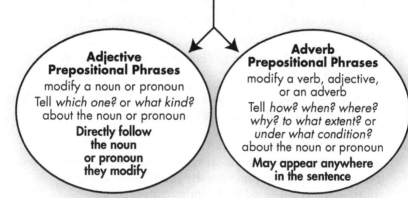

Adjective Prepositional Phrases
modify a noun or pronoun
Tell *which one?* or *what kind?* about the noun or pronoun
Directly follow the noun or pronoun they modify

Adverb Prepositional Phrases
modify a verb, adjective, or an adverb
Tell *how? when? where? why? to what extent?* or *under what condition?* about the noun or pronoun
May appear anywhere in the sentence

The bench *beneath the elm trees* needs a serious repair.

The debate *concerning school vouchers* is scheduled for Friday.

I did not notice any girl *in pedal pushers.*

Kaneisha walked *around the track* sixteen times.

Underneath the open prairie sky, the imposing farm house stood alone.

Mr. Donnegan exercises seriously *because of health problems.*

CONJUNCTION: A WORD THAT JOINS WORDS, PHRASES, OR CLAUSES

Coordinating Conjunctions
Connecting words that join words, phrases, or clauses that are grammatically alike—frequently, though not exclusively, used to join independent clauses

and   but   for   or   nor   yet   so

Correlative Conjunctions
Connecting words that join groups of words that are grammatically alike—sometimes used to join independent clauses

both...and   either...or   neither...nor   not only...but also

Conjunctive Adverbs
Connecting words that are used to join independent clauses

to show contrast: however, nevertheless, instead, on the other hand, still

to add more information on the same subject: furthermore, moreover, in addition

to show the effect or result of a cause: therefore, consequently, as a result

to show similarities: likewise, similarly

to show the opposite of what is intended: otherwise

to emphasize a fact in a stronger or more specific way: in fact, indeed

Punctuation rule: When joining two independent clauses together with a conjunctive adverb, *place a semicolon before* the conjunctive adverb *and place a comma after* it.

Tanya wanted to travel to Florida; *therefore,* she worked all summer to pay for her trip.

You had better arrive before the start of the first act; otherwise, you won't be seated until the intermission.

Subordinating Conjunctions
Subordinating conjunctions are used to form a subordinate clause. By means of the subordinating conjunction, the subordinate clause is appropriately connected to the independent clause. Subordinating conjunctions appear at the beginning of the subordinate clause.

> Subordinating conjunctions begin *adverb subordinate clauses*. Those marked with asterisks may sometimes begin *adjective* or *noun subordinate clauses*.

although	before	provided that	when*
as	even though	since	whenever
as if	if*	so that	where*
as long as	inasmuch as	than	whereas
as soon as	in order that	though	wherever
as though	now that	unless	while
because	once	until	

PARTS OF SPEECH FOR STRUCTURE AND SYNTAX

Nouns

What parts of the sentence can nouns be?	subject, predicate nominative, direct object, indirect object, object of the preposition, appositive, and noun of direct address
What phrases and clauses function as nouns?	gerund phrases, infinitive phrases, and noun subordinate clauses

Pronouns

	can be whatever nouns can be

Verbs

What are the two categories of MAIN verbs?	action verbs and linking verbs
What are the COMPLEMENTS that follow action verbs?	direct objects and indirect objects *What questions do direct objects answer after the action verb?* whom? or what? *What questions do indirect objects answer after the action verb?* to whom? or to what? for whom? or for what?
What are the COMPLEMENTS that follow linking verbs?	predicate nominatives and predicate adjectives
What are the four forms of the verb?	present tense, past tense, present participle, and past participle
What are the two verb forms that require a helping verb in front of them in order to function as a verb in the sentence?	present participles and past participles
What are the 23 HELPING verbs?	am/is/are/was/were/be/been/have/has/had/do/does/did/can/could/shall/should/may/might/must/will/would/being
What is a phrasal verb? .	a main verb PLUS a preposition or an adverb, such as *make up, break down, call for, show off, hang out, drop in, live up to, put up with*

Prepositions

Is a subject or a complement in a prepositional phrase?	no; do not confuse the object of the preposition with either a subject or a complement
When does a comma follow an introductory prepositional phrase?	when an introductory prepositional phrase contains more than four words OR when two or more prepositional phrases begin a sentence

Adjectives

What do adjectives modify?	nouns or pronouns
What are the questions that adjectives answers?	what kind? which one? whose? how many?
What phrases and clauses function as adjectives?	prepositional phrases, participial phrases, infinitive phrases, and adjective subordinate clauses

Adverbs

What do adverbs modify?	verbs, adjectives, other adverbs
What are the questions that adverbs answer?	how? when? where? why? to what extent? under what condition?
What phrases and clauses function as adverbs	prepositional phrases, infinitive phrases and adverb subordinate clauses

RHETORICAL PATTERNS AND VARIATIONS FOR SENTENCES

Anadiplosis Repetition of the ending segment at the beginning of another segment:
- When *I give, I give* myself. —Walt Whitman
- All that *Tracy has stated, she has stated* with her usual zeal.

Anaphora Repetition of the beginnings of sentences or clauses:
- *Let us march* to the realization of the American dream. *Let us march* on segregated housing. *Let us march* on segregated schools. *Let us march* on poverty. —Martin Luther King, Jr.
- *Down fell the* tender saplings, *down fell the* aging sycamore, *down fell the* graceful willow, *down fell the* mighty oak under the battering ram of the storm.

Antithesis Repetition by contrasting of parallel elements:
- That's *one small step for* a man, *one giant leap for* mankind. —Neil Armstrong
- Shelby's elastic voice *dug deeply into the well of* the lyric's pain before it *climbed forcefully into the open air of* the song's ultimate joy.

Asyndeton Deliberately omitting conjunctions between words, phrases, or clauses:
- He has been beaten, tortured, interrogated, manipulated.
- I came, I saw, I conquered.

Epanalepsis Repetition of the beginning at the end of a clause or sentence:
- *Blood* hath bought *blood*, and *blows* have answer'd *blows*. —Shakespeare's *King John*
- The *object* of our quest is not our journey's sole *object*.

Epistrophe Repetition of endings in consecutive clauses or sentences:
- I'll have *my bond!* Speak not against *my bond!* I have sworn an oath that I will have *my bond!* —Shylock in Shakespeare's *Merchant of Venice*.

Parallelism Repetition of like structures:
- I thought that *had I not planned* to have a party while my parents were gone for the weekend, or *had I not gone* to pick up the fourth passenger in a car my parents told me was designed for three teenagers, or *had I not run* the red light ten minutes before the wreck, or *had we not stopped* to buy cigarettes for my friend, I would surely have avoided the entire incident. —Nick Crivello

Polysyndeton Using conjunctions between words, phrases, or clauses:
- A man with no hat, *and* with broken shoes, *and* with an old rag tied round his head. A man who had been soaked in water, *and* smothered in mud, *and* lamed by stones, *and* cut by flints, *and* stung by nettles, *and* torn by briars; who limped, *and* shivered, *and* glared, *and* growled; *and* whose teeth chattered in his head as he seized me by the chin. —Charles Dickens' *Great Expectations*

ADDITIONAL PUNCTUATION FOR CLARITY

The primary comma and semicolon rules have been discussed with the punctuation rules that accompany each explanation for clauses and phrases. While there is no attempt in this text to create a complete list of all punctuation rules, some additional ones helpful to the writer include the following:

Comma   (Exercises, pp. 176-177, 179)

Do not use a comma when the coordinating conjunction *and* joins two verbs or predicates that share a common subject.

* Macbeth stabbed the guards *and* wiped the blood on his arms.
* My dad came home early from work *and* spent the rest of the day tearing down the old shed in the back yard.

Semicolon   (Exercises, pp. 178-179)

Usually a comma is placed before a coordinating conjunction that joins two independent clauses; however, use a semicolon with that coordinating conjunction if there are already several commas in one or more of the independent clauses.

* The hijackers, having repeatedly asked for the jet to be fueled with three times the amount needed to reach Paris, set a 5 p.m. deadline for being allowed to leave the Marseilles airport; but the authorities remained determined to keep the airliner on the ground in Marseilles.
* Troy Aikman, who directed the Dallas Cowboys' offense for twelve seasons until his retirement in early 2001, quarterbacked the Cowboys to three Super Bowl victories in four years; and already there is a generation of football fans who know him only as a television sportscaster.

Use a semicolon to separate items in a series when the items themselves already contain commas.

* Byzantine trade included furs such as sable, mink, and fox; precious stones such as rubies, gold, and ivory; and fabrics such as silk, muslin, and damask.

Colon   (Exercises, pp. 178-179)

Use a colon to introduce a part of a sentence that exemplifies, restates, or explains the preceding part. (*If what follows the colon is a sentence, rather than a fragment, capitalize the first word.*)

* All essays contain portions that need improvement: The paragraphs, sentences, and diction are potential victims of the red pen.

Use a colon to introduce a series or list. What comes before the colon, however, must be an independent clause, a complete sentence.

* **Incorrect** Advance Placement English students will study: *Beowulf, Macbeth, The Tempest, Paradise Lost, Return of the Native,* and *Great Expectations.*
* **Correct** Advance Placement English students will study powerful works of literature: *Beowulf, Macbeth, The Tempest, Paradise Lost, Return of the Native,* and *Great Expectations.*

COMMON PROBLEMS WITH STRUCTURE AND SYNTAX

Comma splices, run-ons, faulty parallelism, fragments, subject-verb agreement, pronoun-antecedent agreement

Comma Splice (CS)

A comma splice occurs when two sentences—that is, two independent clauses—are joined together with a comma only. In such a situation, a coordinating conjunction should follow the comma. You may decide, as well, to correct the comma splice in other ways.

Original

John walked down to the candy store, he decided to buy Jolly Ranchers.

Possible Revisions

John walked down to the candy store, and he decided to buy Jolly Ranchers. [The writer places *a coordinating conjunction after the comma.*]

John walked down to the candy store; he decided to buy Jolly Ranchers. [The writer joins the two independent clauses with a *semicolon.*]

John walked down to the candy store, where he decided to buy Jolly Ranchers. [The writer turns the second independent clause into an ADJSC with the *subordinating conjunction* WHERE, which, as in this case, is one of the subordinate conjunctions that can, at times, begin an adjective subordinate clause. Two other subordinate conjunctions that have this flexibilty are IF and WHEN. The *comma* is required because the adjective subordinate clause is *nonessential.*]

John, deciding to buy Jolly Ranchers, walked down to the candy store. [By changing the verb DECIDED to DECIDING, the writer turns the second independent clause into a **PrPP**.]

Original

Michael loves violent action films, however, his girlfriend enjoys romantic ones.

Possible Revisions

Michael loves violent action films; however, his girlfriend enjoys romantic ones. [Since HOWEVER is a *conjunctive adverb*, the writer changes the *comma* after FILMS to a *semicolon.*]

Michael loves violent action films, but his girlfriend enjoys romantic ones. [The writer replaces the conjunctive adverb HOWEVER with the coordinating conjunction BUT; the only *comma* required is the one after FILMS.]

Although Michael loves violent action films, his girlfriend enjoys romantic ones. [The writer removes the conjunctive adverb HOWEVER and turns the first independent clause into an ADVSC with the subordinating conjunction ALTHOUGH; the *comma* after FILMS remains because a comma is required whenever an adverb subordinate clause begins a sentence.]

Run-On (RO)

A run-on sentence is similar to a comma splice since it contains more than one sentence—more than one independent clause—but, in the case of a run-on, the writer has not added required punctuation to join these two structures.

Original

My uncle retrieves my aunt from her search we start toward the lobby.

Possible Revisions

My uncle retrieves my aunt from her search, and we start toward the lobby. [The writer adds the *coordinating conjunction* AND preceded by *a comma*.]

My uncle retrieves my aunt from her search; we start toward the lobby. [The writer uses a *semicolon* to join the two independent clauses.]

After my uncle retrieves my aunt from her search, we start toward the lobby. [The writer turns the first independent clause into an ADVSC with the *subordinating conjunction* AFTER; a *comma* is necessary as the adverb subordinate clause begins the sentence.]

Faulty Parallelism (//)

Two or more items—a pair or a series—should be PARALLEL (alike, of the same kind, similar) in grammatical structure to avoid faulty parallelism.

Original

John argued forcefully with his teacher and at times with anger.

Revision

John argued forcefully with his teacher and at times angrily. [What was a single-word adverb, FORCEFULLY, and an adverb prepositional phrase, WITH ANGER, has become two single-word adverbs.]

Original

Dorothy asked the teacher what she had to do to improve her grade and about the exam.

Revision

Dorothy asked the teacher what she had to do to improve her grade and what questions he would place on the exam. [The prepositional phrase ABOUT THE EXAM has been changed to a noun subordinate clause, a structure parallel to the other noun subordinate clause.]

Original

Michael asked to have more help on his essay, get to turn it in late, and that he receive an "A" in English.

Revision

Michael asked that he have more help on his essay, that he be allowed to turn it in late, and that he receive an "A" in English. [All three items are now noun subordinate clauses beginning with the relative pronoun THAT.]

Sentence Fragments (SF)

Because sentences must have a subject and a verb, sometimes writers confuse a subordinate clause for a complete sentence because subordinate clauses have a subject and verb. Subordinate clauses must be attached to independent clauses.

Original

Pip accepted an offer to travel to London. Because he wanted to become a gentleman.

Revision

Pip accepted an offer to travel to London because he wanted to become a gentleman.

Sometimes writers think phrases, which do not have a subject and a verb, can stand as an independent clause.

Original

Sending Joe and Biddy a gift that he purchased instead of visiting them.

Revision

Pip sends Joe and Biddy a gift that he purchased instead of visiting them.

Subject-Verb Agreement (SV)

Subjects that are singular require singular verbs, and subjects that are plural require plural verbs. This general practice becomes tricky **when the subject is an indefinite pronoun**. Such indefinite pronouns as *either, neither, each, everyone,* and *everybody* are always singular and take a singular verb.

Original

Either of those girls *are* certain to perform well in the competition.

Revision

Either of those girls *is* certain to perform well in the competition.

Another situation that can cause difficulty in subject-verb agreement occurs **when the subject is followed by a prepositional phrase**. The noun following a preposition is the object of the preposition, and **the object of the preposition is never the subject** of a clause. [For example, GIRLS is the object of the preposition OF in the preceding two sentence examples.]

Original

The singer, along with the other members of the band, *are* always acting silly.

Revision

The singer, along with the other members of the band, *is* always acting silly.

Pronoun-Antecedent Agreement (PA)

When we write sentences, our pronouns and antecedents must agree in number, gender, and person. Remember that a pronoun is a word used in place of a noun; some examples include *I, me, you, he, few, most, their.* A pronoun's antecedent is a word or group of words to which a pronoun refers. See pp. 148-149 for specific examples, a list of indefinite pronouns, and commentary regarding the *his / her* dilemma. Among the problems that arise when using pronouns, and their potential solutions, are these that follow.

Avoid vague, confusing, or ambiguous pronoun reference.

Original

When Michelle purchased some groceries, *they* asked her for her Kroger's discount card.

Revision

When Michelle purchased some groceries, *the cashier* asked her for her Kroger's discount card.

Original

The teacher discussed the student's failing grades with her mother after *she* finished drinking the cup of coffee.

Revision

After the teacher finished drinking the cup of coffee, she discussed the student's failing grades with her mother.

Singular indefinite pronouns (see p. 148) act as singular antecedents.

Original

Each of the students at Englewood Girls' Academy will purchase *their* books Tuesday.

Revision

Each of the students at Englewood Girls' Academy will purchase *her* books Tuesday.

Revision

The students at Englewood Girls' Academy will purchase *their* books Tuesday.

A collective noun takes a singular pronoun when considered a unit; considered in terms of individual parts, the collective noun takes a plural pronoun.

Original

The basketball *team* won *their* opening playoff game 71-63.

Revision

The basketball *team* won *its* opening playoff game 71-63. [In this case, the team acted as a unit.]

EXTENDING ELABORATION WITH MODIFICATION[1]

(Exercise, p. 163)

Analysis Modifiers

Method End the original sentence with a comma, *choose a noun* (with or without modifiers) *that emphasizes details you have just cited*, and then continue your analysis. Study these examples.

- The Pardoner tries to sell a "holy relic" even to the "widow who mightn't have a shoe," a *defilement* of Christian theology that provides further evidence of the Church's corruption.
- Joe extends his "restoring touch" unto Pip, "aiding and comforting [him]…by giving [Pip] gravy," a *benevolent deed* that demonstrates not just his concern for Pip, but his willingness to help and care for him.

Repeat Word Modifiers

Method End the original sentence with a comma, *repeat a key word*, and then continue extending your elaboration. Study these examples.

- By omission, the narrator implies that she possesses something beyond the physical realm that warrants his love, *something* intangible to the five senses.
- Hester chooses to live in the town in which she has sinned, *live* despite the daily ridicule not only from townspeople but also from clergymen.
- The Pardoner is both deceptive and greedy, *deceptive* in his selling of false relics to naïve believers, *greedy* in his desire to make a profit using his position in the church.

Sample Modifications

- Duke Theseus represents a leader who attempts to balance the feminine and the masculine.

Elaboration with repeat word modifier

Duke Theseus represents a leader who attempts to balance the feminine and the masculine, the *masculine* that restores the order King Creon disrupted, the *feminine* that grants clemency to Arcite and Palamon.

Elaboration with analysis modifier

Duke Theseus represents a leader who attempts to balance the feminine and the masculine, a *combination* that allows him to maintain an image of strength along with compassion, a *combination* that places love before violence.

- While living with Pap, Huck is in a dangerous situation.

Elaboration with repeat word modifier

While living with Pap, Huck is in a dangerous situation, a **situation** that requires quick thinking and imagination if he is to survive.

Elaboration with analysis modifier

While living with Pap, Huck is in a dangerous situation, an **environment** that often involves physical and mental abuse.

---

[1] Adapted from Williams, Joseph M. *Style: Ten Lessons in Clarity & Grace*. Boston: Scott, Foresman, 1989. 131–132.

Sentence Combining: Repeat Word Modifiers/Analysis Modifiers

Directions: Combine each group of sentences using one or more *repeat word* or *analysis* modifiers. Underline, italicize, or highlight the modifiers created. You may delete extra words if necessary.

1. Pip, confused by Estella's cruel remarks, begins to feel shame about his home life. At this point in the novel, Pip realizes that his social class will prevent him from achieving happiness.

2. Adding to this self-inflicted torture, Dimmesdale battles Chillingworth. He is a physician who does not abate Dimmesdale's pain but is a "chief actor in the poor minister's interior world." He is able to "arouse him with a throb of agony."

3. Scrooge disdainfully comments about his nephew's monetary status: "You're poor enough." This shows how Scrooge evaluates individuals by their monetary value.

4. Near this prison rests "a portion of the virgin soil…a cemetery." Cemeteries often remind one that death might affect this community, too.

5. In addition, Wealhtheow also presents to Beowulf "two arm-wreaths, with robes and rings also, and the richest collar." These gifts represent Hrothgar and Wealhtheow's gratitude towards Beowulf for killing the notorious Grendel. Beowulf cleanses the hall.

6. Chaucer depicts the knight as a virtuous pilgrim. He is a person who fights for the Church. He rejects extravagance in exchange for humility.

7. Bob Cratchitt's office fire is smaller than Scrooge's. This detail is ironic considering Bob's heart is much warmer than his boss'.

8. Cratchitt's office is described as a "dismal little cell." The word *cell* suggests that he is imprisoned by Scrooge's cruelty.

9. Frankenstein realizes that his experiment, if successful, will transcend all previous scientific discoveries. This accomplishment would exalt the doctor to a position of great fame.

10. Scrooge sees the Christmas season as devoid of tangible value. This is a view of the world that is base and political. His cynicism thwarts a relationship with his nephew.

Sentence Combining with Adverb Subordinate Clauses

The following six words are subordinating conjunctions that may begin adverb subordinate clauses. Three of the subordinating conjunctions suggest a contrasting relationship between the two clauses of the sentence; three are used to indicate a cause and effect relationship.

for contrast	**although**	**even though**	**while**
for cause and effect	**because**	**since**	**as**

Directions: In the following pairs of sentences, COMBINE one sentence with the other BY TURNING ONE OF THE SENTENCES INTO AN ADVERB SUBORDINATE CLAUSE AND ATTACHING IT TO THE OTHER. Attach six subordinate clauses *before the independent clause*. Place six subordinate clauses *after the independent clause*. Be sure your combination makes logical sense; not just any combination will do. Also, be sure to <u>follow the comma rules with regard to adverb subordinate clauses</u>, p. 135. Make *one combination* per pair. *Use all six* subordinating conjunctions by the end. Underline, italicize, or otherwise highlight the adverb subordinate clause.

1. A 1948 law says that women cannot be assigned combat duty. It is possible women will be involved in combat in the next war.

2. The thief will get away with the crime. Someone will report him to the police.

3. The play's director stated that rehearsals begin an hour earlier today. She feels that the actors need much more practice.

4. Michelangelo's sculpture *Pieta* is now displayed only behind a protective glass shield. It was damaged by a lunatic.

5. Over fifteen inches of snow fell during the night. The school district decided to have school anyway.

6. I do not have any money. I'll have to borrow twenty dollars from someone else.

7. Other composers may have been more inventive. None have captured the American spirit like Duke Ellington.

8. Sheryl has practiced vigorously for months. She is ready to win all three track and field events that she's entered.

9. Over ten inches of ice glazed the streets. The school district decided to call off school.

10. People always become ill at one time or another. There is a great demand for students, both female and male, to enter the nursing profession.

11. An innocent man was executed for the crime. The real murderer was eventually caught and signed a confession.

12. The linebacker suffered a hamstring injury in last week's game. The coaches expected him to play Sunday.

Sentence Combining with Adjective Subordinate Clauses

Directions: In the following pairs of sentences, combine one sentence with the other by turning one of the sentences into an adjective subordinate clause that modifies the boldfaced word. Underline, italicize, or otherwise highlight the adjective subordinate clause. Punctuate the new sentence correctly (see p. 136).

1. **Guillermo** is normally very shy in class. He surprised all his peers by delivering an impassioned speech on capital punishment.

2. The award-winning **film** created additional revenue for Steven Speilberg. The film combined actual war footage with fabricated scenes.

3. **Charles Dickens** spent part of his youth working in a shoe factory. Later in life he became a successful writer.

4. The three boys planned a **joke**. The joke involved hiding water balloons in the bottom of the girls' book bags.

5. The **girls** did not realize the balloons were in their bags when they threw them on the ground. The girls became very angry once the water seeped out from the bottom of the bags.

6. The girls decided to plot their **revenge**. The revenge will be much more creative and clandestine than the boys' so-called joke.

7. The governor decided to veto the latest welfare reform **bill**. This piece of legislation would obligate working mothers to work only 20 hours per week, rather than the current requirement of 30.

8. Yvette has a **belief** regarding wealth. Acquiring wealth is extremely necessary for success in life.

9. **Ariel** is an ethereal spirit in Shakespeare's *The Tempest*. Ariel serves the magician Prospero.

10. Disguised as a beggar in his own palace, Odysseus manages to demonstrate **restraint**. This prevents him from prematurely revealing his identity.

Writing Complex Sentences with Adjective Subordinate Clauses

Directions:
- Create five original complex sentences, each one containing a correctly punctuated adjective subordinate clause.
- Each adjective clause must begin with a different relative pronoun. The five relative pronouns to be used are *whose, who, that, whom,* and *which.*
- Underline, italicize, or otherwise highlight the adjective subordinate clause.
- Identify the subject and verb in your adjective subordinate clause.

> **Subject-Verb Combinations**
> With regard to sentence structure exercises, it is recommended that students identify the subject and verb (including any helping verbs) of every clause during any exercise. This repeated practice engrains in each student the two essentials of any clause—be it a subordinate clause or an independent clause—and, therefore, provides a marked contrast to the structure of the phrase. A simple **S** over each subject and a **V** over every verb is all that it takes.

Writing Compound-Complex Sentences with Adjective and Adverb Subordinate Clauses

Directions:

- Create five original compound-complex sentences, each one containing a correctly punctuated adjective and adverb subordinate clause.
- Underline, italicize, or otherwise highlight the adjective and adverb subordinate clauses.
- Identify the subject and verb in both your subordinate clauses and your independent clauses.
- To join together the two independent clauses in each sentence, use either solo semicolons or correctly punctuated conjunctive adverbs.

Noun Subordinate Clauses and Adjective Subordinate Clauses

Directions:

- Identify the subject and verb in every clause, subordinate and independent.
- Underline, italicize, or otherwise highlight each subordinate clause.
- If the subordinate clause is an adjective, identify it as **ADJSC** and draw an arrow to the word it modifies.
- If the subordinate clause is a noun, identify it as **NSC** and write its function in the sentence next to the identification (e.g. **NSC-S** or **NSC-OP**).

1. Sparta was the ancient Greek city-state where physical strength and skill were most highly admired.

2. In Athens, which was Sparta's greatest rival, intellectual achievement was greatly valued.

3. The Athenian belief in democratic values was what the Spartans could never understand.

4. The Athenian whose leadership brought his city-state to pre-eminence was Pericles.

5. That Athens grew economically, culturally, and militarily under Pericles became a threat to Spartan interests.

6. The news that Athens had invaded the Spartan peninsula of Peloponnesus caused the Spartans to prepare for war.

7. The Spartans knew why the Greeks had invaded their territory.

8. They sent a declaration of war to those leaders who were prepared to receive it.

9. From what became known as the Peloponessian War arose the Greek world's first renowned historian, Thucydides.

10. Reading Thucydides will benefit anyone who believes knowledge of the past may prevent problems in the future.

Writing Complex Sentences with Noun Subordinate Clauses

Directions:
- Create five original complex sentences, each one containing a noun subordinate clause.
- Each noun clause must begin with a different relative pronoun. The five relative pronouns to be used are *who, that, what, how,* and *why.*
- Underline, italicize, or otherwise highlight the noun subordinate clause.
- Identify the subject and verb in all of your clauses, both independent and subordinate.

Three Types of Subordinate Clauses: Adverb, Adjective, and Noun

Directions:
- Identify the subject and verb in every clause, subordinate and independent.
- Underline, italicize, or otherwise highlight each subordinate clause.
- If the subordinate clause is an adjective, identify it as **ADJSC** and draw an arrow to the word it modifies.
- If the subordinate clause is an adverb, identify it as **ADVSC** and write the question it answers next to the identification. (e.g. **ADVSC-WHY?**)
- If the subordinate clause is a noun, identify it as **NSC** and write its function in the sentence next to the identification (e.g. **NSC-PN** or **NSC-DO**).

1. After he looked at me for a moment, the man turned me upside down and emptied my pockets.

2. When he came to the low church wall, he got over it like a man whose legs were numb and stiff.

3. She was not a good-looking woman, and I had the general impression that she must have forced Joe Gargery to marry her by hand.

4. That I was going to rob Mrs. Joe almost drove me crazy with guilt.

5. As soon as the great black velvet pall outside my window was shot with gray, I got up and went downstairs.

6. He crammed what little food was left into the breast of his gray jacket.

7. Joe, who had ventured into the kitchen after me, drew the back of his hand across his nose with a conciliatory air.

8. Joe threw his eyes over the handcuffs and pronounced that the job would necessitate the lighting of his forge fire.

9. The cattle turned their heads from the wind and sleet and stared angrily as if they held us responsible for what annoyed them.

10. That the shouting was made by more than one voice soon became apparent.

11. Because one of the soldiers, who carried a basket in lieu of a gun, dropped to his knees to open it, my convict took the opportunity to look round him for the first time and saw me.

12. The "something" I had noticed before clicked in the man's throat.

Simple, Compound, Complex, and Compound-Complex Sentences

Directions:
- Identify the subject and verb in each clause.
- Underline, italicize, or otherwise highlight each subordinate clause.
- Identify each clause as **ADVSC**, **ADJSC**, and **NSC** and explain why it is that type of clause. (Follow directions for such an explanation on the preceding page's directions for "Three Types of Subordinate Clauses.")
- Identify the entire sentence as
    S simple = one independent clause
    CP compound = two independent clauses
    CX complex = one independent clause + one or more subordinate
        clauses
    CPCX compound-complex = two independent clauses + one or more
        subordinate clauses

1. Edmond Dantes, whose marriage to Mercedes was prevented by various villains, spent fourteen years in prison for a crime that he never committed.

2. The unfortunate jeweler was lying on the floor in a pool of blood, which flowed from three large wounds in his chest; a kitchen knife with only its handle showing had been plunged into the fourth wound.

3. He discovered that a slope had been made; moreover, the rock had slid down to its present position, where it had been fixed in place by another rock about the size of a building stone, which had been used as a wedge.

4. Before inviting the two new cardinals to dinner, Cesar Borgia asked his father about a famous key opening a certain cupboard and a ring containing a lion's head.

5. He stopped in the hall and called for a servant to announce him to Noirtier, but nobody answered.

6. They poured some rum down his throat; complaining of a sharp pain, he soon opened his eyes and groaned.

7. As he stood knocking vainly on the door, Maximilien saw his father walking from the bedroom and pressing to his side an object that he tried to conceal beneath his coat.

8. That Dantes spent the years of his captivity planning an all-encompassing revenge against his enemies will not be a surprise to whoever has read about his travails.

9. Villefort buried the evidence of his affair under a full moon and before the curious eyes of a man he did not notice.

10. A novel of deception and desire, *The Count of Monte Cristo* provides the serious reader with a hero, Edmond Dantes, whose adventures require both mental and physical dexterity; however, what may serve as the ultimate cause of his success is his patience.

Sentence Combining with Present Participial Phrases

Directions:
- Combine the following sentences by turning one of them into a present participial phrase.
- Make TWO combinations per pair, *one before* the noun it modifies and *one after* it.
- Underline, italicize, or otherwise highlight each present participial phrase.
- Use commas where necessary.

e.g. Miami's citizens *have* already *experienced* two hurricanes this year. They *are* very well *prepared* for any future catastrophe.

The writer has FOUR OPTIONS for combining these two sentences. Note comma locations.

Miami's citizens, *having already experienced two hurricanes this year*, are very well prepared for any future catastrophe.

Having already experienced two hurricanes this year, Miami's citizens are very well prepared for any future catastrophe.

Miami's citizens, *being very well prepared for any future catastrophe*, have already experienced two hurricanes this year.

Being very well prepared for any future catastrophe, Miami's citizens have already experienced two hurricanes this year.

1. Sergeant Simpson reprimands the private very severely. He forcefully removes one of his stripes.

2. Tamika traveled to the airport in a yellow van. She arrived twenty minutes early.

3. The coach has called two straight running plays with no success. He then decides to signal for a long pass.

4. The philosopher spoke to the English II classes at Garland High. She urged the students to study metaphysics before they graduate.

5. My cat refused to eat any food in his tray. He seemed to be on a hunger strike until we allowed him to lick off the dinner plates.

6. Hiroshima, Japan, had been destroyed by an atomic bomb in 1945. It was rebuilt over a period of fifteen years.

7. The robin eats at the bird feeder each morning. The bird is occasionally joined by a pair of sparrows.

8. The oak was struck by lightning. It split in half and fell to the ground.

9. The Secretary of State flies into Kashmir this weekend. She attempts to work out a peaceful settlement in the region.

10. Michael Stipe promotes the sale of his autobiography. Each weekend he visits bookstores and signs autographs.

Sentence Combining with Past Participial Phrases

Directions:

- Combine the following sentences by turning one of them into a past participial phrase.
- Make TWO combinations per pair, *one before* the noun it modifies and *one after* it.
- Underline, italicize, or otherwise highlight each past participial phrase.
- Use commas where necessary.

e.g. The coach of the basketball team *was concerned* about Randolph's inability to make free throws. He decided to bench him for the second half.

in THIS **example, the writer has** TWO OPTIONS **for combining these sentences.**

The coach of the basketball team, *concerned about Randolph's inability to make free throws*, decided to bench him for the second half.

Concerned about Randolph's inability to make free throws, the coach of the basketball team decided to bench him for the second half.

Hint: When looking at a pair of sentences, you must FIRST FIND A VERB PHRASE CONTAINING A PAST PARTICIPLE. The verb phrase with a past participle is the one that contains a helping verb. TO FORM THE PAST PARTICIPIAL PHRASE, JETTISON THE HELPING VERB AND RETAIN THE PAST PARTICIPLE. In the above case, of the two sentences involving the coach and Randolph, only the first sentence has a past participle in the verb—*was concerned,* with *was* being the helping verb and *concerned* the past participle form of the verb. IF BOTH SENTENCES IN THE PAIR HAVE PAST PARTICIPLES, THEN YOU WILL LIKELY HAVE FOUR OPTIONS FOR COMBINING the sentences because you may select either past participle to begin the past participial phrase.

1. Columbus was exhausted by a series of storms on his fourth voyage. He stayed in his cabin for the duration of the journey.

2. Magellan was enraged by the actions of two mutinous captains on his journey. He executed them posthaste.

3. The caterpillar is denied an opportunity to live. It is swatted onto the floor a few feet in front of me.

4. The free safety for the football team was injured in the play. He writhes helplessly on the ground.

5. Shannon's softball team was defeated in the state championship game. It was awarded the Hollander Trophy for Highest Team Batting Average.

6. Primal Scream's "Exterminator" was played online four times in one hour on 3WK Underground Radio. It drove my little sister out of my bedroom.

7. He was surprised at the violence contained in the news report. He quickly turned the channel to MTV.

8. Odysseus was instructed by Athena to disguise himself in his own house. He dined with the suitors and restrained his outrage at their supercilious behavior.

9. Her finished poems had been placed in a secret drawer by Emily. They were found twenty years after she died.

10. Grendel was easily defeated by Beowulf. The monster fought and yelled but fled to the swamps to bleed to death.

Identifying Present and Past Participial Phrases

Directions:
- Underline, italicize, or otherwise highlight the participial phrase.
- Draw an arrow to the word the participial phrase modifies.
- Identify the phrase as **PrPP** or **PaPP**.

1. Admired by Johann Sebastian Bach, Vivaldi's compositions included instrumental works and operas.

2. The first European explorers arriving in South America had found that many Indian tribes farmed the land.

3. Located at this time in the Cairo museum, Tutankhamen's coffin is made of solid gold.

4. The encyclopedia, containing more than 40,000 entries, provides an enormous range of information.

5. Pip, turning from the Temple Gate as soon as he had read the warning, made his way to Fleet Street, where he obtained a carriage and drove to Covent Garden.

6. Pip, obligated by his sense of duty to his benefactor, puts his life in peril on Magwitch's behalf.

7. The child racing through Aunt Nikita's vegetable garden soon disappeared behind the stone wall encompassing the next-door neighbor's back yard.

8. The building we lived in was gray, as were the streets, filled with slush the first few months of my life there. [Sentence from Judith Ortiz Cofer's "Silent Dancing."]

9. Sometimes I'd come home to find her lounging in the bamboo chair on the back porch, eating melon, or lying on the couch with a bowl of half-melted ice cream balanced on her chest. [Sentence from Naomi Shihab Nye's "Maintenance."]

10. I left the suburb folded in light, the white beams already taking on a grayish glitter, a dog barking somewhere. [Sentence from Eavan Boland's "The Woman, The Place, The Poet."]

Identifying Gerund Phrases and their function

Directions:
- Underline, italicize, or otherwise highlight the gerund phrase.
- Tell if it is used as a subject (**GP-S**), direct object (**GP-DO**), object of the preposition (**GP-OP**), or the predicate nominative (**GP-PN**).

1. Fearing to have the news of Estella's marriage to Drummle confirmed by the newspaper caused Pip to stop his subscription to the local daily.

2. Joe's primary mission in London was restoring me to good health.

3. Composing ragtime piano pieces was Scott Joplin's special talent.

4. Because ragtime musicians did make a practice of writing down their music, some critics did not accept ragtime as a legitimate form of jazz.

5. Imagine telling that to Scott Joplin!

6. Making an errata page is sometimes part of the publishing business.

7. At the age of twelve, Billy the Kid began living a life of crime.

8. Portraying Billy as the Robin Hood of the frontier became common with dime-novel authors of the day.

9. By covering his exploits with glamour, writers turned the story of a vicious murderer into a Wild West legend.

10. A favorite occupation for writers of stories, novels, and films is retelling the legend of Billy the Kid.

Distinguishing Between Gerund and Present Participial Phrases

Directions: Because present participles and gerunds are both verb forms that end in *ing*, it may be tricky to tell them apart unless you keep in mind their function in the sentence: A present participial phrase functions as an adjective; a gerund phrase, of course, functions as a noun. Each sentence below contains either a present participial phrase or a gerund phrase.
- If it is a participial phrase, underline, italicize, or otherwise highlight it and draw an arrow to the word it modifies.
- If it is a gerund phrase, underline, italicize, or otherwise highlight it and tell how it is being used in the sentence (e.g. **GP-DO**).

1. Dancing as a cultural activity probably started with ancient religious ceremonies.

2. Moving into other areas of life, it later became a form of recreation and entertainment.

3. Medieval performers, lacking a stage, danced in a great hall.

4. Members of the audience would enjoy dancing of every description.

5. The only drawback was charging the customer astronomical prices for each performance.

6. After establishing academies of dance, the country's minister for cultural affairs created multiple scholarship opportunities for talented children.

7. The most popular scholarship, paying full tuition for the entire six-year program, is granted to ten students each year.

8. One academy has a renowned year-long course in dance exercise that the country's soccer players, hoping to qualify for the World Cup team, must take and pass.

9. The dancers completing the six-year program in ballet compete for positions with various ballet troupes throughout the continent.

10. Those studying theatrical dance often audition for roles in musicals staged in New York City and London

Identifying Infinitive Phrases and their function

Directions:
- Underline, italicize, or otherwise highlight the entire infinitive phrase.
- Identify the infinitive phrase as **N-IP**, **ADJ-IP**, or **ADV-IP**.
- If the phrase functions as a noun, identify the reason (**N-IP=S**, **N-IP=OP**, etc.). If the phrase functions as an adjective, draw an arrow to the word modified. If the phrase functions as an adverb, identify the reason (**ADV-IP=WHY**, **ADV-IP=WHERE**, etc.) and draw an arrow to the word it modifies.

1. One of the passengers decided to attack the hijacker.

2. To provide myself some necessary relaxation, I rented a cabin at Possum Kingdom Lake for the three-day weekend.

3. If you are interested in receiving a job application, Mrs. Cunningham is the secretary to ask at this time.

4. "To dream the impossible dream" is the first line of my favorite song.

5. The lieutenant's orders were to dismiss the troops forthwith.

6. The best place to view the skyline is near White Rock Lake.

7. Latreisha wanted to take swimming lessons so that she would feel more comfortable when she goes on the Alaskan cruise.

8. Parker listened to *West Side Story* to calm his nerves before the interview with the theater director at the university.

9. Demetria proposed a theory that the Vikings were probably the first to circumnavigate the world.

10. To stop the argument between Jacob and Minh, Julia told them to split in half the hundred-dollar bill they had found.

Infinitive, Gerund, and Participial Phrases

Directions: Each sentence may contain an infinitive, gerund, present participial, or past participial phrase. Some of these sentences contain MORE THAN ONE such phrase.

First, *determine whether a phrase* is a participial phrase or a gerund phrase.
- IF it is a PARTICIPIAL PHRASE, underline, italicize, or otherwise highlight it; identify it as **PrPP** or **PaPP**; and draw an arrow to the word it modifies.

- IF it is a GERUND PHRASE, underline, italicize, or otherwise highlight the phrase and tell how it is functioning (**GP-S**, **GP-OP**, etc.) in the sentence.
- IF it is neither a participial phrase nor a gerund phrase, then it is an INFINITIVE PHRASE. Underline, italicize, or otherwise highlight it and tell its function (**N-IP=DO**, **ADJ-IP**, **ADV-IP=HOW**, etc.).

1. Working overtime is the only way Sara can earn enough money to support her family.

2. The motorcycle parked by the fire hydrant will receive a ticket from the police officer.

3. To part with her collie upset Enriqueta so much that her parents tried to assure her that getting a new dog would be a very high priority in the next few weeks.

4. Francine's primary interest is acting in a community theater.

5. The driver of the blue Chevy pickup was given a ticket for running a stop sign.

6. Concerned about the hurricane, the residents of the island community left their homes.

7. The vacationers, swimming leisurely, had no knowledge of the danger in the water.

8. The authorities wondered whether postponing the concert would be preferable to cancelling it altogether.

9. To activate the community's interest in banning boom boxes in the nearby park, a neighborhood group circulated a petition to bring the matter before the city council.

10. I suppose that finding a pickup painted metallic black was more important to Ricky than the price he would have to pay for it.

11. The loud crying in the next room caused the lady to make an inquiry; however, she soon discovered that to cry loudly does not always signify a serious problem.

Sentence Combining with Absolute Phrases

Directions: Combine the following sentences by creating an absolute phrase out of one sentence in the pair and joining that phrase to the other. Underline, italicize, or otherwise highlight the absolute phrase.

- Removing the "be" verb from the sentence creates an absolute phrase.

Original
Julia listened in stunned silence. Her smile was vanishing from her face.

Revision
Julia listened in stunned silence, *her smile vanishing from her face.*

Original

The furnace was broken. We huddled under blankets and waited for dawn.

Revision

The furnace broken, we huddled under blankets and waited for dawn.

- Turning an active voice verb into a participle creates an absolute phrase.

Original

She looks up and smiles at her uncle. Long strands of silky hair fall limply on her face.

Revision

She looks up, *long strands of silky hair falling limply on her face*, and smiles at her uncle.

1. She cheerfully punches the keys T-H-E E-N-D and looks up with a proud crescent stretching across her lips. Her eyes gleam brightly as she reads over the masterpiece.

2. My mother keeps bellowing names, and soon her friends and relatives converge on the house. Her voice draws life from the dream's dark corners. [from Bernard Cooper's *Maps to Anywhere*]

3. John waited in the classroom. His fingers tapped on the desk nervously.

4. The community was restored. Prospero decides to throw away his magic staff and leave his recent past behind him.

5. The bank robbers fled the scene within minutes. The security guard saw part of the license plate numbers.

6. Mrs. Jones stared at the class. She had two research papers in her hand. She gritted her teeth.

7. John knelt on the fifty-yard line. He looked up at the tied score. He realized the team only had ten seconds.

8. Her heart races as she rushes away from the foreboding footsteps. The freezing wind chills her to the bone.

9. Mark's bedroom was a disaster. He had dirty underwear draped on the waste paper basket. He had soiled socks under the bed.

10. Three rugby players walked into the locker room together. One was soaked in sweat.

Sentence Combining with Appositive Phrases

Directions: Combine the following pairs of sentences by turning one of the sentences in each pair into an appositive phrase. Underline, italicize, or otherwise highlight the appositive phrase.

1. Jerry Jones is the owner of the Dallas Cowboys. He is currently interviewing potential head coaches.

2. Edmond Dantes is a master of disguises. He meticulously plans a variety of strategies for achieving his ultimate goal.

3. The *Pharoan* is a ship owned by the Morrell family. It was decimated during a severe storm at sea.

4. Dr. Gregory wrote a new book on Elizabeth Bishop. She teaches at Harvard University.

5. That student has received scholarship offers from eight different universities. She is a recent immigrant from Tanzania.

6. He subscribes to the *The Georgia Review*. This literary magazine publishes some of the finest nonfiction in the Unites States.

7. Dinah plans to move to New York City and play in the house band at The Blue Note. She has been a jazz pianist since high school.

8. Rod Steiger was an Academy Award-winning actor. He was best known for his roles in *On the Waterfront, The Pawnbroker,* and *In the Heat of the Night*.

9. Chuck Palahniuk is the author of *Fight Club*. He has become Darrell's favorite novelist.

10. Patrice boasts a .355 batting average. She is the starting shortstop on her high school baseball team.

Commas with Introductory Elements

Directions: Place commas after the introductory elements in each sentence. Introductory elements that require commas include the following: introductory ADVERB SUBORDINATE CLAUSES, introductory PRESENT AND PAST PARTICIPIAL PHRASES, introductory ADVERB INFINITIVE PHRASES, an introductory GROUP (TWO OR MORE) OF PREPOSITIONAL PHRASES, and any INTRODUCTORY WORDS.

1. After the principal entered the classroom everyone became uncomfortably quiet.

2. With the fall of Rome in A.D. 476 the empire crumbled.

3. Continuing to plan out his strategies Odysseus rests against the doorway as he listens to the heaving noises coming from Polyphemus' throat.

4. Provided that his ship is able to pass by Charybdis safely Odysseus and his mariners will take a chance on a moderately more successful encounter with Scylla.

5. If you had seen Polyphemus milking his ewes you might have carried away a somewhat different impression from that of Odysseus.

6. Yes it is difficult to excuse the eating of six of Odysseus' men.

7. Closed for a week of overdue repairs to its facilities my favorite pizza parlor was unavailable for a visit by my English class.

8. Although I have not seen the movie *The Client* I heard the book was much better.

9. To defend his client effectively the lawyer hired a private investigator.

10. Because Vivian was always making people laugh she decided to use her natural clumsiness as a stepladder to a career in comedy.

Using Commas with Coordinating Conjunctions: Compound Sentences vs. Compound Predicates

Directions:
- If the coordinating conjunction is used in order to join independent clauses to form a compound sentence or a compound-complex sentence, *place a comma before* it.
- If the coordinating conjunction is used in order to join compound parts of a predicate, *do not place a comma before* it.
- To be sure whether you have a compound sentence or a compound predicate, *identify the subject and verb in each clause*, both independent and subordinate clauses. (Remember that all verbs in the compound predicate will have the same word as the subject; all verbs in the compound sentence will have different words as the subject.)
- Underline, italicize, or otherwise highlight any subordinate clauses.
- Identify each sentence as simple (**S**), compound (**CP**), complex, (**CX**), and compound-complex (**CPCX**).

1. Theseus held out his hand to Hercules and hoped that his cousin would rethink his plan to kill himself.

2. Walking in the parade before the sacrifice, Ariadne noticed the Athenian hero and immediately fell in love with him.

3. Theseus leapt toward the hideous animal and grasped its bulging throat.

4. It took not only his strength to accomplish this arduous task but also his intelligence.

5. Hercules could not seem to control his emotions effectively and he often felt penitent about the resulting actions.

6. Theseus was sometimes a little bit supercilious and, therefore, convinced that he could do whatever he wanted to do whenever he pleased.

7. Atlas came back with the apples but did not give them to Hercules.

8. Psyche betrays her husband's wishes and proceeds to take a quick glance at him.

9. This shouldn't come as much of a surprise because the Athenians admired knowledge over brawn and believed that wit vanquished any enemy.

10. Hercules destroyed every member of his family with implacable fury but he would not have contemplated such a gruesome action if he were in his right mind.

11. Heroes might be those people who rescue passengers from a grisly plane crash or simply rescue a pet cat from a tree.

12. Although Psyche never wandered without purpose, she traveled great lengths on many of her journeys and she would have been hopelessly lost without succor.

Using Semicolons

Directions: Apply the rules for usage of semicolons, pp. 157 and 138, to the following sentences. Be prepared to explain why using the semicolon in each sentence is necessary. Whatever punctuation already appears in the sentence is appropriately used.

1. The pastel drawings are lovely nevertheless, they should be sprayed with a fixative.

2. The weather is very strange we should have had a hard frost at least three weeks ago.

3. Cooking in front of television cameras can be embarrassing for example, I have seen cooks spill batter all over the stove and drop food on the floor.

4. The story of the woman with multiple personalities shows the disease's brutal cause, bizarre symptoms, and strange development but the woman's tale is not ever sensationalized.

5. The most significant dates of the Civil War were April 12, 1861 July 3, 1863 and April 9, 1865.

6. The participants in the exhibit are Judi Parker, who paints in water color Simon Rogers, who is a potter and Peter Mondavian, who sculpts in transparent plastic.

7. Paper airplanes are not airplanes at all they should be called paper gliders.

8. I want to get a roommate who makes up the bed and understands the proper use of hangars consequently, I filled out a questionnaire to help determine roommate compatibility.

9. Blenders, food processors, and instant food have eliminated most slicing, dicing, and pureeing yet the time required for putting together a meal seems the same.

10. California, Texas, and New York are the three most populous states and Florida and Arizona are the fastest growing.

Why are the uses of the semicolon in these three sentences that follow incorrect? Revise and explain.

11. Even though Sophocles wrote 124 plays; only seven plays by him still exist.

12. I have checked the following sources; encyclopedias, almanacs, indexes, and periodicals.

13. Stacey has to leave basketball practice for his ballet rehearsal at five o'clock, otherwise; the director will have to assign his role to another dancer.

Using Colons and Semicolons

Directions: Place colons and semicolons where they belong in the following sentences. All commas currently in these sentences are correct and should be left alone.

1. The following items appeared in error on our credit card bill twelve folding chairs, which we did not order one automatic juice squeezer, which we returned and three Christmas tree ornaments, for which we paid cash.

2. Tuition for the music school is not high moreover, many scholarships are available.

3. Paris, Venice, and Amsterdam are all beautiful cities but my favorite city anywhere in the world is Cairo.

4. Perhaps inspired by Diego Rivera's work, artist Judith Baca helped create the world's longest mural the one-mile-long piece, entitled *The Great Wall of Los Angeles*, shows the contributions made by ethnic groups to the city.

5. In the Olympics the first-place winner gets a gold medal second-place, a silver medal and third-place, a bronze medal.

6. It's obvious why you're tired you've been staying up too late.

7. Jim enjoys history, literature, and psychology yet his ambition is to become a math professor.

8. Before you paint, gather the necessary supplies paint, a palette, and brushes.

9. Remove the cable clamps in the reverse order from the way you connected them first, disconnect one of the black cable's clamps from the engine block then, disconnect the other from the assisting battery finally, disconnect the red cable's clamps from the positive terminals.

10. He admits he doesn't know yet what he will do with his life, how he will do it, or where he will do it but he is sure his life hereafter will have nothing to do with football.

Using Commas, Colons, and Semicolons

Directions:
- Identify all subjects and verbs in each clause, subordinate and independent.
- Underline, italicize, or otherwise highlight all subordinate clauses.
- Place punctuation where it belongs.

1. In the prologue to his epic Homer asks a muse to sing through him.

2. The mariners who ate the lotus were eventually plucked from the ship by a ravenous twelve-necked hyenamaid an odious creature that even the brave Odysseus feared.

3. Telemachus the only son of Ithaca's king searched for his father for a year being unable to find any information about him he returned to his mother's palace so that he could help her with keeping the suitors under control.

4. In order that everyone have an opportunity to listen to the sirens Odysseus decided that his mariners disturbed by the idea that only he might listen to their song should remove the beeswax from their ears for a maximum of ten seconds.

5. Circe who was enchanted by this man who did not fear her granted

Odysseus' request for help that would put him on the road home.

6. To discern the values of Greek culture from a study of Homer's epics all Greek school children were required to read both the *Odyssey* and the *Iliad* from an early age therefore the primary curriculum of the nation was centered on these two texts.

7. Odysseus' largest ship destroyed by one of Zeus' lightning bolts was unable to survive the voyage home.

8. The reunion of Odysseus with his son which was assisted by the goddess Athena produced a flood of tears and a plan for reclaiming their kingdom.

9. The slaughter of the suitors reminds the careful reader of an earlier Homeric simile like the monster Scylla from which six of his mariners could not escape Odysseus is compared to a fisherman pulling his prey in by a net.

10. Penelope the woman who resisted the pressure of the suitors to abandon Odysseus for dead and choose one of them as her new husband refuses to disarm herself until the conqueror of these men has passed a final test.

Imitating Syntax and Style of Authors

Directions: Write your own sentence, purposely imitating the syntax and style of each of the following sentences composed by other authors.

e.g. **author** Ito Romo *El Puente*
Lola tripped, and when she did, she leapt forward, falling flat on her face, her nose against the pavement.

Imitation of syntax and style
Macbeth reflected, and after he decided to kill the king, he proceeded with his plan, condemning his soul to hell, the earth about to tremor.

1. **Author** Kyla Dunn "Cloning Trevor"
A human egg, retrieved just hours earlier from a young donor, was positioned under a microscope, its image glowing on a nearby video monitor.

2. **Author** Philip Roth "My Baseball Years"
It was different, however, on Sundays out at Ruppert Stadium, a green wedge of pasture miraculously walled in among the factories, warehouses, and truck depots of industrial Newark.

3. **Author** Annie Dillard *An American Childhood*
He chased us silently over picket fences, through thorny hedges, between houses, around garbage cans, and across streets.

4. **Author** Charles Bowden "Teachings of Don Fernando"
His voice courtly, his face calm, his body singing of ease, I will trust him completely.

5. **Author** Robert Fagles *Iliad*
Lord marshal Agamemnon rose up in their midst, streaming tears like a dark spring running down some desolate rock face, its shaded currents flowing.

Directions:
- Examine each sentence and identify all the subject-verb combinations—in other words, identify all the clauses, independent and subordinate.
- Identify each sentence as **S**, **CP**, **CX**, or **CPCX**—and explain why.
- Identify each subordinate clause as **ADVSC**, **ADJSC**, or **NSC**—and explain why your response is correct.
- Identify each **PrPP**, **PaPP**, **GP**, **IP**, and **AbP**—and identify its function.

1. That Bob Ewell acted pusillanimously in this story is further evidence that cowardice and bigotry go hand in hand.

2. To give Tom Robinson an opportunity to have his side of the story fairly presented to the jury, Judge Taylor decides that Atticus Finch should defend him.

3. Because Miss Havisham had been jilted, she began teaching Estella to treat men with contempt; to give her adopted daughter the chance to sharpen her skills is the reason why the wealthy lady issued Pip an invitation to play.

4. Whoever is Pip's benefactor has hired Mr. Jaggers to act as Pip's guardian when the former apprentice arrives in London.

5. Seeing the neighborhood from Arthur Radley's point-of-view becomes a major learning experience for Scout.

6. Boo Radley, disturbed by what he observes from behind his window, runs into the kitchen and grabs a knife; the only idea on his mind is defending his children from Bob Ewell.

7. Biddy, tears tumbling down her cheeks, watched Pip turn away.

8. Although the jury decides that Tom Robinson is guilty, a few of Maycomb's judicious people understand what has really happened; taking hours to deliberate Tom's fate is a small step forward in a town that has seen no progress since the Civil War ended.

9. His destruction imminent, the protagonist has remained a selfish, haughty, and ultimately ill-fated individual who long ago stopped growing as a human being.

10. The passion with which the lawyer for the defense presented her client's case to the jury distracted her listeners from the subtle thread of irrationality tying her case together.

USING PARALLEL GRAMMATICAL STRUCTURES IN YOUR WRITING

When a writer repeats the same grammatical structure [a part of speech, a phrase, or a clause] within a sentence, those structures are said to be parallel. These grammatical structures are joined by various types of words, such as coordinating conjunctions, correlative conjunctions, and other words that naturally link or compare specific words, phrases, or ideas.

Coordinating conjunctions
and, but, or, for, nor, so, yet

Correlative conjunctions
either...or, neither...nor, not only...but also, not...but, more...than, both...and, whether...or, as...as

Words of comparison
while, than, as well as, also, rather than; from...to; instead of ; less than; with... without; for...against [The word THAN is one example of a supple word choice for making comparisons requiring parallel structures. Whenever you write A is QUICKER THAN B or A is MORE CHALLENGING THAN B etc., you are naturally creating a situation where both A and B must be parallel grammatical structures.]

Linking verbs
is, am, are, was, were,

No matter the joining word or words a writer selects, the first requirement for parallelism to work in a sentence is that THE SAME GRAMMATICAL STRUCTURE BE REPEATED.

Writers can make parallel the same parts of speech (nouns, verbs, adjectives, etc.), the same type of phrase (gerund phrases, infinitive phrases, etc.), and the same type of clauses (noun subordinate clauses, adverb subordinate clauses, etc.). Exercises, pp. 186-187.

A. Words of Comparison and Nouns

Parallel: Michael enjoys all types of activities, from sports to music. [Here the *correlative conjunctions* FROM...TO join two *nouns*.]

Not parallel: Michael enjoys all types of activities, from sports to playing music. [The *gerund* PLAYING MUSIC is not the same structure as the single *noun* SPORTS.]

Parallel: Michael enjoys all types of activities, from playing sports to playing music. [Here two *gerund phrases* are parallel.]

B. Correlative Conjunctions and Adverbs

Parallel: The new president of the student council spoke not only eloquently but also passionately. [Here two *adverbs* are joined by *correlative conjunctions*.]

Not Parallel: The new president of the student council spoke not only eloquently but also with passion. [The single *adverb* ELOQUENTLY cannot be parallel with the *prepositional phrase* WITH PASSION.]

Parallel: The new president of the student council spoke not only with eloquence but also with passion. [Here two *adverb prepositional phrases* are parallel.]

C. Coordinating Conjunctions and Predicates

Parallel: Tiffany read the text message, shared it with her friend, and responded to it. [Here three *predicates*—a PREDICATE being the verb and its complements, such as direct and indirect objects as well as any modifiers—are joined by commas and the *coordinating conjunction* AND.]

Not parallel: Tiffany read the text message, shared it with her friend, and her response was sent. [The parallelism is broken when the writer does not add a third *predicate* but instead adds an *independent clause.*]

Parallel: After Tiffany read the text message and after she shared it with her friend, the two of them cleverly prepared a response, quickly sent it, and patiently waited for a reply. [Here the sentence begins with parallel *adverb subordinate clauses.* Can you identify what other grammatical structures are also parallel in this sentence?]

Each grammatical structure must be in balance with any other grammatical structure with which it is parallel. The completed sentence should reflect a sense of stylistic harmony and wholeness, with all parts of the sentence in rhetorical equilibrium.

D. Linking Verbs and Infinitive Phrases

Parallel: To walk in this rain with neither a raincoat nor an umbrella is to invite a reprimand from your mother and ridicule from your father. [Here *infinitive phrases* are parallel. Note how each infinitive phrase is balanced appropriately on either side of the linking verb IS. Note, as well, the parallelism within the infinitive phrases, in the first, the *correlative conjunction* NEITHER...NOR joins two *nouns*; in the second, a *coordinating conjunction* AND joins two *direct objects of the infinitive* TO INVITE, each *direct object* being modified by an *adjective prepositional phrase.*]

Not parallel and out of balance: To walk in this rain with neither a raincoat nor an umbrella is an invitation for your mother to reprimand you and to invite ridicule from your father. [The writer disrupts the parallelism after the linking verb by introducing a *noun phrase*—AN INVITATION FOR YOUR MOTHER—instead of an *infinitive.*]

Parallel: A walk in the rain with neither a raincoat nor an umbrella is an invitation for your mother to reprimand you and for your father to ridicule you. [Here two *nouns*—WALK and INVITATION—are parallel. Note that what follows each noun contributes to the balance on both sides of the linking verb IS.]

E. Words of Comparison and Gerunds

Parallel: Moving an army by train was, of course, much faster than moving one by foot. [*Gerund phrases* joined by MUCH FASTER THAN are parallel.]

Not parallel and out of balance: Moving an army by train was, of course, much faster than the army's previous custom of walking. [The opening *gerund phrase* MOVING AN ARMY is out of balance with the *noun phrase*, THE ARMY'S PREVIOUS CUSTOM, that follows MUCH FASTER THAN.]

Parallel: The army's movement by train was, of course, much faster than its progress by foot. [Here two *noun phrases*, ARMY'S MOVEMENT and ITS PROGRESS, both modified by *adjective prepositional phrases*, BY TRAIN and BY FOOT, are parallel.]

F. Coordinating Conjunction and Infinitive Phrases

Parallel: Rachel decided to finish her math homework, to read another chapter of a novel, and to look over her notes from this morning's biology class. [Here we have three parallel *infinitive phrases*, each of them functioning as the direct object in the sentence, the final one joined by a *coordinating conjunction*.]

Not parallel and out of balance: Rachel decided to finish her math homework, then reading another chapter of a novel and the notes from this morning's biology class. [The writer creates imbalance by beginning with an *infinitive phrase*, "to finish...," with the infinitive TO FINISH having as a direct object HOMEWORK, then shifts to a *gerund phrase*, "reading...," with the gerund READING having two direct objects, CHAPTER and NOTES.]

Parallel: Rachel finished her math homework, read another chapter from a novel, and looked over her notes from this morning's biology class. [Here three verbs and their *predicates* are parallel.]

G. Correlative Conjunctions and Independent Clauses

Parallel: Either I read Charles Dickens or I read Thomas Hardy. [Two *independent clauses* are parallel.]

Not parallel and out of balance: I read either Charles Dickens or I read Thomas Hardy. [Note that what follows EITHER, a proper *noun*, is not in balance with what follows OR, an *independent clause*.]

Not parallel: Either the reading of Charles Dickens should be required or English educators should make students read Thomas Hardy.

Parallel: Either English educators should require their students to read Charles Dickens or they should make them read Thomas Hardy. [Two *independent clauses* are now parallel. Note that balance of idea is achieved even when the wording in the two parallel structures are not exact.]

H. Coordinating Conjunctions and Clauses

Parallel: Although Patrick fumbled the football four times during the game and although he fumbled three of those times in the red zone, his team still managed to eek out a 7 – 6 victory. [Two *adverb subordinate clauses* are parallel.]

Not parallel and *out of balance*: Patrick fumbled the football four times during the game, and three of those times the ball was lost in the red zone, but his team still managed to eek out a 7 – 6 victory. [This sentence contains three independent clauses, the subjects of each clause having little or no relation to each other. Moreover, the passive voice verb in the second independent clause is not parallel with the active voice verbs in the other clauses.]

Parallel: Patrick, who fumbled the football four times during the game and who lost the ball three times in the red zone but who did manage to carry the ball over the goal line once, was likely the main reason for a tough 7 – 6 victory over what had been considered a pretty weak opponent. [Three *adjective subordinate clauses* are parallel.]

I. Coordinating Conjunction and Clauses

Parallel: That the defense lawyer paid a witness to lie for his client, that the prosecutor created evidence to incriminate the defendant, and that the judge neglected his responsibility to instruct the jury caused a major scandal in the community that cost three people their jobs. [Three *noun subordinate clauses* are parallel.]

Not parallel: It was eventually revealed that the defense lawyer bribed a witness to lie for his client, the evidence that incriminated the defendant had been created by the prosecutor, and the jury's instructions were not completely read to them by the judge, and all of this created a scandal that cost three people their jobs. [The second and third noun subordinate clauses have passive voice verbs while the first has an active voice verb.]

Parallel: The defense lawyer paid a witness to lie for his client, the prosecutor created evidence to incriminate the defendant, the judge neglected his responsibility to instruct the jury, and the resulting uproar led the community to demand that all three be fired. [Four *independent clauses* are parallel.]

J. Semicolon and Infinitive Phrases

Parallel: To play the fool because you are a fool is one matter; to act it when you are not, another indeed. [Two *infinitive phrases* are parallel. (The second independent clause omits the verb IS, the comma implying its existence.]

Not parallel: To cheat on the test because you did not study is one thing; that you deny it after having bragged about it to your friends, quite the other. [Make the grammatical structure after the semicolon—currently a *noun subordinate clause*—parallel to the *noun infinitive phrase* before the semicolon.]

Forming Parallel Grammatical Structures

1. Complete one of the sentences below with a series of adjective subordinate clauses that begin with WHO. Make sure that clauses are in balance.

    He is my best friend, a friend who…

    or

    She is my best friend, a friend who…

2. Finish this sentence with a series of adverb subordinate clauses that begin with IF. Make sure the clauses are in balance.

    The teacher has agreed to reconsider your failing grade if…

3. Compose a sentence that ends with a noun modified by two *absolute phrases*. Make sure the phrases are in balance. (e.g.. He admired the cake, its icing dripping along the sides, its chocolate sprinkles inviting him to partake.)

4. Finish this sentence with a series of *noun infinitive phrases*. Make sure the phrases are in balance.

    The point guard for our basketball team tried to…

    or

    The prosecuting attorney asked the jury to…

    or

    The student in the last row suddenly decided to…

5. Finish this sentence with a series of *noun subordinate clauses* that begin with THAT. Make sure the clauses are in balance.

    When he finally reached the police station, he declared that….

    or

    After everyone had left, she noticed that…

    or

    When they arrived home from the parent-teacher conference, my parents told me that….

6. Compose a sentence that begins with a series of *gerund phrases* followed by ARE MY PRIMARY GOALS FOR THIS YEAR. Make sure the phrases are in balance.

7. Compose a sentence that begins with a series of *noun subordinate clauses* that begin with THAT. Since they begin the sentence, they will be considered the compound subject of the sentence; therefore, you must conclude your sentence with a verb and its predicate. Make sure your noun subordinate clauses are in balance. See **Example I** if you wish a model.

8. Compose a sentence combining two parallel grammatical structures using EITHER/OR or NEITHER/NOR. Models can be found at **Example G**.

9. Compose a sentence modeled on **Example J**, but be sure to use different infinitive phrases.

10. Finish one of these sentences by ending it with a series of *prepositional phrases* that begin with one of the following prepositions: WITH, ABOUT, or TO.

> Within minutes, it was clear to me that his sermon would be about...
>
> or
>
> At last, I left home for good with...
>
> or
>
> Overjoyed by the news, Stacy told it to...

11. Compose a sentence in which a series of *vivid verbs and their predicates* are parallel and balanced.

12. Compose a sentence that contains structures out of balance and provide an explanation for the error.

13. Write a sentence that contains multiple parallel grammatical structures. Underline, italicize, or otherwise highlight each area of the sentence that contains similar structures. In addition, clearly identify the parallel structures.

14. In a speech, you will not only discover parallel grammatical structures within a single sentence but often within entire paragraphs. Orators use parallelism to create a rhythm that makes the speech easier on the ear, a pleasure to hear. Parallelism is, for any writer, a hallmark of style and an invitation to your reader: you will enjoy reading what I have written.

Go to the American Rhetoric website at http://www.americanrhetoric.com. Select one or more of the 100 famous speeches in its archive to read. Identify the speaker, the date of the speech, the audience for it, and its title (if any). Within the first five or so paragraphs of the speech, locate and explain examples of parallelism and cut and paste at least three distinct examples (either isolated sentences or a group of sentences purposefully placed in parallel structure) for your classmates. For each example, explain the elements that are parallel.

6

EDITING SYMBOLS

FIXING THE PARAGRAPH PROBLEMS

This chapter consists of an explanation of the various editing marks, or symbols, teachers may use as they read and evaluate the various drafts of student composition. The symbols are placed here in alphabetical order for ease of use. Students should consult this section if they are unsure how to respond to the teacher's use of a symbol. In addition, teachers may wish to have students use these editing marks during peer editing work. The instructor's editing symbol key is listed as well in the appendix, pp. 263-264.

A = ADD A TRANSITIONAL PHRASE OR SENTENCE

Editing Symbol

A

A1 = After the initial topic sentence, add a transitional sentence that further clarifies and identifies the path the paragraph intends to take, that is, the organization of material: time, place, idea.

A2 = Add a phrase or clause acting as a modifier to the end of the topic sentence to further define and specify a general word that appears in the topic sentence. Then apply this definition to the text.

A3 = Add a transitional phrase or clause, indicating how you plan to organize the evidence, to the beginning of the sentence after the topic sentence.

Original A1, A2

Dickens reveals Scrooge's rudeness and anger. For instance, Scrooge's nephew says, "A Merry Christmas, Uncle! God save you."

Revised

Dickens reveals Scrooge's rudeness and anger towards the people around him, **particularly his nephew and his employee Bob Cratchit. Such an attitude is reflected in his words and actions.** For instance, approached by his nephew who wishes him "A Merry Christmas, Uncle," Scrooge rudely sputters out "Bah! Humbug!"—his temper numbing the seasonal joy.

Original A1

Through examples in gesture and conversation, Dickens depicts Scrooge as selfish, stubborn, and pessimistic. For example, he keeps his door "open so that he might keep an eye upon his clerk" (13; ch. 1).

Revised

Through examples in gesture and conversation, Dickens depicts Scrooge as selfish, stubborn, and pessimistic. **Scrooge displays his selfishness in his treatment of his employee.** For example, he keeps his door "open so that he might keep an eye upon his clerk" (13; ch. 1), a devious eye that enjoys watching his employee freeze next to a dying fire.

Original A1

Besides utilizing bird imagery to depict physical qualities, Shakespeare also employs such imagery to illustrate emotional characteristics of man. For example, Romeo says that "love's light wings" (2.2.67) enable him to conquer the barrier that separates them.

Revised

Besides utilizing bird imagery to depict physical qualities, Shakespeare also employs such imagery to illustrate emotional characteristics of man. **Clearly, one recognizes the depth of Romeo's love when he scales the walls of Juliet's home to testify of his love for her.** Questioned by Juliet as to how he got there, Romeo answers that "love's light wings" (2.2.67) enable him to conquer the barrier that separates them.

Original A1, A2

The Christmas dinner scene at Bob Cratchit's that Scrooge observes depicts the ideal family. Mrs. Cratchit is dressed in "ribbons, which are cheap and make a goodly show for sixpence" (77; ch.1).

Revised

The Christmas dinner scene at Bob Cratchit's that Scrooge observes depicts the ideal family, **a family that celebrates despite ill fortune, that encourages all its members to share in responsibility, that practices acts of selflessness.** For example, despite their poverty, Mrs. Cratchit is dressed in "ribbons, which are cheap and make a goodly show for sixpence" (77; ch.1), for she is able to express joy and celebration within their economic means.

Original A2

Donne uses metaphors to remind us of man's communal nature. He compares the church to one body. He needs the church, "whereof [he is] a member" (10), as a form of support just as the head, "ingrafted into that body" (10), needs the help of the body, the larger group or structure that provides life. He compares man to a book, demonstrating that they are both "of one author" and that man naturally belongs to a community as a book belongs to a "volume."

Revised

Donne uses metaphors to remind us of man's communal nature, **metaphors that reveal man's need to belong to a larger group. First,** the poet compares the church to one body. He needs the church, "whereof [he is] a member" (10), as a form of support, just as the head, "ingrafted into that body" (10), needs the help of the body, the larger group or structure that provides life. **Next,** Donne compares man to a book, demonstrating that they are both "of one author" and that man naturally belongs to a community as a book belongs to a "volume."

> Organized by time and idea; note that, at the end of the topic sentence, the repeat word modifier serves as a transition to the first supporting detail.

Original A1

In chapter one the details and diction prepare us for a "tale of human sorrow and frailty" (38; ch.1). For example, the people gather in front of a prison, "a wooden edifice, the door of which was heavily timbered with oak and studded with iron spikes" (38; ch.1).

Revised

In chapter one the details and diction prepare us for a "tale of human sorrow and frailty" (38; ch.1). **The details direct us to objects that evoke sorrow and depression.** For example, the people gather in front of a prison, "a wooden edifice, the door of which was heavily timbered with oak and studded with iron spikes" (39; ch.1).

> This second sentence provides a transition from the topic sentence to the first supporting detail.

Original A1

Accepting the consequences of one's actions demonstrates courage. In *The Scarlet Letter*, the protagonist Hester Prynne has committed adultery.

Revised

Accepting the consequences of one's actions demonstrates courage. **The hero commits a sin or violation against the community, but instead of resisting punishment, he or she acknowledges the transgression and proceeds with life.** In *The Scarlet Letter*, the protagonist Hester Prynne must face the results of her adultery everyday.

Original A3

The distorted civil life in *1984* serves as a warning against the loss of human compassion. Winston describes the popular nature of hangings, occurring "about once a month," the "popular spectacle [that] children always clamored to be taken to see it."

Revised

The distorted civil life in *1984* serves as a warning against the loss of human compassion. **The reader first sees this cold and uncaring future** when Winston describes the popular nature of hangings, occurring "about once a month," the "popular spectacle [that] children always clamored to be taken to see it."

Original A3

In Bridges' poem, the poet presents a noble depiction of Eros, but over time humans have forgotten this illustration. The speaker lists images of the god of love calling him an "idol of the human race" and a "tyrant of the human heart" (2-3).

Revised

In Bridges' poem, the poet presents a noble depiction of Eros, but over time humans have forgotten this illustration. **In the very first stanza**, the speaker lists powerful images of the god of love, calling him an "idol of the human race" and a "tyrant of the human heart" (2-3).

Original A2. A3

Achilles, however, is a man different from the average person. Achilles nearly comes to blows with the Greek army's leader, Agamemmon.

Revised

Achilles, however, is a distinguished man **exempt from the standards of the average person. Homer makes this clear in the first scene of epic**, in which Achilles nearly comes to blows with the Greek army's leader, Agamemmon.

B = BLENDING TEXTUAL SUPPORT

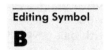

Editing Symbol

B

B1 = Blend text more smoothly with the analysis.
B2 = Blend needs to be grammatically correct.
B3 = Explain the text you are quoting by wrapping the conceptual associations you have made [the explanation] around the text you are directly quoting so that the reader understands how the text proves your point. For more detail about conceptual associations, see Chpt. 1, pp. 20-22: Level Two of the ANALYTICAL VOICE CHART.
B4 = Don't blend too early, without first setting up the aspect of the topic sentence the quotation is supposed to support. It is not clear how this supports the topic sentence or previous statement.
B5 = First explain the context of the quotation.

Three methods for blending

There are three methods for blending direct quotations in paragraphs. Ideally, the writer might use a combination of two or three of the methods.

METHOD ONE

Blend the text as if the words were already a natural part of the sentence.

Original B1, B2, B3

The seasonal atmosphere opens in dialogue between Scrooge quoting, "every idiot who goes about with 'Merry Christmas' on his lips should be boiled with his own pudding" (14; ch. 1), to his nephew.

Revised

Scrooge insolently interrupts the seasonal dialogue **by exclaiming to his nephew that "every idiot who** goes about with 'Merry Christmas' on his lips should be boiled with his own pudding" (14; ch. 1).

Original B1, B3

Another trait that exemplifies his virtue of loyalty is in a passage that states "he had done nobly in war" (11). This shows not only his physical brawn and strength, but also his loyalty and beliefs toward God by going on the crusade.

Revised

Not only has the Knight "done nobly in war" (11), proving his loyalty to both God and country, but also he dispels a myth that all brawny warriors prefer killing to traveling on pilgrimages.

Original B4, B5

Without compassion, Scrooge says, "Those who are badly off must go there." He even says, "They cost enough" (19; ch. 1).

Revised

Without compassion, Scrooge asserts that the poor deserve their plight; **if this means living in prisons, "those who are badly off must go there."** In fact, he even appears to resent these establishments, **lamenting, "They cost enough"** (19; ch. 1).

Original B3, B4, B5

One sees how Scrooge possesses an extreme dislike, almost hatred, for his fellow man. "'Don't be cross, Uncle,' said the nephew. 'What else can I be,' returned the uncle, 'when I live in a world of fools as this?'" (14; ch. 1).

Revised

Scrooge's rude manner, combined with his quick, snide replies, acts as an instant indicator of Scrooge's true personality. For example, his conversation with his nephew demonstrates his disdain for others. Even Scrooge's nephew **scolds him: "Don't be cross, Uncle!"** Scrooge is inexorable, refusing to reflect on his own behavior and **instead blaming others "in a world of fools as this"** (14; ch. 1).

Original B1

The Friar doesn't like to hang out with the peasants. This is shown in the quote, "nothing good can come of commerce with such slum-and-gutter dwellers" (246–47).

Revised

Those with no gifts to give are not worthy of the Friar's eminent service, **for he knows "nothing good can come of commerce** with such slum-and-gutter dwellers" (246–47).

Original B2, B3

"I thought it out for two or three days, and then I reckoned I would see if there was anything in it. I got an old tin lamp and an iron ring and rubbed until I sweat like a injun…" (6; ch. 1) shows us that Huck would believe anything that was told to him at first.

Revised

In the beginning especially, Huck believes what people tell him; he believes, as Tom says, that, **if he "got an old tin lamp** and an iron ring and rubbed" (6; ch.1) it, a genie would appear. Soon, however, Huck realizes, **after he "rubbed until** I sweat like a injun" (6; ch. 1), that Tom may be full of lies.

Original B1

The quotation "So then I judged that all that stuff was only just one of Tom Sawyer's lies. I reckon he believed in the A-rabs and elephants, but as for me, I think different" (6; ch. 1) supports this idea.

Revised

Soon Huck begins to separate his thinking from Tom, perhaps realizing that Tom's world is not the same as his, **judging "that all that stuff was only just one of Tom Sawyer's lies"** (6; ch.1). If they are lies, according to Huck, he knows **he has the option to "think different"** (6; ch.1).

Original B3

Like Eveline, Mrs. Kerner, in the story "Grace," becomes entrapped by an overwhelming responsibility to family life. She is married to a man and the text says "never seems to think he has a home at all" (104). Mrs. Kerner has been married for twenty-five years. "For twenty-five years…[has] kept house shrewdly." This is "irksome" and "unbearable" (105).

Revised

Like Eveline, Mrs. Kerner, in the story "Grace," becomes entrapped by an overwhelming responsibility to family life. Married **to a man who "never seems to think he has a home at all," (104) Mrs. Kerner "for twenty-five years…[has] kept house shrewdly" in her husband's frequent absence,** an onerous burden that leads to an "irksome" and "unbearable" (105) life at home.

Original B3, B4

Stryver tells Carton, "I want to get all the preliminaries done with." He hopes that he should give her "his hand a week or two before Michaelmas Term, or in the little Christmas vacation between it and Hilary" (108; bk. 2, ch. 12). Here he is very cold and calculating.

Revised

Cold and calculating, Stryver treats his marriage to Lucie as a business transaction: he is concerned more about trivial preliminaries and contingency plans than he is about Lucie herself. **His first thought is to propose "to get all the preliminaries done with,"** so they could then **"arrange at their leisure whether he should give her his hand** a week or two before Michaelmas Term, or in the little Christmas vacation between it and Hilary" (108; bk. 2, ch. 12).

Original B3

Banquo tells Macbeth that the witches are "the instruments of darkness." These are entities that deceive us and "oftentimes, to win us to our harm tell us truths."

Revised

Shakespeare depicts Banquo as a **cautious and shrewd observer, a soldier recognizing how the witches function** as "the instruments of darkness," the tools or devices ("instruments") the devil uses to deceive and "oftentimes, to win us to our harm," the word "win" **suggesting that the vulnerable, particularly Macbeth in this context, are prizes for Satan.**

Original B1, B2, B3, B4, B5

The setting is described as "unprosperous and bare." There is no wealth here and it describes very much Mr. Wilson. Even his car is covered in dust, a "dust-covered wreck of a Ford." It is not even placed in a prominent location but "in a dim corner." And Mr. Wilson isn't clean because he is "wiping his hands on a piece of waste." "Spiritless man, anemic, and faintly handsome" these describe a man hapless.

Revised

The **bleak details of Wilson's auto shop**, both "unprosperous and bare," reflect the **hapless condition of its proprietor, a financial prosperity absent and barren**. Even the faint hope of success—"the dust-covered wreck of a Ford"— remains elusive, for it almost cowers from sight, merely "crouched in a dim corner," the **repetition of** "dust" and "dim" **further emphasizing the failed, ruined, and spoiled ambitions of Wilson. In fact, these spoiled aspirations shroud Wilson**, who wipes "his hands on a piece of waste," a gesture that **both underscores the futility of his efforts and functions, through the selection of the word** "waste," metaphorically to illustrate a life of despair. Lastly, Wilson's description as a man "spiritless" and "anemic," whose looks are now merely "faintly" apparent, **connote the mortality and frailty of his hopes, hopes barely "visible" to Nick when he enters the garage.**

Original B3

At the beginning of the battle, Grendel's mother immediately recognizes "a human observing her outlandish lair," so she brutally "lunge[s] and clutch[es] him" (1499-1501). Beowulf knows "that for all his courage he could never use the weapons he carried" (1508-1509). Only having seconds to adjust, he quickly "heaved his war-sword and swung his arm," but his new plan is also unsuccessful because "the shining blade refused to bite" (1520-1524).

Revised

At the beginning of the battle, **Beowulf must quickly adapt to Grendel's** mother, who immediately recognizes "a human observing her outlandish lair," and hence brutally "lunge[s] and clutch[es] him" (1499-1501). Beowulf, **with little time to think shrewdly, quickly analyzes his limitations, and despite** recognizing "that for all his courage he could never use the weapons he carried" (1508-1509), he nonetheless recognizes he must respond, anticipating that "the shining blade refused to bite" (1520-1524), **yet a second challenge to his warrior instincts.**

Original B3

The spider is like the soul. It, too, is "ceaselessly musing, venturing, throwing, seeking the spheres to connect them."

Revised

The image of the **spider's perseverance is juxtaposed with the soul, who likewise requires an outward movement to sustain its life,** "ceaselessly musing, venturing, throwing, seeking the spheres to connect them."

Original B4, B5

Scrooge refuses to help the poor with "some meat and drink, and means of warmth."

Revised

Scrooge's lack of **compassion contrasts with those of his altruistic guests,** men seeking to assist the poor with "some meat and drink, and means of warmth."

METHOD TWO

Use a colon. The sentence that precedes the colon explains the writer's point; what follows is his evidence.

Example

By excluding himself from humanity and working with incredible devotion, Frankenstein discovers how to generate life: "I pursued knowledge to her hiding places... [and] I became myself capable of bestowing animation upon lifeless matter" (50; ch.4).

Example

This violation of nature is also evident in the monster's horrible inhuman countenance: "His watery eyes seemed almost of the same colour as the dun-white sockets in which they were set.... Oh! no mortal could support the horror of that countenance" (56; ch.5).

METHOD THREE

Identify the speaker of the dialogue before the quotation.

Example

The king sadly emits, "He was my closest counselor, he was keeper of my thoughts.... Men of birth and merit all should be as Ashhere was!" (1062).

C = COMBINE SENTENCES

Editing Symbol

C

Combining sentences helps eliminate wordiness, helps extend the elaboration of a single idea, and helps remove unnecessary breaks in thought. Use present and past participial phrases, infinitive phrases, gerund phrases, absolute phrases, appositive phrases, subordinate clauses, repeat word/ analysis modifiers, parallel grammatical structures, solo semicolons, and conjunctive adverbs to make combinations.

Original C

A virtuous man exhibits high moral standards, leads an ethical life ~~and does not lose sight of life by becoming engulfed in his material possessions. In order to have high moral standards, one must~~ be truthful, possess honor, be generous ~~to those around him~~, and be courteous to all people. (50 words)

Revised

A virtuous man exhibits high moral standards, leading an ethical life that does not lose sight of Christian values. These values demand truth, generosity, and courtesy towards all people. (29 words)

Original C

Two knobby, sand-caked digits point down toward the rust-colored clay, signaling the breaking ball. ~~Background to the sign are~~ his blue pinstripe baseball ~~pants I often focus on so intensely that I can define the middle seam of his long~~, dusty knickers. (44 words)

Revised

Two knobby, sand-caked digits, set against dusty blue pinstripe knickers, point down toward the rust-colored clay, signaling the breaking ball. (22 words)

Original C

Driven with concentration, he pictures ~~himself reacting the fastest and diving out the farthest in the start of the race. He sees himself~~ enter the water in a tight streamline position to begin his underwater kick ~~which boosts~~ him ahead of the other swimmers. ~~Then he sees himself come up out of the water and take a powerful first stroke~~. (60 words)

Revised

Driven with concentration, he pictures himself departing the starting block seconds before his opponents, entering the water in a tight streamline position, already set to begin his underwater kick, catapulting himself ahead of the other swimmers, and emerging to start his first stroke. (43 words)

Original C

He lifts his right leg to the first step. ~~He~~ proceeds with his left leg to the top of the block. ~~Then~~ his right leg rises to the top of the block. (32 words)

Revised

He lifts his right leg to the first step and proceeds with his left to the top of the block, his right soon following. (24 words)

Original C

He turns his head back to stare at the sweatshirt ~~on the swimmer he is following. The sweatshirt's colors, reminding him of the other schools which are competing~~, radiate green, red, and blue into his face. (36 words)

Revised

He turns his head back to stare at the adversary's sweatshirt two feet in front of him, its green, red, and blue colors glaring into his face. (27 words)

Original C

The nation is out of control. Its morals ~~are~~ thrown around in the storm of lost ethics. ~~The~~ society ~~has been~~ overridden by their own lack of virtue and the malevolence has developed into a catastrophic event.

Revised

The nation out of control, its morals thrown around in the storm of lost ethics, a society overridden by its own lack of virtue, this young country finds itself beset by a malevolence that has led to catastrophe.

Original C

This vicious storm of dishonor has "waves of swift dissension" swarming, illustrating the rapidly declining moral state of the culture. ~~The particular~~ image of a wave ~~illustrates~~ the inevitab~~ility of the~~ damage caused by this declination of values.

Revised

This vicious storm of dishonor has "waves of swift dissension" swarming, illustrating the rapidly declining morality of the culture, the image of a wave illustrating the inevitable damage caused by this declining values.

E = EXTEND YOUR ELABORATION OF IDEAS

Editing Symbol

E

E1 = The writer needs to elaborate and incorporate additional textual support.

E2 = The writer is missing some important textual examples.

E3 = The writer should extend the elaboration of details, commenting further on this point before moving to the next item.

E4 = The elaboration is vague, shallow, or merely restates the quotation.

Extending the elaboration of ideas is a challenging skill; it requires the writer to reflect on and to identify the *conceptual associations connected to the diction, images, and details cited as evidence* (Level Two of the ANALYTICAL VOICE Chart). The writer can also discuss *whether the evidence cited is a significant REPETITION, a noteworthy CONTRAST, a pivotal SHIFT, or a revealing JUXTAPOSITION* that generates a central idea (Level Three of the ANALYTICAL VOICE Chart). This level of analysis moves beyond plot summary and is one of the defining marks of a sophisticated writer.

Original E3

The second stanza establishes the analogue between spider and soul by repeating images of a tension between alienation—"detached in measureless oceans of space"—and connection—"till the bridge you will need be formed." This is a spider who is "ceaselessly musing, venturing, throwing, seeking the spheres to connect them."

Revised

The second stanza establishes the analogue between spider and soul by repeating images of a tension between alienation—"detached in measureless oceans of space"—and connection—"till the bridge you will need be formed." **Moreover, the repetition of "ceaselessly," "tirelessly," "need," and "patient"** suggests that the gesture to move out of the self is innate, a natural occurrence that is not a burden but a requirement for nourishment.

Original E3

Banquo not only intuitively recognizes the witches as evil, but also articulates their strategy, namely, to "tell us truths"—statements of "honest" fact, though mere "trifles," or insignificant comments.

Revised

Banquo not only intuitively recognizes the witches as evil, but also articulates their strategy, namely, to "tell us truths"—statements of "honest" fact, though mere "trifles," or insignificant comments. **Both "truths" and "honest" deceptively lure the individual into a feigned trust, ultimately allowing these ambassadors of darkness to "betray's / In deepest consequence," the modifier "deepest" poignantly reminding that, in contrast, the consequences won't be mere "trifles" but grave outcomes.**

Original E3

Scrooge refuses to respond to the men soliciting for the poor. He is perfectly content with letting the prisons take care of the poor, and he quickly tells them to leave. "'It's enough for a man to understand his own business, and not to interfere with other people's. Mine occupies me constantly. Good afternoon, gentlemen!'"

Revised

Scrooge's lack of **compassion contrasts with those of his guests, men seeking to assist the poor with** "some meat and drink, and means of warmth." Scrooge, however, asserts that the poor deserve their plight; if this means living in prisons, "those who are badly off must go there," **a statement abdicating any level of social responsibility. Moreover, his final statement, seeking to be left alone with "his own business," where "Mine occupies me constantly," reinforces an abject selfishness, his repetition of "own," "mine," and "me" indicating his interest in withdrawing from society rather than joining it.**

Original E3

Consequently, Macbeth's noble image is blemished, and he intensifies the doubt about his character's true nature by showing an uncommon attachment and fondness for war when Ross refers to him as "Bellona's bridegroom"(1.2.56).

Revised

Consequently, Macbeth's noble image is blemished, and he intensifies the doubt about his character's true nature by showing an uncommon attachment and fondness for war when Ross refers to him as "Bellona's bridegroom"(1.2.56). **By calling him the husband of the Roman goddess of war, Ross communicates Macbeth's true passion for war, an intimacy similar to a husband's love for his wife, an unusual and hyperbolic image that undercuts Macbeth's revered nobility, the comparison suggesting an abnormality in his character.**

Original E3

On Juliet's balcony, Romeo says that "love's light wings" (2.2.67) enable him to conquer the barrier that separates them.

Revised

Clearly, one recognizes the depth of Romeo's love when he scales the walls of Juliet's home to testify of his love for her. **Questioned by Juliet as to how he got there**, Romeo answers that "love's light wings" (2.2.67) enable him to conquer the barrier that separates them. **This image of a bird's flight reinforces the idea that Romeo's love is invincible and unfettered, a love soaring beyond all limitations.**

Past participial phrase.

Original E4

In response to his nephew's felicitous greeting, Scrooge retorts, "What reason have you to be merry? You're poor enough" (13; ch. 1), a statement that shows how Scrooge points out that his nephew is poor.

Revised

In response to his nephew's felicitous greeting, Scrooge retorts, "What reason have you to be merry? You're poor enough" (13; ch. 1), **a response showing how Scrooge thinks happiness can be measured by monetary wealth.** Ironically, Scrooge demonstrates the opposite because he is wealthy and not happy.

Absolute phrase.

Original E4

To his nephew, he exclaims of Christmas, "much good it may do to you! Much good it has ever done you!" (14; ch. 1). His view of Christmas remains warped, and he refuses to acknowledge the spirit of the season.

Revised

To his nephew, he exclaims of Christmas, "much good it may do to you! Much good it has ever done you!" (14; ch. 1). Once again, Scrooge sees the season as devoid of tangible value, **a view of the world that is base and political**. Moreover, his cynicism thwarts a relationship with his nephew.

Analysis modifier.

Original E3, E4

Again, this self-centered side of his character becomes extremely obvious when he concludes, "I wish to be left alone" (19; ch. 1), and ushers them out with another "Good afternoon, Gentlemen." Scrooge acts with no concern for others and does so in a manner that ruins other people's good cheer, making himself look glum.

Revised

Again, this self-centered side of his character becomes extremely obvious when he insists, "I wish to be left alone" (19; ch. 1), and ushers them out with another "Good afternoon, Gentlemen." **These statements emphasize Scrooge's desire to isolate himself from society, not simply physically, but emotionally and socially, refusing to recognize any communal responsibility for those less fortunate.**

Original E3

In a fit of anger and grief, Juliet declares that Romeo is "a dove-feathered raven" (3.2.74). Certainly, Shakespeare masterfully applies bird imagery to demonstrate the emotional complexities of man.

Revised

In a fit of anger and grief, Juliet declares that Romeo is "a dove-feathered raven" (3.2.74). **This image reflects Juliet's feelings of betrayal by Romeo, a man who on the outside seems honorable but on the inside is despicable; however, Juliet's unending love calms her tumultuous emotions, and she forgives the sin of Romeo. Without a doubt, human emotions of the sixteenth century were as volatile and unpredictable as they are today.** Certainly, Shakespeare masterfully applies bird imagery to demonstrate the emotional complexities of man.

Original E2

"I shall help you" (68), Wyglaf yells as he goes to help defend Beowulf's life in the battle of the dragon. He fights "alongside the king, the brave soldier" (68).

Revised

Wyglaf rushes to defend Beowulf's life in the battle against the dragon as he shouts, "I shall help you" (68). **Risking his own life, Wyglaf "fights along-side the king" (68), and through their combined effort, "they had downed their foe by common action, the atheling pair." Only with the aid of Wyglaf is Beowulf able to achieve "the last victory in the list of his deeds and works in the world" (69).**

Original E1, E3

For example, "she had little dogs" she would be feeding with roasted flesh, or milk, or fine white bread. Furthermore, she has a cloak with a "graceful charm" and "[wears] a coral trinket on her arm, / a set of beads, the gaudies tucked in green," and a "golden broach of brightest sheen" (153–155).

Revised

For example, she **has** little dogs **she feeds** with roasted flesh, or milk, or fine white bread, **an abhorrent ownership that shows her lack of consideration for the starving people of this epoch.** Furthermore, **for one who should be living a simple life as a nun,** she has a cloak with a "graceful charm," and "[wears] a coral trinket on her arm, / a set of beads, the gaudies tucked in green," and a "golden broach of brightest sheen" (153–155).

Original E2, E3

Another vice Chaucer illustrates is greed. Chaucer begins his description of the doctor as a man who "had a special love of gold" (426). Rather than serve the individual, the doctor has forgotten his oath and pursues his work with an ardent desire for material wealth. He takes advantage of those in need of his services and works with the apothecary.

Revised

Another vice Chaucer illustrates is greed. Chaucer begins his description of the doctor as a man who "had a special love of gold" (426). Rather than serve the individual, the doctor has forgotten his oath and pursues his work with an ardent desire for material wealth. **Knowing "no one alive could talk as well as he did / on points of medicine and of surgery" (400–401),** he takes advantage of those in need of his services. Manipulating his position, **he "made money from other's** [apothecaries with whom he dealt] **guile," never forgetting that "gold stimulates the heart"** (415–416).

Original E2, E3

Even when her husband does come home, he returns drunk after spending the "money in his pocket" (104) at the local tavern, irresponsible behavior that creates many problems for Mrs. Kerner. She has to take care of her kids alone and she has to take care of her husband when he's sick. He's little help to her.

Revised

Even when her husband does come home, he returns drunk after spending the "money in his pocket" (104) at the local tavern, irresponsible behavior **that presents Mrs. Kerner with two problems. First, she alone must deal with the pressures of mature life, pressures caused by the adult responsibility of making sure that the human necessities of nutrition and shelter are fulfilled, both of which are provided by finances. Because her husband spends some of the family income on alcohol, Mrs. Kerner obviously must worry that her family may not receive what they need and, therefore, must work harder in order to ensure that this does not occur. Second, she must heal her husband "dutifully whenever he [is] sick" (105) while simultaneously watching over "two girls and a boy" (104) and, previously, "her two eldest sons" (105), a handful of children that obviously presents her with the arduous task of raising them also. Furthermore, because she does not receive any help from her husband, Mrs. Kerner must raise the children as both their mother and father, a strong indication that all her time and efforts are restricted to her family.**

IP= IMPROVING INTRODUCTORY PARAGRAPHS

Editing Symbol

IP

IP1 = The analogy for the introduction is not effective; too many aspects of the situation re-created are not applicable to the paper's thesis.

IP2 = Not all of the showing details in the introduction are necessary; remove those that are not associated with the concepts in the thesis.

IP3 = The writer needs to interpret and comment on the details employed in the introduction, highlighting specifically those associations truly similar to the thesis. See pp 110-112.

Original IP2, IP3

A scout for the Red Army peers through his binoculars for any suspicious activity. What he sees makes his heart start pumping fast. Ferocious German Panzers, ready for an attack, line up along the snow-capped plains outside of Kharkov, Russia. The scout reports back to his division commander, Vasily, calmly sipping his hot coffee in an abandoned building. The commander cursing wildly, he throws down his cup and orders his troops to take up their positions. Vasily instructs his soldiers that they will not surrender, regardless of what might happen. Killing thousands of Soviets, the Germans heavily pummel Kharkov with artillery hours later. Furious and flustered, Vasily tries to think of a plan to save his division. He does not want to retreat from the city, but he has no other choice; if he refuses to give up, the Germans will annihilate his force. Changing his original plan, Vasily decides to withdraw his division from the city and allow the Germans to move in. Leaders often have to alter their decisions because of changing circumstances in order to avoid defeat.

Revised

A scout for the Red Army peers through his binoculars for any suspicious activity. What he sees makes his heart start pumping fast: ferocious German Panzers, ready for an attack, line up along the snow-capped plains outside of Kharkov, Russia. The scout reports back to his division commander, Vasily, **who immediately decides to order his troops to take up their positions, insisting they would never surrender, regardless of the danger. Unfortunately, the German Panzers pummeled the Soviets**, killing thousands of Red soldiers. Furious and flustered, Vasily searches for a plan to save his division, **refusing to retreat from the city, but soon acknowledging that the Germans will likely annihilate his force. To avoid complete destruction, Vasily alters his initial decision and now orders a withdrawal, saving his men. Vasily illustrates the flexibility necessary for successful leadership.** The most effective leaders often have to alter their decisions when circumstances change in order to avoid defeat.

Original IP1

Cheers erupt from the crowd. The muscular yet underfed lion roars victoriously, the sweat dripping from its fangs, white as pearls. The lean gladiator coughs blood, falling to his knees, the briefness of his life flashing before his eyes. The audience begins to rise, anticipating the action. A quick lunge, a spray of blood, and quickly the lion is already devouring its newly-found prey. The crowd instantaneously sits back down, yet no feeling of

> The analogy being made in the Original focuses on the reaction of the crowd, the writer then trying to connect the crowd's desensitized connection to violence with that of Perry Smith's. Most of the showing details involved are superfluous to the writer's actual purpose. In the Revision below, the writer's focus turns to the gladiator, the singular figure then being compared to the singular figure of Perry Smith. The commentary regarding the gladiator and violence leads into the writer's purpose regarding Perry Smith and the adverse effects of a violent upbringing.

remorse or sympathy can be found anywhere in the Coliseum; in fact, excitement engulfs the arena. The crowd never hears of peaceful times; they only hear of foreign wars and gladiator battles. The lack of similarities between the crowd and the gladiators cuts these two groups apart, and the audience shows no compassion to the sub-society of gladiators who suffer from this social fissure. Similarly, the process of the minimization of the feelings of guilt and sorrow can also be applied to Perry Smith in Truman Capote's novel, *In Cold Blood*. Similar to the crowd, Perry experiences a life plagued with violence, and, as a result, feels no remorse for the pain he causes. Because of Perry's hateful and violent upbringing, he uses these as channels to solve conflicts.

Revised

An olive-skinned muscular man, wearing a deep purple toga shouts into the air, his voice indiscernible from the thousands of other spectators, each cheering for a single gladiator, the crowd's excitement crackling through the arena. His eyes, fixed upon a starved, aggressive lion devouring a still living gladiator, **express neither remorse nor sympathy for his fellow human; he's a gladiator, trained to be disconnected from the violence, influenced by a culture of violence that has taught him that not all human life has intrinsic value and that some human life can be used for sport. Individuals from all cultures are susceptible to forming distorted beliefs about violence against their fellow man.** Similarly, the life of Perry Smith, in Truman Capote's *In Cold Blood*, manifests how a violent upbringing can produce a moral confusion allowing for aggression without concern for human dignity. Because of Perry's hateful and vicious upbringing, he develops a twisted morality that accepts violence as an appropriate method for conflict resolution.

Original IP3

"You think my daughter should what?!" screams the red-faced mother. Opposite her, the teacher, who is holding parent-teacher conferences, replies calmly, "I think your daughter should drop down to regular geometry. I say this because she has not passed any of her tests, does not complete her homework, and never participates in class." Fists clenched, the mother shrieks "absolutely not! You're just a rotten teacher who wants my Melanie to fail! You're no good at all!" Taking a deep, calming breath, the teacher replies, "Mrs. Vera, I think that your daughter would do better in a class with a slower pace and more hands-on instruction. In fact, I think that with the knowledge she has already gained while in honors geometry, she will do very well in regulars." This trend occurs in *Twelve Angry Men* when debating the validity of the old man's testimony, the eighth juror's logical arguments defeat the third juror's flawed emotional appeals.

Revised IP3

"You think my daughter should what?!" screams the red-faced mother. Opposite her, the teacher replies calmly, "I think your daughter should drop to regular geometry. I say this because she has not passed any of her tests, does not complete her homework, and never participates in class." Fists clenched, the mother shrieks ,"Absolutely not! You're just a rotten teacher who wants my Melanie to fail! You're no good at all!" Taking a deep, calming breath, the teacher replies, "Mrs. Vera, I think that your daughter would do better in a class with a slower pace and more hands-on instruction. In fact, I think that with the knowledge she has already gained while in honors geometry, she will do very well in regulars." **The logic that her daughter would succeed in a different class finally dawning on her, Mrs. Vera nods her head, slowly at first, then with increasing intensity, "Yes, you're right." In this situation, dispassionate, logical arguments prevail over fiery, emotional outbursts.** This rhetorical strategy occurs as well in *Twelve Angry Men* as two jurors debate the validity of the old man's testimony, the eighth juror's logical arguments overcoming the third juror's flawed emotional appeals.

L = LISTING PLOT DETAILS

Editing Symbol

L

The student is merely listing details without elaborating or explaining why these details or quotations provide support for the topic sentence. The writer, in this case, is forgetting about the reader, who has not viewed the evidence in the same manner or with the same degree of reflection as the writer.

Original L

"What right have you to be dismal? What reason do you have to be morose? You're rich enough" (14; ch. 1), says the nephew. Scrooge replies with a remark saying, "Humbug." Scrooge even refuses to help the needy. "At this festive time of the year, Mr. Scrooge, it is more than desirable that we should make some slight provision for the poor and destitute, who suffer greatly at the present time" (17; ch. 1). Mr. Scrooge blatantly and bluntly says no and shows them out.

Revised

Scrooge attempts to lower the spirits of his nephew by asking, "What right have you to be merry? You're poor enough" (14; ch. 1). His attempts to deride his nephew fail, for the nephew quickly retorts, "What reason do you have to be morose? You're rich enough" (14; ch. 1), **an attempt to make Scrooge confront his own logic. Unfortunately,** Scrooge's "Humbug" reply **not only demonstrates his unwillingness to engage in a logical debate but also demonstrates another example of his desire to isolate himself. In a similar manner, Scrooge seeks to separate himself from the social obligation to donate to those less fortunate. For example,** two men approach Scrooge requesting "some slight provision for the poor and destitute" (19; ch.1).

Original L

Besides utilizing bird imagery to depict physical qualities, Shakespeare also employs such imagery to illustrate emotional characteristics of man. Climbing up to Juliet's balcony, Romeo answers that "love's light wings" (2.2.67) enable him to conquer the barrier that separates them. Along with the stirring picture of Romeo's desire, one observes the passion of Juliet in the balcony as she compares herself to a spoiled child who refuses to release a bird. She says, "I would have thee gone—/And yet no farther than a wanton's bird,/That lets it hop a little from his hand" (2.1.221–223) and then plucking it back again. Again, in her room, Juliet's mercurial emotions are vividly demonstrated with bird imagery; we feel Juliet's turmoil as she discovers that Romeo has killed her cousin Tybalt. In a fit of anger and grief, Juliet declares that Romeo is "a dove-feathered raven" (3.2.74).

Revised

Besides utilizing bird imagery to depict physical qualities, Shakespeare also employs such imagery to illustrate emotional characteristics of man. **Clearly, one recognizes the depth of Romeo's love when he scales the walls of Juliet's home to testify of his love for her. Questioned by Juliet as to how he got there, Romeo answers that "love's light wings" (2.2.67) enable him to conquer the barrier that separates them. This image of a bird's flight reinforces the idea that Romeo's love is invincible and unfettered, a love soaring beyond all limitations.** Along with the stirring picture of Romeo's desire, one observes the passion of Juliet in the balcony as she compares herself to a spoiled child who refuses to release a bird. **The image shows a small bird in captivity, while a young child holds tightly to the beloved** possession, letting "it hop a little from his hand," (2.2.179) and then plucking it back again. **Likewise, Juliet protests the release of Romeo but later relents and frees him because she realizes that her grasp will kill him if he stays.** Again, in her room, Juliet's mercurial emotions are vividly demonstrated with bird imagery; we feel Juliet's turmoil as she discovers that Romeo has killed her cousin Tybalt. In a fit of anger and grief, Juliet declares that Romeo is "a dove-feathered raven" (3.2.74). **This image reflects Juliet's feelings of betrayal by Romeo, a man who on the outside seems honorable but on the inside is despicable; however, Juliet's unending love calms her tumultuous emotions, and she forgives the sin of Romeo. Without a doubt, human emotions of the sixteenth century were as volatile and unpredictable as they are today. Certainly. Shakespeare masterfully applies bird imagery to demonstrate the emotional complexities of man.**

Original L

The narrator in "To His Coy Mistress" demonstrates a keen knowledge of persuasion. He uses this knowledge to convince his mistress to consummate their relationship. To achieve this goal, he uses many methods: speaking about her beauty, mentioning that he may die soon, and saying that they must seize the day. First, he mentions her appearance: "Thine eyes, and on thy forehead gaze / Two hundred to adore each breast" (12–13). Moreover, if there were enough time, he says, he would spend "an age, at least, to every part" (16), for she "deserve[s] this state" (17). Unfortunately, he does not have time for such adoration, nor does she, for "at my back, I always hear / Time's winged chariot hurrying near" (19–20). With death's imminent arrival comes additional fears: If she dies tomorrow, "Thy beauty shall no more be found" (23). She will be found alone, he tells her, without his love, without his "echoing song"—alone in that "private place / But none, I think, do there embrace" (29–30). Once finished with these potential scenarios, he beseeches her to seize the day, carpe diem: "while the youthful hue / sits on thy skin like morning glow… / Now let us sport us while we may" (31–33). He hopes that after this begging, they will "roll all our strength, and all / our sweetness, up into one ball" (34–35).

> The student is merely summarizing and listing the details of the poem, not explaining what's persuasive about them.

Revised

The narrator in "To His Coy Mistress" demonstrates a keen knowledge of persuasion, a carefully plotted strategy of seduction: first, secure trust; second, create discomfort; and third, provide relief. **He begins with flattery, necessary to gain trust and to prove his devotion, not simply to her physical appearance**—"Thine eyes, and on thy forehead gaze / Two hundred to adore each breast" (12–13)—**but to her spiritual appearance as well**—"And the last age should show your heart / For, Lady, you deserve this state" (16–17). **Here the narrator highlights a love that transcends the mere physical and reaches the spiritual. Once she trusts these intentions, the narrator begins to**

> Notice the change. The writer explains the persuasive technique of flattery; what follows is text to support this claim. After going further to point out two types of flattery—physical and spiritual—the writer continues beyond summary to provide his analysis of the details.

create discomfort: "But, at my back, I always hear / time's winged chariot hurrying near / And yonder, all before us lie/deserts of vast eternity" (19–22). **He goes beyond this imminence of death to list specific possibilities, scenarios especially disconcerting to a woman: first,** "thy beauty shall no more be found" (23); **second, she'll die a virgin and be subject to the** "worms [that] shall try that long preserved virginity" (26); third, she'll be alone, for "the grave's a fine and private place, / But none, I think, do there embrace" (29–30). **The narrator quickly leaves these ghastly images, and he introduces relief, a solution much more pleasant, one that will eliminate this fear of potential waste of beauty and purity. His mistress only needs to act now** "While the youthful hue/sits on thy skin like morning glow" (31–32). **If she acts now, the two of them can enjoy their youth,** "like amorous birds of prey,/rather at once our time devour, / than languish in his slow-chapped power" (36–38). **Now with his plot complete, the narrator is ready to** "tear our pleasures, with rough strife, / through the iron gates of life" (41–42).

Original

He rests himself on a Disney World t-shirt and stares into Mickey Mouse's eyes. He sees a yellow Penn 6 tennis ball peeking around the side of the Snoopy wastepaper basket. Next to the basket sits a half-eaten slice of pepperoni pizza with ten ants running along the burnt crust.

Revised

He rests himself on a Disney World t-shirt and stares into Mickey Mouse's eyes. Intimidated **by Mickey's grin, Bernie begins to swipe him with his black furry paw. After ten swipes, Bernie, realizing Mickey** poses no further threat, yawns, rests his left cheek on his two front legs, closes his eyes, and falls asleep.

Original

Peering into the tight, dark closet, my nose, prying for clues, searches the room as it vacuums the air. My left hand reaches out and touches a suede suit. Next, I touch a cold aluminum baseball bat, the rubber part frayed.

Revised

Peering into the tight, dark closet, my nose, prying for clues, searches the room. **As it vacuums the air, sniffing left and right, a pungent odor reaches its attention. Cringing itself upwards, the nose attempts** to hide from this smell as I retreat quickly because of my sudden antipathy for this place.

Original

Finding evidence of gluttony one could point out, "He was a fat and personable priest," and "He liked a fat swan best, and roasted whole" (200–202).

Revised

At a time when food was scarce for many medieval people, Chaucer portrays a "fat and personable priest…[who] liked a fat swan best and roasted whole" (200–202), a religious who clearly demonstrates gluttony as a mortal sin.

O = OFF-TOPIC

Editing Symbol
●

O1 = This evidence doesn't support the topic sentence.
O2 = Not completely off-topic, but the writer is either slipping into plot summary or failing to explain adequately how the evidence supports the topic sentence.

Original O1

In the opening dialogue of *A Christmas Carol*, Dickens creates Scrooge's shallow personality through the repetition of diction associated with money. Almost every comment Scrooge makes includes economic diction. For example, Scrooge's nephew first arrives and says, "A Merry Christmas, Uncle" (13; ch.1). The narrator describes his nephew as "all in a glow; his face was ruddy and handsome; his eyes sparkled" (13; ch.1).

Revised

In the opening dialogue of *A Christmas Carol*, Dickens creates Scrooge's shallow personality through the repetition of diction associated with money. Almost every comment Scrooge makes includes economic diction. For example, when Scrooge's nephew first arrives to greet him a "Merry Christmas," **he disdainfully comments about his nephew's monetary status. "You're poor enough" (13; ch.1), he retorts, a statement that shows how Scrooge evaluates individuals by their monetary value.**

Original O2

[TOPIC SENTENCE of the paragraph: In the opening dialogue of *A Christmas Carol*, Dickens creates Scrooge's shallow personality through the repetition of diction associated with money.]

Finally, Scrooge says to his clerk that he will "want all day tomorrow, I suppose?" (21; ch.1). He then says, "If I was to stop half-a-crown for it, you'd think yourself ill used…and yet you don't think me ill-used, when I pay a day's wages for no work" (21; ch.1).

Revised

Finally, Scrooge's conversation with Bob Cratchit, his clerk, **revolves around money. Scrooge moans that Bob will** "want all day tomorrow, I suppose?" (21; ch.1). **He continues to explain how Christmas has created an economic problem for him:** "If I was to stop half-a-crown for it, you'd think yourself ill used…and yet you don't think me ill-used, when I pay a day's wages for no work" (21; ch.1). **Here Scrooge demonstrates that he cannot even perceive Cratchit as a human being but as an economic possession, swindling him unfairly.**

Original O2

In "Sonnet 29," William Shakespeare uses many images that illustrate love is the power that helps man move out of his despondency. The character says, "outcast state" (2). Next, he says he wants to be like "one more rich in hope / featured like him with friends possessed" (5–6). He has antipathy for his life because he isn't as fortunate as others. Then "haply I think on thee, and then my state / like to the lark at break of day arising from sullen earth"(10–11). He finally says, "That then I scorn to change

> Writer must explain how these details support the topic sentence.

my state with kings"(14).

Revised

In his "Sonnet 29," William Shakespeare uses many images that illustrate love is the power that helps man move out of his despondency. **Feeling melancholy, the character disdains his "outcast state" (2), a state he curses because he cannot** be like "one more rich in hope / featured like him with friends possessed" (5–6). He has antipathy for his life because he isn't as fortunate as others. **However, his despondency—his "self almost despising" (9)—is ephemeral, for another person's "sweet love" (13) brings him from despair into a new day, a day in which he sees the value of his life and knows the power of love. He now is like "the lark at break of day arising / from sullen earth" (11–12), a man who can arise and sing with contentment despite any troubles. Furthermore, he realizes that love is more valuable than changing his "state with kings" (14).**

Original O1

Though the Victorian Age is filled with potential, many poets recognized that all is not well with society, for society may appear, as the sea, "calm tonight" (1), but if one "listen[s] you hear the grating roar" (9). The roar comes from a people with confused values and unmet spiritual needs, a people who lost "the sea of Faith," faith in a God, faith in human relationship. In Browning's "My Last Duchess," the Duke calls the portrait of his wife a "piece of wonder" (3). In addition, Arnold's narrator says, "ah, love, let us be true" (29). Arnold recognizes that it is only this love that will battle against the "ignorant armies [that] clash by night" (37). By contrast, Housman says, "smart lad, to slip betimes away" (9), the lad who still has his "defended challenge cup" (24). It is this culture that says "I shot him dead because— / because he was my foe" (9–10), a culture that does not value the potential for human love, but a culture that values a push to "strive, to seek, to find, and not to yield" (70).

> Confusing details. Not clear how they are on topic.

Revised

Though the Victorian Age is filled with potential, many poets recognized that all is not well with society, for society may appear, as the sea, "calm tonight" (1), but if one "listen[s] you hear the grating roar" (9). The roar comes from a people with confused values and unmet spiritual needs, a people who lost "the sea of Faith," faith in a God, faith in human relationship. **Their faith, rather, is in material— superficial—accomplishments; art, for example, is a "piece of wonder" (3), says the Duke in Browning's "My Last Duchess."** The genuine wonder, **however, is man and his power to form relationships: "Ah, love, let us be true" (29). Here, in Arnold's "Dover Beach," the narrator recognizes that it is only this love that will battle against the "ignorant armies [that] clash by night" (37). Rather, this culture cares more, as Housman says, about the "smart lad, to slip betimes away" (9), the lad who still has his "defended challenge cup"** (24). It is this culture that says "I shot him dead because— / because he was my foe" (9–10), a culture that does not value the potential for human love, but a culture, as Tennyson says, that values a push to "strive, to seek, to find, and not to yield" (70).

Original O2

In chapter one, the details and diction prepare us for a "tale of human sorrow and frailty" (38; ch. 1). The details direct us to objects that evoke sorrow and depression. For example, the people gather in front of a prison, "a wooden edifice, the door of which was heavily timbered with oak and studded with iron spikes" (38; ch. 1). Revealing an aspect of humanity that often brings suffering to the community, this "prison house somewhere in the vicinity of Cornhill" (38; ch. 1) reminds us of the consequence of our sinful nature. Moreover, there is a "grass plot, much overgrown with burdock, pigweed, apple peru, and such unsightly vegetation" (38; ch. 1). Near this prison rests "a portion of the virgin soil...a cemetery" (38; ch. 1). In addition to these gloomy details, the diction adds to the despondency of the setting, providing words that remove life and energy from this environment. For example, the "gray, steeple-crowned hats," the prison "with weather stains [and its] beetle-browed and gloomy front," and "the black flower of civilized society" (38; ch. 1) Along with the absence of color, visually suggesting sorrow, there are the objects of touch, such as the door "heavily timbered with oak and...iron spikes" and the "rust on the ponderous iron-work" (38; ch. 1).

Revised

In chapter one, the details and diction prepare us for a "tale of human sorrow and frailty" (38; ch.1) The details direct us to objects that evoke sorrow and depression. For example, the people gather in front of a prison, "a wooden edifice, the door of which was heavily timbered with oak and studded with iron spikes" (38; ch.1). Revealing an aspect of humanity that often brings suffering to the community, this "prison house somewhere in the vicinity of Cornhill" (38; ch. 1) reminds us of the consequence of our sinful nature. **Moreover, a "grass plot, much overgrown with burdock, pigweed, apple peru, and such unsightly vegetation" (38; ch. 1), creating a place few would find inviting, suggests that there is little beauty to be seen. Near this prison rests "a portion of the virgin soil...a cemetery" (38; ch. 1), reminding the reader that death, a sorrowful event, will soon affect this community.** In addition to these gloomy details, the diction adds to the despondency of the setting, providing words that remove life and energy from this environment. For example, **dark colors dominate the chapter:** the "gray, steeple-crowned hats," the prison "with weather stains [and its] beetle-browed and gloomy front," and "the black flower of civilized society" (38; ch. 1). Along with the absence of color, visually suggesting sorrow, the objects of touch, such as the door "heavily timbered with oak and...iron spikes" and the "rust on the ponderous iron-work" (38; ch. 1), **reveal the hardness and coldness that often accompanies a mood of sorrow and frailty.**

P = PARAGRAPH NEEDS REVISION

Editing Symbol

P

P1 = The organization (time, place, idea) of main points that support the topic sentence needs to be identified or emphasized more clearly.

P2 = This collection of sentences doesn't provide complete coherence; check logic and word glue, and topic string.

P3 = Paragraph could use more textual support and analysis; look for additional examples.

P4 = Tie to thesis needs to be stronger.

Original P1, P2, P3

Scrooge and his nephew have an interesting discussion in chapter one. His nephew greets his uncle, but Scrooge only says, "Bah Humbug!" (13; ch. 1). The narrator describes the nephew as very jovial. Even Scrooge recognizes his nephew's ebullient appearance as he wonders, "What reason have you to be merry?" (13; ch. 1). Scrooge asks, "What right have you to be dismal? What reason have you to be morose?" (14; ch. 1). Scrooge thinks money governs everything, "bills without money…a time for finding yourself a year older, and not an hour richer" (14; ch. 1). His nephew, however, admits that he has 'not profited" from Christmas but describes it as "a kind, forgiving, charitable, pleasant time…when men and women seem by one consent to open their shut-up hearts freely, and to think of people below them as if they really were fellow passengers to the grave" (15; ch. 1). His nephew pleads, "Why cannot we be friends?" and Scrooge ignores the request for relationship and dismisses him with "Good Afternoon" (16; ch. 1). When men come to solicit money, Scrooge says, "It's enough for a man to understand his own business, and not to interfere with other people's. Mine occupies me constantly" (19; ch. 1). Scrooge's repetition of "own," "mine," and "me" shows his interest in withdrawing from society rather than joining it.

Topic sentence needs to be more precise.

Revised

Scrooge's nephew is his uncle's foil, a character whose qualities contrast with the qualities of another character. First, unlike Scrooge, his nephew uses language and is described by the narrator with language that is sociable and friendly. For example, after his initial greeting to his uncle, the narrator describes the nephew's voice as "cheerful." **This diction is immediately opposite to Scrooge's** response, "Bah Humbug!" (13; ch.1). **The narrator continues to use diction and imagery of friendliness, describing the nephew** as "all in a glow," with a face "ruddy and handsome," with eyes that "sparkled" (13; ch.1). **Even Scrooge recognizes his nephew's ebullient appearance** as he wonders, "What reason have you to be merry?" (13; ch.1). Scrooge, however, is described with diction of harshness and unsociability, his nephew asking, "What right have you to be dismal? What reason have you to be morose?" (14; ch.1). **Second, Scrooge defines wealth in life as monetary accumulation, whereas his nephew defines wealth in terms of relationship.** For example, Scrooge sees Christmas as a time when others pay "bills without money…a time for finding yourself a year older, and not an hour richer" (14; ch.1). His nephew, however, admits that he has "not profited" from Christmas but describes it as "a kind, forgiving, charitable, pleasant time…when men and women seem by one consent to open their shut-up hearts freely, and to think of people below them as if they really were fellow passengers to the grave" (15; ch.1). **Here his nephew views life's wealth as developing relationships rather than developing economic riches. This contrast occurs again with Scrooge's language of selfishness as opposed to his nephew's language of invitation. Whereas his nephew pleads**, "Why cannot we be friends?" Scrooge ignores the request for relationship and dismisses him with "Good Afternoon" (16; ch.1). **Scrooge's**

*Paragraph is organized by idea—contrast. Note the second sentence as transitional **A1**.*

Notice that the writer explains how the quoted material supports the topic sentence.

isolation appears later when he turns away the two gentlemen who are soliciting funds for the poor; Ebenezer uses language of the self. He says "it's enough for a man to understand his own business, and not to interfere with other people's. Mine occupies me constantly" (19; ch.1). **Scrooge's repetition of "own," "mine," and "me" shows his interest in withdrawing from society rather than joining it.**

Original P3

Many characters are loving. In *Beowulf,* Wiglaf washes the hero after he kills the dragon. "Then that excellent thane with his own hands washed his battle-bloodied prince, bathed with water the famous leader, his friend and lord" (120). The prologue of *The Canterbury Tales* has loving characters, too. The parson, for example, "was a good man of the priest's vocation" (120). The parson also has a large parish that covers several miles. "Wide was his parish, with houses far asunder, / but he would not be kept by rain or thunder, / if any had suffered a sickness or a blow, from visiting" (121–23). He visits his parishioners even in bad weather.

> Problems with transitional **A2** and topic sentence.

Revised

The comic and epic worlds depict characters who demonstrate **an ability to love others, to "move beyond self-interest" (120), and to serve their fellow man.** In *Beowulf,* Wiglaf places his king's needs before his own, taking "that excellent thane with his own hands" and washing "his battle-bloodied prince" (120), preparing the king for a dignified death. Here Wiglaf stands in contrast to the selfish thanes who previously fled from the flames of the dragon. Likewise, Chaucer's parson equally acts to help **serve others'** needs before his own. This "good man of the priest's vocation" ignores the difficulties of his job, serving a parish "with houses far asunder" (120–121). More important than distance is his desire to help those who "had suffered a sickness or a blow"; for them "he would not be kept by rain or thunder" (125–126).

> Writer will apply this expanded definition of love to his examples.

> Notice words from topic sentence.

Original P1, P2, P3

The comic and tragic worlds have characters who have an appetite for knowledge. In Chaucer's prologue, the Oxford cleric says "he much preferred to have beside his bed / his twenty volumes bound in black or red" (210–11). In addition, "For though he knew what learning had to offer, / there was little coin to jingle in his coffer. / On books and learning he would promptly spend" (298–300). He says that "his scholarship was what he truly heeded" (229). His dress is reflected by this knowledge: "He rode a mount as skinny as a rake, / and he was hardly fat. / He wore an outer cloak of threadbare stuff" (224–26). In addition to the comic world, the tragic world has characters who illustrate this point. Victor Frankenstein says he "explore[s] unknown powers, and unfold[s] to the world the deepest mysteries of

> What are the main points that support **TS**?

> Transition problems after the topic sentence and here, when moving from the comic to the tragic worlds.

> Writer is listing and summarizing throughout this paragraph.

creation" (39; ch. 2). His friend Henry says, "How very ill you appear; so thin and pale; and look as if you had been watching for several nights" (60; ch. 5). Henry thinks Victor looks sick. Often, Victor "nearly sank to the ground through languor and extreme weakness" (54; ch. 4), but his desire "could not tear my thoughts from my employment, loathsome in itself, but which had taken an irresistible hold of my imagination" (56; ch. 4). Victor admits that he has an appetite: "If the study to which you apply yourself has a tendency to weaken your affections, and to destroy your taste for those simple pleasures in which no alloy can possibly mix, then that study is…not befitting the human mind" (41; ch. 3). This is what is important about Walton. He also is an example of a person who has an appetite for knowledge. He is interested in "the marvelous, a belief in the marvelous, intertwined in all my projects" (42; ch. 3), a life shaped by "a steady purpose, a point on which the soul may fix its intellectual eye" (42; ch. 3).

Revised

Both the comic and tragic worlds depict characters whose appetite for knowledge **becomes obsessive.** In Chaucer's prologue, the Oxford cleric's **pursuit of knowledge, his desire** "to have beside his bed / his twenty volumes bound in black or red" (210–211), **demonstrates an imbalance, a lack of restraint** that is **reflected in his physical form**, a young man "hardly fat…. He wore an outer cloak of threadbare stuff" (220, 226). Instead of attending to his physical needs, he would "for learning's sake, let himself look hollow and sober enough" (228), preferring "his scholarship, [which] was what he truly heeded" (229). **This physical decay occurs in Victor Frankenstein, who, like the cleric, seeks to** "explore unknown powers, and unfold to the world the deepest mysteries of creation" (39; ch. 2). **He pursues these intellectual goals impetuously, paying the price physically. Even Clerval notices** "how very ill you appear; so thin and pale; and look as if you had been watching for several nights" (60; ch. 5). **Unfortunately, even though Victor, at one point,** "nearly sank to the ground through languor and extreme weakness" (54: ch. 4), **his deleterious desire "could not tear** my thoughts from my employment, loathsome in itself, but which had taken an irresistible hold of my imagination" (56; ch. 4). Victor justifies this obsession for knowledge, since often "we [are] upon the brink of becoming acquainted" with a discovery, but our "cowardice or carelessness" restrains "our enquiries" (42; ch. 3). Later, when Victor meets Walton, he sees that Walton, too, craves "the marvellous, a belief in the marvellous, intertwined in all my projects," a life shaped by "a steady purpose, a point on which the soul may fix its intellectual eye" (42; ch. 3).

> Writer makes the topic sentence more specific. His second sentence contains commentary that clearly ties back to the idea of obsessiveness.

> Now, the writer transitions smoothly from a comic character, the Oxford cleric, to a tragic charcater, Victor Frankenstein, with the words "This physical decay" and "who, like the cleric, seeks to…." He uses diction that suggests an obsession—"pursues," "impetuously," and "deleterious"—and thus makes his argument more coherent in this revision.

Original P4, P2, P3

Hawthorne introduces Dimmesdale with some strength and weakness.

Addressing the crowd during Hester's ignominy, Dimmesdale stands with a very "striking aspect" (46, ch.3). This "striking" appearance garners the admiration of the community and represents his "high eminence" (46, ch.3) in the view of society. Further examples include his "large, brown, melancholy eyes, and tremulous mouth" (46, ch.3) creating a sense of a "vast power of self-restraint" (46, ch.3) and knowledge. Even on the scaffold, he affects "the people like the speech of an angel" (46, ch.3), clearly showing how he influences his congregation. He pleads with a voice "tremendously sweet, rich, deep, and broken" (47, ch.3). Yet the passion in his "broken" voice represents his equally caring personality, which further grabs the appeal of the community. Another side of Dimmesdale also emerges as the narrator describes him as "apprehensive, a startled, [and] a half frightened look" (46, ch.3). As he watches Hester tormented upon the scaffold for their shared sin, he appears "as a being who felt himself quite astray from and at a loss in the pathway of human existence" (46, ch.3). He's clearly beginning to change.

> In the essay from which this body paragraph is taken, the writer compares two characters from **The Scarlet Letter**, Arthur Dimmesdale and Roger Chillingworth. The writer's thesis statement is as follows: *In **The Scarlet Letter** by Nathaniel Hawthorne, the physiognomies of Dimmesdale and Chillingworth parallel their various physiological states and the destructive effects of sin.* Compare this original paragraph to the revised paragraph that follows and discuss why the writer has made the changes that appear.

Revised

Hawthorne introduces Dimmesdale **with a positive correlation between his outward appearance and inward confidence; however, subtle hints of trepidation in his appearance reveal the first signs of his consuming guilt.** Addressing the crowd during Hester's ignominy, Dimmesdale stands with a very "striking aspect" (46, ch.3), **an aspect that demonstrates confidence and establishes a commanding presence on the stage.** This "striking" appearance garners the admiration of the community and represents his "high eminence" (46, ch.3) in the view of society. Further **emphasizing his poise and equanimity,** his "large, brown, melancholy eyes, and tremulous mouth" (46, ch.3) create a sense of a "vast power of self-restraint" (46, ch.3) and knowledge. **His powerful appearance on stage, accompanied by his strong speaking prowess,** "affect[s] the people like the speech of an angel" (46, ch.3), **demonstrating his ability to earn the veneration of others through his appearance and manner.** He pleads with a "tremendously sweet, rich, deep, and broken" (47, ch.3) voice, **showing confidence and poise with "rich, deep" undertones that "vibrate within [the] hearts" of the people.** Yet the passion in his "broken" voice represents his equally caring personality, which further grabs the appeal of the community. **However, despite this eloquent manner, the first degree of his guilt emerges through an ever-present sense of anguish that overshadows his features with "** an apprehensive, a startled, [and] a half frightened look" (46, ch.3). **These faint, yet disgruntling, physical attributes abruptly contrast his mostly confident stature, tainted by the guilt of his adultery.** As he watches Hester tormented upon the scaffold for their shared sin, he appears "as a being who felt himself quite astray from and at a loss in the pathway of human existence" (46, ch.3), **physical indications of his growing guilt and emotional turmoil. These negative physical attributes mark the beginning of a transformation from his true, confident, and composed self, to a morally conflicted man unable to find his place in society and "human existence" (46, ch.3).**

S = SUMMARIZING PLOT

Summarizing here rather than explaining how these details support the topic. This problem is similar to listing (L). See those examples, pp. 205-207. A thorough study of Chapter One, "Close Reading Strategies That Develop an Analytical Voice," is highly recommended.

Original S

A silent spider sits alone on a promontory, a piece of land projecting into the sea or water or a bluff. He is apart from the mainland. The spider glances at the emptiness around him and begins making its web, spinning its string. The spider works on producing his web without tiring, quickly projecting something from within himself to something outside of him. Moreover, the spider is patient, waiting.

Revised

The spider launches "forth filament, filament, filament, out of itself," indicating a desire to connect outside of oneself, a response to isolation. The steady "unreeling" of filament, "tirelessly speeding them" to produce a web, manifests the spider's natural commitment to its own survival.

Original S

The Eighth Juror talks about the el train, which, he says, "takes about ten seconds to pass a given point." He points out that "the woman saw the stabbing through the last two cars." He concludes that "we can assume that the body fell to the floor just as the train passed by." He takes these details to make a final conclusion: "Therefore, the el train had been roaring by the old man's window for a full ten seconds before the body fell. The old man, according to his own testimony, hearing "I'm going to kill you" and the body falling a split second later, would have had to hear the boy make this statement while the el was roaring past his nose. It's not possible that he could have heard it."

Revised

Juror Eight demonstrates his apt ability to think logically and hence to demonstrate his own ethical stature. Consistently making appeals to logos, Juror eight inductively concludes that "it's not possible that [the old man] could have heard" either a falling body or the boy's alleged statement, "I'm going to kill you." This logical argument emerges from a series of observed details, namely, that the train "takes about ten seconds to pass a given point," "the body fell to floor just as the train passed by," and the "train had been roaring…for a full ten seconds." Moreover, what provides the structure for this claim is causality, the careful sequencing of events [causes] that descend upon an ultimate effect—the old man merely thought he heard an ominous statement and subsequent fall of a body. Finally, the juror's narrative uses language unmodified by emotional appeals—the "body fell," "the body falling," "for a full ten seconds before the body fell" rather than exclaiming "the bloody corpse collapsed" or "the helpless father was ruthlessly stabbed." Here Juror Eight's language demonstrates restraint and a desire to focus solely on facts. Even the repetition of "ten seconds" and "split second" evoke a mathematical precision reflecting the juror's own phronesis.

Original S

The Toyota ad wants to persuade readers to buy a Corolla. The ad shows five Corollas on a roller coaster, coming off of a large loop, with several passengers smiling and extending their hands into the air. The colors are vibrant, the yellow roller coaster, the red Corollas, and the blue sky.

Revised

Toyota's ad seeks to persuade consumers that its Corolla inherently possesses a sense of youthful power and exhilaration. The ad's primary rhetorical strategy, a chimeric analogue, juxtaposes a Corolla on a roller coaster, one designed to shift the audience's probable impression of the Corolla as lackluster to one more energetic. The ad, adorned with images of joy and thrill—smiling twenty-year olds, multiple hands extended without stress into the blue sunshine, and a text built out of vibrant, primary colors—reinforces Toyota's claim that purchasing the Corolla will produce a fanciful experience not physically possible with other automobiles.

SH = SHOW CONCRETE IMAGES

Editing Symbol

SH

SHOW rather than *tell* these details. The reader can't see any images. SHOWING text includes direct excerpts—quotation, paraphrase, etc.—from the literary text, along with the writer's commentary. See Chapter 3, especially pp. 38-39.

Original SH

My room has so much junk in it I can barely move.

Revised

Pushing open my bedroom door, I kick aside the stack of dirty underwear, which soon covers my copies of *Hamlet*, *Macbeth*, and *Othello*, their pages open from last night's comparative reading.

Original SH

When Hester **leaves prison, she faces harassment** from the town, but she does not run away.

Revised

From the moment she exits from behind the prison door, Hester, **holding her head high, confronts the accusing eyes of the community,** all of whom, including at times her daughter Pearl, serve as the agents for her punishment. **Forced to wear a scarlet letter "A" upon her chest, Hester does not flee from the town that has so harshly judged her; rather, she chooses to remain close to the community, living in a small cottage just outside the town limits.**

Original SH

During the feasts, the scop tells **important stories** that affect his audience.

Revised

The feast also allows the scop to tell important tribal stories—tales of heroic idealism, such as that of **Sigemund and Fitela, and tales of warning, such as** that of Heremod and his greed.

Original SH

The knight is a very humble person; **he doesn't wear fancy clothes.**

Revised

Chaucer illustrates the knight's humility through his appearance: **"He possessed / fine horses, but he was not gaily dressed"** (24–25). In fact, not only does he avoid "fine" clothes, but he does not care about trivial aspects of his appearance, arriving at the pilgrimage **"with smudges where his armour had left mark"** (30).

Original SH

The Parson lives **a simple life and tries to share with others.**

Revised

The Parson goes beyond his individual poverty, **living simply, by sharing his own paltry resources, "giving to poor parishioners both from Church offerings and his property"** (60).

Original SH

The monk loves the **pleasures of the material world.**

Revised

This material world beckons the monk with its offerings of **fashionable gold, fine clothing, food, and beer.**

Original SH

The Friar only loves to hang around people who are rich.

Revised

The Friar loves only those who have money to give, **for he knows "nothing good can come of commerce with such slum-and-gutter dwellers"** (75).

T = TRANSITIONS ARE WEAK

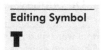

Editing Symbol

T

T1 = Check word glue and logic glue between each sentence.
T2 = Revise transition so there is a closer link between these two sentences.
T3 = The transition could be less wordy.
T4 = Maintain topic string.

THERE MUST BE A TRANSITION BETWEEN THE DIRECT QUOTATION AND THE PREVIOUS SENTENCE; OTHERWISE, THE READER DOES NOT UNDERSTAND WHY THE WRITER HAS PRESENTED THE QUOTATION. Therefore, the writer should not begin a sentence with a direct quotation because this could confuse the reader.

Original T2 T4

Scrooge deals with a great deal of money that he is unwilling to give away. Two gentlemen come to ask for donations for the "poor and destitute."

Revised

Scrooge deals with large amounts of money that he is unwilling to give away. **For example, he refuses to donate money** to the "poor and destitute" despite the pleas of two gentlemen.

Original T1

To keep his penny-pinching ways, "Scrooge kept the coal-box in his own room" (13; ch. 1) to ensure that his clerk cannot replenish his single ember should it burn out. Dickens illustrates Scrooge's attitude towards his nephew's financial situation when he responds to a comment from his nephew.

Revised

To keep his penny-pinching ways, "Scrooge kept the coal-box in his own room" (13; ch. 1) to ensure that his clerk cannot replenish his single ember should it burn out. **Scrooge is also parsimonious** with his speech, as illustrated in his terse conversation with his nephew.

Original T2, T4

Huck is resourceful, an ability to look around and use everything he has to complete **tasks. "An old rusty** saw without any handle; it was laid in between a rafter and the clapboards of the roof" (33; ch. 7). This is a good example of resourcefulness.

Revised

Huck is resourceful, an ability to look around and use everything he has to complete tasks. **For example, when Huck is locked up in his one-room shack, wondering if his father has left for good, he cannot find a way out until he looks closer at the wall and finds "an old** rusty saw without any handle; it was laid in between a rafter and the clapboards of the roof" (33; ch.7). **Here Huck uses his keen sense of survival, his ability to find a way out of the house, to create a plan to fake his death to get away from his father.**

Original T1

Dimmesdale, carrying the burden of his ignominious sin within his heart, has suffered for seven years. He often beats himself "with a bloody scourge [which he] had plied...on his own shoulders" (141; ch. 11). On Sundays, he tells his parishioners that he is "utterly a pollution and a lie!" (140; ch. 11). Chillingworth is "a chief actor in the poor minister's interior world," one who could "arouse him with a throb of agony" (137; ch. 11). The narrator says Dimmesdale is "looking like pure fallen snow" before his parishioners, men and women who label him "the saint on earth" (140; ch. 11). Dimmesdale says his heart is "all speckled and spotted with iniquity" (130; ch. 11).

> Transitional word glue is missing, and the Chillingworth example is off-topic.

Revised

Dimmesdale, carrying the burden of his ignominious sin within his heart, has *suffered* for seven years. **He, more than anyone, knows that he is guilty of a crime,** *punishing* himself physically "with a bloody

> The words in italics are transitional WORD GLUE, repeating the idea of suffering established in the topic sentence.

scourge [which he] had plied…on his own shoulders" (141; ch. 11) **and mentally** with his Sunday reproach: "I, your pastor, whom you so reverence and trust, am utterly a pollution and a lie!" (140; ch. 11). **Adding to this self-inflicted** *torture*, Dimmesdale battles Chillingworth, not simply a physician helping to abate Dimmesdale's pain but "a chief actor in the poor minister's interior world," one who could "arouse him with a throb of agony" (137; ch. 11). **Even beyond these forces,** Dimmesdale **must face an** *agonizing* **duplicity**—"looking like pure fallen snow" before his parishioners, men and women who label him "the saint on earth," (140; ch. 11) and knowing that his heart is "all speckled and spotted with *iniquity*" (130; ch. 11). **His soul** *besieged* **by forces on every side,** Dimmesdale cannot hide the truth from Hester; she recognizes that he stands "on the verge of lunacy," that "a *deadlier* venom [has] been infused into him by the hand that proffered relief" (160; ch. 13).

Original T2 T4

The second and, perhaps, most vital event that marks Roger's descent to savagery is his abdication of order and logic for acts of evil. Piggy, the remnants of the old society, "the rational mind opposed to intuition and insight" (Delbaere-Garant 190) is killed by Roger who frees himself through the act.

Revised

The second and, perhaps, most vital event that marks Roger's descent to savagery is his abdication of order and logic for acts of evil. **Here, Roger** frees himself of the remnants of the old society through the killing of Piggy, who exists as "the rational mind opposed to intuition and insight" (Delbaere-Garant 190).

Original T3

When the narrator describes her smell, he first allows us to dream of the sweet scent of perfume, but then surprisingly emphasizes how his mistress' breath "reeks." **Disgusted by her visage and scent that smells so bad,** the reader then reads about the voice of the narrator's mistress as he wonders if she could be decent in any way.

Revised

When the narrator describes her smell, he first allows us to dream of the sweet scent of perfume, but then surprisingly emphasizes how his mistress' breath "reeks." **The reader disgusted,** he then reads about the voice of the narrator's mistress as the reader wonders if she could be decent in any way.

Original T2

One will regret and "forever tarry" (17) once one is old because there is not enough time to go out and do what one has already passed up. In addition, Herrick says, "Old Time is still a-flying" (3); time keeps on going whether you want it to or not.

Revised

One will regret and "forever tarry" (17) once one is old because there is not enough time to go out and do what has already been passed up. **For time, as Herrick reminds, does not exhibit this lethargy but is always "still a-flying" (3).**

Original T2

His professor, M.Waldman, gives him many scientific books, all of which Frankenstein "read with ardour" (44; ch. 3). Frankenstein's obsessive work habits keep him "engaged in [his] laboratory" for such long periods of time that "the stars often disappeared in the light of morning" (52; ch. 4).

Revised

His professor, M.Waldman, gives him many scientific books, all of which Frankenstein "read with ardour" (44; ch. 3). **This ardour quickly becomes obsessive** as Victor is "engaged in [his] laboratory" for such long periods of time that "the stars often disappeared in the light of morning" (52; ch. 4).

Original T3

In addition to expressing this honorable valor, Darnay embodies the second aspect of virtue demonstrated by John the Apostle, a natural tendency towards loyalty and righteousness.

Revised

His valor honorable, Darnay embodies the second aspect of virtue demonstrated by John the Apostle, a natural tendency towards loyalty and righteousness.

Original T3

Unfortunately, Scrooge's "Humbug" reply not only demonstrates his unwillingness to engage in a logical debate but also demonstrates **an example of his desire to isolate himself. In another example of his desire to isolate himself,** Scrooge seeks to separate himself from the social obligation to donate to those less fortunate.

Revised

Unfortunately, Scrooge's "Humbug" reply not only demonstrates his unwillingness to engage in a logical debate but also demonstrates **another example of his desire to isolate himself. In a similar manner,** Scrooge seeks to separate himself from the social obligation to donate to those less fortunate.

TS = REVISE THE TOPIC SENTENCE

Editing Symbol

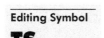

TS1 = Need a stronger focus so that all sentences clearly connect to this topic sentence; this will help coherence.

TS2 = Topic sentence contains an example, that is, a plot detail rather than an ORGANIZING IDEA + ASPECT OF THESIS.

TS3 = Connect the topic sentence to the thesis of the paper more clearly, perhaps adding actual words or synonyms from the thesis. Although the thesis for the essay makes a coherent argument, the writer's diction in one or more of the topic sentences does not yet clearly articulate a necessary component in the argument of the thesis.

TS4 = This is too broad or vague—not sure the reader will understand what is meant. The writer's language in the affected topic sentence does not specify why the paragraph helps prove the larger argument found in the thesis.

TS5 = The diction is imprecise.

NOTE: The examples that follow are topic sentences, some of which are followed by partial paragraphs.

Original TS5

Dickens also demonstrates the theme of forgiveness in the New Testament through moral dilemmas, imitating the catharsis of New Testament tax collectors, particularly Zaccheus, with his character Jerry Cruncher.

Revised

Dickens also **depicts the forgiveness found** in the New Testament through moral dilemmas, imitating the catharsis of **tax collector Zaccheus through Jerry Cruncher.**

Original TS4, TS5

Dickens is showing Scrooge's absolute cold heart.

Revised

Dickens **shows** Scrooge's **unsympathetic and selfish heart.**

Original TS4, TS5

Scrooge's nephew is not like his uncle.

Revised

Scrooge's nephew is his uncle's **foil, a character whose qualities contrast with the qualities of another character.**

Original TS2

The knight has decided to go immediately from the battlefield to the journey toward Canterbury. Even his tunic is still dirty; he doesn't bother to look good. Later, we meet the parson who also, we know through the narrator, will put service ahead of his needs.

Revised

The first class deals with the "most holy" people, those who put the Lord as well as their fellow man in front of their own needs and desires, men and women who possess many of the qualities of Christ. For example, the knight, uninterested in resting after fighting in the Crusades, immediately joins the pilgrimage to worship his God.

> A category is now defined in the topic sentence. The student will then apply this definition to the characters, such as the **knight,** who serve as examples of the definition.

Original TS4, TS5

Shakespeare has a lot of bird imagery, and it means various things.

Revised

Shakespeare uses bird imagery **to create portraits of man's physical and emotional qualities.**

Original TS3, TS2

During the Christmas dinner, Joe gives Pip gravy and throughout the book does things like this.

Revised

Pip's surrogate father, Joe, frequently safeguards Pip when Pip is in desperate need, demonstrating that a servant must be an active participant in restoring community.

Observe how the topic sentence involving Joe and Pip is revised to connect it more clearly to this thesis statement: *Just as Jesus taught us to serve others, Charles Dickens, in* **Great Expectations**, *reveals that, through the caring example of a fallen community's servants, the community can be restored to a state of love.*

Original TS4, TS5

Some characters are greedy.

Revised

Some of the minor characters in *Great Expectations*, people who devote their lives procuring a higher social status and acquiring material wealth, illustrate the greed and hypocrisy inherent in infernal comedy.

The two original topic sentences having to do with GREED and HONOR are from a paper whose thesis statement is as follows: *In* **Great Expectations** *we meet many minor characters whose parts in the story are rather transitory, but who play a major role in the thematic development of the novel, personifying the virtues and vices of infernal comedy.*

Original TS4, TS5

Some characters are honorable.

Revised

While such vices, however, are the prevailing forces of infernal comedy, not everyone is so despicable and odious; we see characters who represent the virtues of honor and integrity, characters who help to push the novel towards community.

Original TS2, TS3

Pip begins to hate life at the forge after he visits Miss Havisham and Estella.

Revised

Shortly after early childhood, Pip begins to grow into the more contemplative stage of preadolescence, a stage in which he begins to question his surroundings as well as draw conclusions about them.

The original topic sentence is merely a plot detail. Note that the revision sets the remainder of the paragraph up for the inclusion of that plot detail from the original. This paper's thesis statement focuses on the various stages of Pip's growth in the novel and the revision uses diction that connects to that key idea.

Original TS2, TS3

The poem opens with the narrator standing before the ocean.

Revised

The sea depresses the narrator into a cheerless mood of isolation.

The three topic sentences having to do with the sea and faith are original TS for a paper containing the following thesis statement: *Matthew Arnold's sea metaphor allows him to complete a political commentary on the Victorian Age, a time in which man is isolated and void of religious conviction, a situation that can only be rectified by human love.*

Original TS2, TS4

The narrator remembers the faith of the Greeks.

Revised

Arnold changes the speaker's concentration from the physical sea to the metaphorical sea to reflect on the condition of humanity's spiritual faith.

Original TS2

Love is the answer.

Revised

The isolation and loss of faith compel the author even more to move toward personal love.

Original TS2

The mariner attempts reconciliation right after shooting the albatross.

Revised

Man's first step after sin is to move toward reconciliation.

> The three topic sentences that focus on the mariner are from a paper whose thesis statement is as follows: *Coleridge's "Rime of the Ancient Mariner" illustrates man's proclivity since the Fall to sin without cause, to possess the opportunity of reconciliation, and to have the option to do penance, all in hopes of receiving forgiveness.*

Original TS2

The mariner's misfortunes begin by abruptly and without cause killing the albatross.

Revised

Since the Fall, man often discovers himself sinning without cause and sometimes without explanation.

Original TS2

The narrator learns that the mariner must now tell his tale.

Revised

With reconciliation comes penance, another stage on the path to forgiveness.

Original TS1, TS5

The unhappy nature of life in *1984* is bleak.

Revised

The distorted civil life in *1984* serves as a warning against the loss of human compassion.

Original TS5

Standing up for values and moral beliefs despite social and emotional dangers also makes people courageous even though they are free from physical threats.

Revised

Standing up for moral beliefs despite social and physical danger requires courage.

TH = THESIS PROBLEMS

Editing Symbol

TH

TH1 = Make minor adjustments in style and clarity.

TH2 = Thesis contains only a subject, not an opinion.

TH3 = The idea in the thesis is unclear. The thesis does not adequately articulate, and thus communicate to the reader, the type of argument the essay seeks to prove, namely, one of Aristotle's categories of arguments, a discussion found on pp. 95 - 103: arguments by definition, classification, comparison, or relationship. Because the thesis fails to identify a recognizable argument, the reader may become confused about the function of the topic sentences in the essay.

See Chapter 4, pp. 95 - 109 for additional examples of thesis statements.

Original TH2, TH3

Scrooge has to encounter three ghosts who make him confront issues of his past, finally resulting in Scrooge attending his nephew's Christmas dinner.

Revised

Scrooge's encounter and journey with the three ghosts depicts the requirements necessary for spiritual growth.

Original TH3

In Homer's *Odyssey*, the suitors Antinoos and Eurymachos create several problems for Telemachos.

Revised

In Homer's *Odyssey*, the grip on power held by the suitors Antinoos and Eurymachos is analogous to that possessed by twentieth century tyrants.

Original TH1 TH2

Athena has Telemachos visit Menelaos because she knows this king can be helpful and is impressive.

Revised

Menelaos represents the ideal balance between the spiritual concepts of the yang and the yin.

Original TH3

Minor characters help the theme of the infernal realm in *Great Expectations*.

Revised

In *Great Expectations* we meet many minor characters whose parts in the story are rather transitory, but who play a major role in the thematic development of the novel, personifying the virtues and vices of infernal comedy.

Original TH2

Dickens repeats images of "hands" throughout the novel.

Revised

In *Great Expectations* the motif of the hands indicates Pip's location in the journey toward maturity.

Original TH3

In Dickens' *A Christmas Carol*, Bob Cratchet and Ebenezer Scrooge are two sides of a coin.

Revised

In Dickens' *A Christmas Carol*, Bob Cratchet and Ebenezer Scrooge reflect the tension between virtue and vice.

Original TH3

Matthew Arnold's sea metaphor plays a significant role in the poem.

Revised

Matthew Arnold's sea metaphor allows him to complete a political commentary on the Victorian Age, a time in which man is isolated and void of religious conviction, a situation that can only be rectified by human love.

Original TH2

The narrator in Coleridge's "Rime of the Ancient Mariner" must tell his tale of sin to everyone he meets.

Revised

Coleridge's "Rime of the Ancient Mariner" illustrates man's proclivity since the Fall to sin without cause, to possess the opportunity of reconciliation, and to have the option to do penance, all in hopes of receiving forgiveness.

Original TH1

The images in "Kubla Khan" are very significant and tell us something about Coleridge.

Revised

The imagery in "Kubla Khan" represents Coleridge's vision of conceiving and writing poetry.

Original TH1

When Mary Shelley creates her monster and Victor Frankenstein, she is influenced by Milton's Satan and God and uses their characteristics.

Revised

In creating the monster and Victor, Mary Shelley borrows from Milton's *Paradise Lost*, using aspects of both Satan and God interchangeably.

V = VAGUE DETAILS

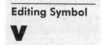
Editing Symbol
V

V1 = This comment needs to be more specific, precise; avoid plurals.

V2 = This comment does not really say anything.

Original V2

In response to his nephew's felicitous greeting, Scrooge retorts, "What reason have you to be merry? You're poor enough" (13; ch. 1), a response that shows the cold-heartedness of Scrooge.

Revised

In response to his nephew's felicitous greeting, Scrooge retorts, "What reason have you to be merry? You're poor enough" (13; ch. 1), **a response showing Scrooge thinks happiness is measured by monetary wealth.**

Original V1

Scrooge rejects his invitation and shows he is not a very festive person.

Revised

Scrooge rejects his invitation and reveals his desire to **isolate himself from situations that would require not only monetary generosity but also spiritual.**

Original V2

The nephew displays kindness toward his cruel uncle and invites him to Christmas dinner: "Dine with us tomorrow. I want nothing from you" (15; ch. 1), an example of his unselfish deeds that he performs towards his uncle.

Revised

The nephew displays kindness toward his cruel uncle and invites him to Christmas dinner: "Dine with us tomorrow. I want nothing from you" (15; ch. 1), **an invitation that not only attempts to use the power of community to change Scrooge, but also anticipates Scrooge's suspicion of his nephew's possible monetary motives.**

Original V2

The king and his warriors are brought together in a **friendly atmosphere,** where a spiritual connection known as *comitatus* is formed.

Revised

Feasting helps bring the community closer together. **Hrothgar** knowing this, he commands the **construction of Heorot** so that he may **"share the gifts God had bestowed on him upon its floor with folk young and old" (67).**

Original V1

Feasting, one of the most recurrent themes in *Beowulf*, helps the reader understand the significant elements of the Anglo-Saxon culture. One such element is gift-giving, which is an example of *comitatus*. For example, Hrothgar gives Beowulf **many gifts**. In addition, Wealhtheow, the queen and Hrothgar's wife, also **gives presents** to Beowulf .

Revised

Feasting, one of the most recurrent themes in *Beowulf*, helps the reader understand the significant elements of the Anglo-Saxon culture. <u>One significant element</u> is **gift-giving**, not simply a sign of monetary remuneration but a spiritual symbol of appreciation and fulfillment of the sacred *comitatus* bond that maintains order in the tribe. <u>For example,</u> Hrothgar **bestows "on Beowulf a standard worked in gold, a figured battle-banner, breast and head armour" (69).** <u>In addition,</u> Wealhtheow, the queen and Hrothgar's wife, also presents to **Beowulf "two arm-wreaths, with robes and rings also, and the richest collar the monk has ever heard of in all the world" (69).**

> Note the underlined transitional words.

Original V1

Dimmesdale, carrying the burden of his ignominious sin within his heart, has suffered for seven years. He frequently **beats himself** and even **tells his parishioners, amazingly, the truth,** but they don't believe it.

Revised

Dimmesdale, carrying the burden of his ignominious sin within his heart, has suffered for seven years. He, more than anyone, knows that he is guilty of a crime, for he punishes himself **physically "with a bloody scourge [which he] had plied...on his own shoulders" (141; ch. 27) and mentally with his Sunday reproach: "I, your pastor, whom you so reverence and trust, am utterly a pollution and a lie!" (140; ch. 27).**

W = WORDY STRUCTURES

Editing Symbol

W

W1 = This phrase is unnecessary. Do not write, for example, "In chapter one it says, 'Hester walked down the path.'" Instead, blend text with the writer's analysis. See **B1**.

W2 = Use fewer words: transform longer phrases into single concrete words; turn prepositional phrases into single adjectives.

W3 = Be careful about piling adjectives or adjective phrases one after another; this slows down the rhythm of the sentence. Either eliminate unnecessary adjectives or reposition some in participial phrases.

W4 = Remove redundant words within the sentence.

Original W2

The reader could possibly argue here that Scrooge is unaware ~~of the uncomfortable state of his employee~~; however, the text ~~goes on to show how little care Scrooge does have for the well being of~~ his employee. (37 words)

Revised

The reader could possibly argue here that Scrooge is unaware of **Cratchit's discomfort**; however, the text **provides more evidence** of **Scrooge's lack of concern** for his employee. (27 words)

Original W1

~~In further~~ expression of his lust for money, ~~the Pardoner goes on to say~~, "But let me briefly make my purpose plain; / I preach for nothing but for greed of gain" (4–5). (31 words)

Revised

The Pardoner again states his lust for money: "But let me briefly make my purpose plain; / I preach for nothing but for greed of gain" (4–5). (25 words)

Original W2

Furthermore, the Friar ~~was a man who~~ put money ahead ~~of anything else in his life, who did not work~~ for the poor, ~~but only the rich~~; he didn't even go into areas that were inhabited by poor people. (39 words)

Revised

Furthermore, the Friar puts money ahead of his religious obligation, helping the poor. In fact, he makes a deliberate point not to enter impoverished neighborhoods, but only those of the rich. (31 words)

Original W2

Keeping the sock company ~~from their vantage point several~~ inches away near the closet door, two ~~dilapidated~~ gray Nike track spikes smell of the trials and tribulations of a long, full athletic career. (33 words)

Revised

Keeping the sock company, two Nike track spikes, inches away near the closet door **and dappled with mud streaks and gashes in the faded leather,** smell of sweat and dried grass. (31 words)

Original W2

As I hastily walk down the hall, ~~I see some~~ gray ~~shirts that have turned almost completely white after several~~ bleachings creeping out of my doorway; ~~one shirt in particular looks like~~ a Dalmation except it is gray with white spots instead of white with black spots. (47 words)

Revised

As I hastily walk down the hall, a gray shirt, spotted with bleach stains like a Dalmation's coat, creeps out of my doorway. (23 words)

Original W3

He adjusts his red and white-billed helmet with his ~~left black~~ Reebok batting ~~glove-clad hand.~~ (17 words)

Revised

With his left hand, covered by a Reebok batting glove, he adjusts his red and white-billed helmet. (18 words)

Original W2 / W4

Its **movement journeys toward a recapturing of** virtue.

Revised

It seeks to recapture virtue.

Original W2, W4—409 words

~~The grim, unhappy nature~~ of life in *1984* serves as a warning against the loss of human compassion. The reader first sees this cold and uncaring future when Winston describes the popular nature of hangings, ~~which people now treat as a public event. He testifies that "[A hanging] happened~~ about once a month and was a popular spectacle. Children always clamored to be taken to see it" (23; bk. 1, ch. 2). The description of children, typically considered innocent and harmless, as "clamoring" for violence hints at a twisted, unnatural childhood. Winston continues to delineate the bizarre upbringing of Oceanian children society when he describes the play of two children as "like the gamboling of tiger cubs which will soon grow up into man-eaters" (23; bk. 1, ch. 2) This strangely ominous characterization of their antics ~~communicates the perversion of childish exuberance in Oceania. By superseding the parent-child relationship, the Party has succeeded in redirecting the zeal and enthusiasm of childhood into~~

~~the animosity of the Party, thus ensuring another generation of adherents to Big Brother.~~ However, Winston has also fallen victim to this hostility that ~~pervades~~ his society. For example, after a bomb hits a nearby area, in its aftermath he sees ~~a bright streak of red in the dust and "when he [gets] up to it he [sees] that it [is]~~ a human hand severed at the wrist … [and] he kick[s] the thing into the gutter" (84; bk. 1, ch. 8). ~~Here Winston reveals his own desensitization by treating the remains of another (presumably dead) person not with sorrow or respect, but with apathy by treating the hand like a piece of garbage. His neutral and uncaring response to what would typically be a traumatic and horrible event speaks to the cold and impersonal nature of 1984's future.~~ Winston again ~~shows us this calmly violent and desensitized side~~ when, after a female party member sees him in a possibly incriminating area, he contemplates "keep[ing] on her track till they were in some quiet place, and then smash[ing] her skull in with a cobblestone" ~~but ultimately concludes that~~ "the thought of making any physical effort was unbearable" (102; bk. 1, ch. 8). ~~Disquietingly, his primary deterrent against beating the woman to death is not his conscience, nor sympathy, but that he simply lacks the strength to do so. The frightening~~ rationality ~~and ease with which Winston considers this act illustrates the pervasive brutality which characterizes~~ Oceania.

Revised—327 words

The **distorted civil life** in *1984* serves as a warning against the loss of human compassion. The reader first sees this cold and uncaring future when Winston describes the popular nature of **hangings, occurring "about once a month," the "popular spectacle [that] children always clamored to be taken to see it"** (23; bk. 1, ch. 2). The description of children, typically considered innocent and harmless, as "clamoring" for violence hints at a twisted, unnatural childhood. Winston continues to delineate the bizarre upbringing of Oceanian children when he describes the play of two children as "like the gamboling of tiger cubs which will soon grow up into man-eaters" (23; bk. 1, ch. 2) This strangely ominous characterization of **childhood antics—compared to "tiger clubs" and identified as "man-eaters"—underscores the violent perversion of the family and calls attention to the Party's interest in supplanting the parental role with a zeal for the policies of Big Brother.** Winston, however, has also fallen victim to this hostility that **desensitizes** him to humanity. For example, after a bomb hits a nearby area, **he dispassionately sees** "a **human hand** severed at the wrist … [and] he kick[s] the thing into the gutter" (84; bk. 1, ch. 8), **a disregard for the human, his reaction absent of sorrow or respect, merely treating the remains of another like a piece of garbage, a shockingly apathetic response to what would typically be a traumatic and horrible event but now a common gesture in Orwell's dystopia.** Winston again **displays a distorted reaction** when, after a female party member sees him in a possibly incriminating area, he contemplates "keep[ing] on her track till they were in some quiet place, and then smash[ing] her skull in with a cobblestone." **What stops Winston is not a moral code but** "the thought of making any physical effort was unbearable" (102; bk. 1, ch. 8), **a disquietingly rationality that highlights the moral disorder created within Oceania and supported unconsciously by its citizens.**

Original W2, W4

Like John the Apostle, Charles Darnay demonstrates this New Testament theme of virtue in his own moral dilemma. ~~Specifically, Darnay exemplifies moral~~ ~~fortitude as he ruminates whether~~ to aid his imperiled servant, Gabelle, and return to France, leaving his wife and child behind. ~~First of all,~~ Darnay ~~illustrates~~ ~~the courageous aspect of virtue as "he knew~~ very well the force of these circumstances" in the French Revolution, yet still bravely faces this "course of confiscation and destruction," transcending this setting of chaos to help one in need (238-239; bk. 2, ch. 24).

Revised

Like John the Apostle, Charles Darnay demonstrates this New Testament theme of virtue in his own moral dilemma, **his reflection of whether** to aid his imperiled servant, Gabelle, and return to France, leaving his wife and child behind. Darnay **courageously recognizes** "very well the force of these circumstances" in the French Revolution, yet still bravely faces this "course of confiscation and destruction," transcending this setting of chaos to help one in need (238-239; bk. 2, ch. 24).

Original W2, W4

His valor honorable, Darnay embodies ~~the second aspect of virtue demonstrated~~ ~~by~~ John the Apostle, ~~a~~ natural tendency towards loyalty and righteousness. ~~For~~ ~~example, Dickens demonstrates, with a simile, Darnay's habitual propensity to~~ ~~do good and remain loyal.~~ Just as "the winds and streams" typically influence the path of "the mariner in the old story," ~~Darnay's natural sense of virtue and~~ loyalty , like that of John the Apostle, ~~compel him to accompany his servant in France,~~ ~~instinctively "drawing him" to assist despite the adversity and turmoil found~~ ~~there (239; bk. 2, ch. 24). Furthermore, Dickens also depicts Darnay's natural~~ ~~tendency towards goodness, as~~ "that glorious vision of doing good…arose before him" (240; bk. 2, ch. 24). Here, this imagery of virtue in his dreams, clearly seeing "himself in the illusion with some influence to guide this raging Revolution," emphasizes again how natural morality is for the virtuous Darnay, innately part of his subconscious (240; bk. 2, ch. 24).

Revised

His valor honorable, Darnay embodies John the Apostle's natural tendency towards loyalty and righteousness, **a dedication similar to "the mariner in the old story" whose "winds and streams" push him to action, telling him "he must go." This loyalty eschews "his latent uneasiness" and causes him to see "hardly any danger," both Darnay and John the Apostle "recognizing "that glorious** vision of doing good…[that] arose before him" (240; bk. 2, ch. 24). Here, this imagery of virtue in his dreams, clearly seeing "himself in the illusion with some influence to guide this raging Revolution," emphasizes again how natural morality is for the virtuous Darnay, innately part of his subconscious (240; bk. 2, ch. 24).

Original W2, W4

Through this the Party ~~begins a concise plan to~~ extract all meaningful relationships from Oceania.

Revised

Through this the Party extracts all meaningful relationships from Oceania.

WC = WORD CHOICE

Editing Symbol

WC

Word here is **not the best choice**. Avoid bland language, jargon, colloquialisms.

Original WC

The negative details of Wilson's auto shop, both "unprosperous and bare," reflect the bad condition of its proprietor, someone who doesn't have any money.

Revised WC

The **bleak** details of Wilson's auto shop, both "unprosperous and bare," reflect the **hapless** condition of its proprietor, a **financial prosperity absent and barren**.

Original WC

Scrooge doesn't care about others, which is different from the men who knock at his door, men who seek to assist the poor with "some meat and drink, and means of warmth."

Revised WC

Scrooge's **lack of compassion** contrasts with those of his **altruistic solicitors**, men seeking to assist the poor with "some meat and drink, and means of warmth."

Original WC

His physical choice to write makes clear his rebellious thoughts.

Revised WC

His physical choice to write **manifests** his rebellious thoughts.

Original WC

Toyota's ad seeks to persuade consumers that its Corolla is fun and exciting.

Revised

Toyota's ad seeks to persuade consumers that its Corolla **inherently possesses** a sense of **youthful power and exhilaration**.

X2 = REVISE FOR CLARITY AND CONCISENESS

Editing Symbol

X2

Prescriptions for Healthy Sentences

- Avoid EXCESSIVE NOMINALIZATION WITHIN A SENTENCE, where verbs and adjectives have been employed as nouns or noun phrases. Sentences built predominately with nouns rather than verbs will lose energy. Often nominalizations occur <u>after</u> articles (*a, an, the*) or <u>within</u> prepositional phrases. You'll find these nominalizations as subjects, direct objects, objects of prepositions, and predicate nominatives.

Verbs	Nominalization
acknowledge	acknowledgement
agree	agreement
conclude	conclusion
depend	dependent
exclude	exclusion
investigate	investigation
tolerate	tolerance

Adjectives	Nominalization
elegant	elegance
intense	intensity
careless	carelessness

Original

The utilization of domesticity, such as the production of knitting a shroud, is employed by Madame Defarge for the <u>terrorization</u> of the French citizenry and aristocracy.

Revised

Madam Defarge **terrorizes** the French peasants by knitting names into a shroud.

Original

The <u>intention</u> of the suitors is to bring about the <u>demoralization</u> of the household of Odysseus, a locale unable to bring about the cessation of chaos.

Revised

The suitors **intend** to **demoralize** Odysseus' household, its members unable to **end** the chaos.

- Look for a stronger verb that might be acting as a noun or part of a weak verb phrase

Original

In this way the party is able to <u>bar</u> relationships among its citizens.

Revised

In this way the party **bars** relationships among its citizens.

Original

These heartless acts, praised by the government, are the children's duty to the Party, and <u>polarize</u> them from their parents.

Revised

These heartless acts, praised by the government, **polarize** children from their parents.

Original

Homes <u>are filled</u> with controlling youths who <u>have deceit and treachery instilled</u> in them.

Revised

Homes **contain** deceitful and treacherous youths, **brainwashed** by Big Brother.

- BALANCE ABSTRACT DICTION WITH CONCRETE DICTION.

Original

His location, perhaps more importantly, provides the space for his psychological resistance, the writing in a diary, his documentation of treasonous thoughts within his mind his a wish to be alone, an act forbidden by the Party. There he writes a diary, a psychological portrayal of solitary resistance, a reflection of his condemnatory views on the Party's corruption of individual freedom. His physical choice to write manifests his rebellious thoughts, in fact, makes his psychological reflections explicit, a gesture of individual expression certainly punishable by death or at least an extreme prison sentence.

Revised

His location, in the **alcove of his kitchen,** provides the space for his psychological resistance, the writing in a diary, his documentation of treasonous and forbidden thoughts condemning the Party's tyranny.   His physical choice to write makes his illicit thoughts explicit, first a random reflection of **attending a violent movie the previous evening, his memory of the lower class Proles objecting to the macabre film**, a reflection leading to Winston's recognition that the Party cares little for the welfare of these citizens. These written musings lead him to discern more treasonously the manipulative function of the **Two Minutes Hate, recognizing how the images of Goldstein critiquing Big Brother** produces the emotional frenzy of party members, unified in their hatred toward **Goldstein** and in their commitment to the Party. The result of his cognitive violation manifests in more written transgressions, Winston's penning multiple times the phrase **"Down with Big Brother,"** tangible proof of his willful defiance against the party's restrictions on psychological freedom.

[ ] = VARY YOUR SENTENCE BEGINNINGS

Editing Symbol

[ ]

Vary some of these sentence beginnings. Use adverb or noun subordinate clauses; absolute phrases; adverb or noun infinitive phrases; present and past participial phrases; prepositional phrases; gerund phrases, etc.

Original

Hector, likewise, **is** lauded for his bountiful skills in military leadership. **Hector has** no love for war, which is different from Achilles. Achilles fought ferociously. **He does** it out of a sense of responsibility to his community. Furthermore, **he is** noted for his compassion and gentleness, which we witness when we observe his loving farewells to his wife and baby son prior to his departure for the final battle. **He earns** the esteem not only of the men under his command, because he is the leader of all the Trojan armies, but also of his adversaries; nevertheless, no one mistakes him for Achilles.

Revised

Hector, likewise, is lauded for his bountiful skills in military leadership. **Unlike Achilles,** Hector has no love for war. **While he fights ferociously,** he does it out of a sense of responsibility to his community. Furthermore, he is noted for his compassion and gentleness, which we witness when we observe his loving farewells to his wife and baby son prior to his departure for the final battle. **Being leader of all the Trojan armies,** he earns the esteem not only of the men under his command but also of his adversaries; nevertheless, no one mistakes him for Achilles.

◯ **= VIVID VERB USAGE**

Editing Symbol	◯ 1 = Revise this "be" verb with a more vivid, active verb.
◯	◯ 2 = Avoid the passive verb in this context. (p. 151)

Original 2
The next example of selfishness is shown towards Scrooge's clerk.

Revised
The next example of selfishness **occurs** towards Scrooge's clerk. *Or recast the sentence:* Scrooge **aims** his next act of selfishness at his clerk.

Original 2
Instead of being kind and caring towards his fellow man in this season, all of his feelings during Christmas are directed towards money. This is shown when he is speaking to his nephew about the wonderful events of Christmas.

Revised
Instead of being kind and caring towards his fellow man in this season, Scrooge **focuses** on money. For example, when he **speaks** to his nephew about Christmas, Scrooge **insists**, "It is a time for paying bills without money" (14; ch. 1).

Original 2
The scene is opened with a great look at the coldness of Scrooge.

Revised
The scene **opens** with an image of Scrooge's lack of compassion for others.

Original 1
In not sharing his coal with others, he is symbolically not sharing the warmth that he has inside of him, warmth that everyone is capable of sharing.

Revised
In not sharing his coal with others, Scrooge symbolically **imprisons** the warmth he has inside, warmth each person's soul possesses.

Original 1
His hands are massaging Johnny's aching back muscles. The fingers are dancing nimbly, and they are digging into the quivering brawn and kneading the soft white dough.

Revised
Strong hands violently **massage** Johnny's aching back muscles. Ebony fingers, **dancing nimbly, dig** into the quivering brawn and **knead** the soft white dough.

APPENDIX

GENERAL COMPOSITION ASSIGNMENT AND REVISION DIRECTIONS

These directions should be followed for paragraphs, essay test revisions, and major compositions, unless otherwise modified by the teacher.

MAJOR COMPOSITION REQUIREMENTS

1. Composition must be **typed double-spaced.**
2. Composition should use the correct **MLA heading,** pp. 120, 123, 125, 128.
3. Composition should be written in **present tense** when discussing literary topics.
4. Students must **turn in all drafts with the final copy.**
5. All **new additions to final** copy—revised words, sentences, phrases—that did not appear in drafts must be highlighted with a highlighter marker.
6. Students must write a SHOWING-**telling introduction,** p. 110.
7. **When students directly quote from the literary text,** the direct quotation must be followed with a citation in parentheses. For a novel, the parenthetical citation is *page number semicolon chapter number* (450; ch.5); for long poems, such as epics, the citation is *book* or *part period line numbers* (3.45–48); for shorter poems, the citation is *line numbers* (45–46); for a play, the citation is *act period scene period line numbers* (2.3.45–49).

e.g. PIP LOWERS HIS HEAD AND ASKS JOE "TO FORGIVE ME FOR THE WRONGS I'VE DONE YOU" (56; CH.4).

Notice that the parenthetical citation for the direct quotation *comes after* the end quotation marks *but before* the end punctuation.

8. **A Works Cited** page should be placed at the end of the composition. If a student's only entry is the original text, he or she may place the entry, with "Works Cited" preceding it, after the conclusion. (See sample papers at the end of chapter three.)

9. Each body paragraph should contain **extensively elaborated** details.

10. Students should highlight and label one example of the following **sentence structures** that the teacher requires for the particular composition. (Teachers will modify this list per assignment, DEPENDING ON THE STRUCTURES COVERED IN CLASS HERETOFORE, but if they do not, students are expected to include all required structures.)

    a. compound sentence w/conjunctive adverb (p. 138)

    b. compound-complex sentence (p. 138)

    c. present participial phrase (pp. 139-140)

    d. past participial phrase (pp. 139 - 140)

    e. absolute phrase (p. 141)

    f. repeat word modifier (p. 162)

    g. analysis modifier (p. 162)

    h. noun subordinate clause (p. 137)

    i. adjective subordinate clause (p. 136)

    j. adverbial subordinate clause (p. 135)

    k. infinitive phrase (pp. 142 - 144)

    l. gerund phrase (pp. 141-142)

    m. appositive phrase (p. 144)

    n. a sentence with consecutive parallel structures: two or more noun clauses, adverb clauses, present participial phrases, etc. (pp. 182+)

11. Student must highlight and use appropriately ___ SAT **words** from the vocabulary list. (Insert number of SAT words required on blank space.)

12. A student's **conclusion** should avoid summary or mere restatement of the thesis statement; instead, the conclusion ought to connect the thesis to one larger issue: a) to the community; b) to the writer of the composition; c) to other works of literature. See p. 116.

MLA DOCUMENTATION

PARENTHETICAL CITATIONS are placed within the paper itself rather than as foot- or endnotes. Observe how each reference within a parenthetical citation is punctuated.

For lines of **short poetry**: line numbers (45–46).

For lines of **longer poetry or epic**: first, refer to the book or part (or canto); next, IF there are individual stanzas, refer to the stanza number; finally, refer to the line numbers. (1.2.5–7) refers to book 1, stanza 2, lines 5 to 7. (3.117-121) refers to book 3, lines 117 to 121.

For lines of a **play**: act.scene.line numbers (1.2.5–6).

For a **novel**: include the chapter with the page number (34; ch. 4); if the novel has book / section divisions, include that number as well (34; bk.

1, ch. 4).

For a **source** WITHOUT **mention of the author's name** in the writer's essay: include the author's last name and the page number (Gower 41).

For a **source** WITH **mention of the author's name** in the writer's essay: include the page number only (4).

For a **source with more than one author, neither of whom are mentioned** in the writer's essay: include both authors' last names and the page number (Connors and Roberts 45).

For an **author with more than one entry in the works cited page**: include the last name of the author, and the title of the source followed by the page number (Stevenson, *The Poetry of Elizabeth Bishop* 67).

For a **quotation cited indirectly in another source**: include *qtd. in* and the last name of the author of the other source (the indirect source) and the page number (qtd. in Miller 304).

For a **quotation containing a question mark or an exclamation point**: retain this punctuation within the closing quotation mark and place a period after the parenthetical citation. *Mr. Lorry hopes to "see such a night again!"* (94; bk. 2, ch. 6).

For a **book or article with no author**: use the title and a page number ("Poetry of Donne" 65).

For **two authors with the same last name**: include the first initial of each author (or the entire first names if the initials are the same) and the page number (J. Jones and H. Jones 76).

For **a sacred text**: (Gen. 3.15), (2 Cor. 2.16), (John 2.1–4)

Example paragraph with parenthetical documentation

Telemachos is similarly pushed forward by his father's spirit. He tells Athene, after she questions him about his father, that "I for my part do not know. Nobody really knows his own father" (1.215–216). Telemachos must strive, however, to know his father, his past, in order to function in the present. In fact, "to know one's own father is to be part of the continuum of the human race and to see one's place in its future" (Gower 41). Telemachos must then seek to know his father. Athene recognizes this spiritual need: "Oh, for shame. How great your need is now of the absent / Odysseus" (1.253–4). Moreover, as Mary Lou Hoyle states, the entire "first five books of *The Odyssey* reveal the desperate conditions in Ithaka and thus the need for Odysseus the husband and father to return" (66). As a result of this deficit, Telemachos must "fit out a ship with twenty oars, the best you can come by, / and go out to ask about your father who is so long absent" (1.280–281).

Works Cited

Gower, Dona. "Athena and the Paradigm of the Teacher." *Classic Texts and the Nature of Authority*. Ed. Donald and Louise Cowan. Dallas: Dallas Institute of Humanities and Culture, 1993. 36–49.

Hoyle, Mary Lou. "The Sword, the Plow, and the Song: Odysseus' Great

Wanderings." *The Epic Cosmos*. Ed. Larry Allums. Dallas: Dallas Institute of Humanities and Culture, 1992. 59–88.

MLA Works Cited Format

GENERAL RULES FOR DOCUMENTING TEXT-BASED SOURCES
1. Order of information and the punctuation that follows each item: Author's last name, author's first name. Title. City of publication: publisher, date published.
2. Place titles of books, epics, and plays in italics; place titles of articles, chapters, and short poems in quotation marks.
3. Use only first city of publication listed and the latest copyright date.
4. Because the Modern Language Association updates its guidelines frequently, consult your instructor for the latest information. For additional information regarding WORKS CITED formatting, see www.easybib.com

Book w/one author
Orwell, George. *Animal Farm*. New York: Signet, 1946. Print.

A translation
Homer. *The Odyssey*. Trans. Robert Fagles. New York: Penguin, 1996. Print.

A book whose author is unknown
Encyclopedia of Virginia. New York: Somerset, 1993.

Book w/two or more authors
Pressley, Michael, and Vera Woloshy. *Cognitive Strategy Instruction That Really Improves Children's Academic Performance*. Cambridge, MA: Brookline Books, 1995.

An article in a reference book/multivolume work/encyclopedia
Cassidy, James. "The Great Dickens." *Nineteenth Century Literary Criticism*. 10 vols. Chicago: UP of Chicago, 1954.
Pettigrew, Thomas F. "Racism." *The World Book Encyclopedia*. 1998 ed.

An introduction, a preface, a foreword, or an afterward to a text
Drabble, Margaret. Introduction. *Middlemarch*. By George Eliot. New York: Bantam, 1985. vii–xvii.

Article in a scholarly journal
Fitzgerald, John. "The Misconceived Revolution: State and Society in China's Nationalist Revolution, 1923–26." *Journal of Asian Studies* 49 (1990): 323–43.
Baum, Rosalie Murphy. "Alcoholism and Family Abuse in *Maggie* and *The Bluest Eye*." *Mosaic* 19.3 (1986): 91–105.

An essay reprinted in an anthology or book

①   ②   ③

Frye, Northrop. "The Mysticism of Macbeth." *Shakespearean Journal*

④ ⑤ ⑫ ⑥   ⑦   ⑧

99 (1984): 990–95. Rpt. in *Shakespeare*. Ed. Robert D. Denham.

⑨   ⑩   ⑪ ⑫

Charlottesville: UP of Virginia, 1990. 18–27.

①	Author
②	Title of Article
③	The article originally appeared in this journal. You'll find this source at the end of the article or on the bottom of the first page.
④	Volume number
⑤	Date of article
⑥	Rpt. = Reprinted
⑦	This is the book where you found the article, the place where it has been reprinted.
⑧	Edited by Denham
⑨	City of publication
⑩	Publisher
⑪	Year
⑫	Page numbers.

Roberts, Sheila. "A Confined World: A Rereading of Pauline Smith." *World Literature Written in English* 24 (1984): 232–38. Rpt. in *Twentieth Century Literary Criticism*. Ed. Dennis Poupard. Vol. 25. Detroit: Gale, 1988. 399–402.

Article in a newspaper

Feder, Barnaby J. "For Job Seekers, a Toll-Free Gift of Expert Advice." *New York Times* 30 Dec. 1993: A38.

Article in a magazine

Bazell, Robert. "Science and Society: Growth Industry." *The New Republic* 15 Mar. 1993: 13–14.

GENERAL RULES FOR DOCUMENTING ONLINE SOURCES

1. Follow the "order of information and punctuation" that is used when documenting text-based sources.
2. Add the following additional information WHEN IT IS AVAILABLE: the name of the website where the source appeared, the publisher of the website, page numbers, date published on the website., date accessed by you.
3. Because the Modern Language Association updates its guidelines frequently, consult your instructor for the latest information. For additional information regarding WORKS CITED formatting, see www.easybib.com

Article in online newspaper or magazine

Lodge, David. "Dickens Our Contemporary." *The Atlantic Online* May 2002. 14 June 2002.

Material from a scholarly project online

Wollstonecraft, Mary. *A Vindication of the Rights of Woman*. London, 1892. *The Electronic Text Center*. Ed. David Seaman. 2002. Alderman Lib., U of Virginia. 29 July 2002.

Article in online reference database

Doreski, C.K. "Proustian Closure in Wallace Stevens' 'The Rock' and Elizabeth Bishop's 'Geography III.'" *Find Articles*. 2002. 10 pp. Look Smart and The Gale Group. 19 April 2002.

BASIC CLASSICAL RHETORIC[1]

Persuasion

One of the four modes of discourse, **persuasion** seeks to convince the audience to adopt the writer's point of view, his argument. Today, persuasion occurs not only in print media, daily conversation, and public oratory, but also in visual media as well—billboards, TV ads, films, etc. What follows is a brief introduction to how persuasion works, ACCORDING TO ARISTOTLE; it is designed to focus on persuasive strategies for effective writers. Knowledge of these strategies for convincing another can prove advantageous for any student. For one thing, understanding persuasion provides another method for analyzing both fiction and nonfiction; students may, for example, explore the persuasive appeals used by the speaker in the poem "To His Coy Mistress" or examine with greater insight a commentator's advocacy of a specific solution to a national issue. Moreover, as students become more adept at recognizing various methods of persuasion, they can incorporate these strategies into their own argumentation. Finally, recognizing persuasive techniques, along with the common fallacies associated with them, assists students in responding sensibly to the daily bombardment of solicitations and opinions.

For more about rhetoric, see www.telemachospublishing.com

Aristotle and Persuasion

The successful persuader, according to Aristotle, uses three types of appeals to convince others to change their opinions:

logos	the appeal to the audience's reason
pathos	the appeal to the audience's emotions
ethos	the appeal of the persuader's character

LOGOS

When we appeal to logic, to the audience's reason, we may argue using
• INDUCTION beginning with specific details and proceeding to draw a general conclusion

---

[1] MOST OF THE INFORMATION IN THIS SECTION IS ADAPTED FROM CORBETT, EDWARD P.J., AND ROBERT J. CONNORS. *CLASSICAL RHETORIC FOR THE MODERN STUDENT*. NEW YORK: OXFORD UNIVERSITY PRESS. 1999.

- DEDUCTION beginning with a general statement and proceeding to show specific examples as proof
- AUTHORITATIVE SOURCES government research, statistics, expert opinion
- DEFINITION arguing that something meets the definition; a writer says what something is
- DIVISION AND CLASSIFICATION to arrange multiple like items into categories
- ANALOGY arguing that one item is similar to another item
- CONSEQUENCE arguing cause and effect, positing that A causes B or that Y is the effect of (is caused by) X

PATHOS

When we appeal to the emotions of the audience, we may argue using
- sensory images and metaphors that build rapport, create fear, evoke sympathy
- storytelling and narration
- diction that is emotionally connotative.

The emotional appeal can, of course, be misused by some writers for nefarious purposes, to make the audience act in a manner that contradicts what they would otherwise know to be logically sound; therefore, caution is needed by both writers and their audiences. However, the appeal to emotion ought not be discarded, for, *when judiciously employed, it can provide motivation to change and act in a manner that supports reason.*

ETHOS

When writers make an ethical appeal, they communicate to the audience their good character. Aristotle divides this appeal into three types: *phronesis,* that the writer is sensible; *arête,* that the writer has high moral character; *eunoia,* that the writer is benevolent. Ethos, therefore, involves the type of impression the writer creates in the mind of the audience. Any part of the discourse that causes the audience to question the judgment or integrity of the writer can have devastating effect on the persuasive success of the writer's argument.

Successful writers who become skilled persuaders make choices, based on their audience and the occasion of their argument, as to how they arrange the three types of appeals. Reason alone, they know, does not often convince an audience to change. To spur change, or action, the writers must also appeal to emotion. Likewise, if the audience does not trust the judgment and good will of writers, the arguments these writers have made will not be convincing.

DISPOSITIO: ARRANGEMENT OF THE CLASSICAL ARGUMENT

- *EXORDIUM:* the introduction, where the writer/speaker introduces the topic, establishes its importance, and establishes the writer's ETHOS with the audience.
- *NARRATIO:* outlines the current situation, or the basic facts
- *DIVISIO:* explains the argument
- *CONFIRMATIO:* explains the evidence in support of the argument
- *CONFUTATIO:* refutes the opposing arguments
- *PERORATIO:* conclusion

A **non sequitur** is any conclusion that "does not follow" logically from the premises of an argument. Knowledge of such logical fallacies allows careful writers not only to counter arguments opposing their positions but also to avoid faulty reasoning on behalf of their own opinions.

- **Cause-effect** *[post hoc, ergo propter hoc;* "after it, therefore, because of it"]: arguing that because situation B followed situation A, A caused B. e.g. After Mark moved into the neighborhood, the crime rate increased.

- **Slippery slope:** arguing that one action will SURELY lead to a more serious consequence. e.g. Requiring trigger locks will result in guns being banned.

- **Strawman:** first, distorting the opponent's position/argument, thus fashioning it in more easily refuted terms; then, criticizing this distortion. e.g. My opponent's plan to reform Medicare means senior citizens will no longer have access to health care when needed, which is unconscionable.

- **Either-or:** arguing that there exist only two options when, in fact, the issue is not a "black-or-white" one in which other options have been exhausted. e.g. You either support clean air standards, or you support the auto industry.

- **Faulty analogy:** arguing that because two things are alike in some ways, they are also alike in others, with no consideration given to their dissimilarities. e.g. Andy and John are from rural America. John doesn't like the city; Andy probably doesn't like the city either.

- **Begging the question** *[petitio principii]:* "circular reasoning," occurring when something is assumed as true that has yet to be proven. e.g. Michelle didn't steal the ice cream bar because she is an honest person. *To state that Michelle is honest begs the question about her involvement in the theft of the ice cream, neither proving her fundamental honesty nor demonstrating that she has been honest at every moment of her life, including at the time of the theft.*

- *Ad hominem* argument [to the man]: use of an appeal to emotion in a devious manner that, instead of addressing and refuting the argument made by the opponent, finds the writer attacking the character of the opponent. e.g. How can anyone take seriously Henry's so-called moral argument against abortion? After all, he's a man, a chauvinist pig who can't bear children nor possibly understand what a woman does about her own body.

- *Ad populum* argument [to the people]: a type of "bandwagon" approach wherein the assertion is made that, because most people believe X, then Y must be true or Y must be good. Persons advancing an *ad populum* argument often, by employing emotion-charged language and anecdotes, manipulate a concept [justice, equality, patriotism, fairness] that has universal favorability in order to create support for what might otherwise be a controversial or problematic position. e.g. We believe in treating people fairly in this community, so it's only right that anyone who enlists in the military at 18 should be able to buy liquor at 18.

- **Hasty generalization:** arguing that, because a member of a group has a certain quality, all members of the group have that quality. e.g. All English teachers will correct your bad grammar.

- **Red herring** *[ignoratio elenchi;* "ignorance of the refutation"]: a term deriving from the practice of hunters "dragging a herring across the trace in order to lead the hounds away from their pursuit of the prey," a red herring is used by writers who argue by drawing attention to an irrelevant point. e.g. So what if I cheated on the exam? So did Fernando and Pauline.

GRADING RUBRICS

ESSAY RUBRIC

Students receive a copy of this rubric with their graded papers so that they can focus on areas of weakness. The teacher circles those items that pertain to the student's paper.

A–,A / 90, 95, 100 Clearly Outstanding

Content Introduction grabs attention with appropriate concrete details and effectively transitions into the thesis; thesis articulates a persuasive, original opinion, providing insight into the topic; topic sentences articulate precise component of argument, indicating an effective overall organizational structure to the paper; body paragraphs contain creative/original ideas and precise associative statements exploring how meaning emerges from the text's language and details with apt and extensive evidence for support of topic sentences and thesis statement; conclusion effectively discusses the significance of the paper topic; documentation requirements complete.

Style Language and syntax of thesis statement and topic sentences includes suitably precise vocabulary; coherence is created by effective transitions (particularly after topic sentences), clear topic strings, and concise word and logic glue; sentences exhibit a pleasing variety of structures, with accurate punctuation and grammar, appropriately sophisticated diction, and an emphasis on vivid verbs; the writer's analytical voice emerges convincingly.

B–,B,B+ / 80,85,88 Above Average

Content Strong idea for introduction but more concrete detail needed to grab attention and/or more helpful transition to the thesis statement required; thesis statement contains a legitimate, plausible opinion, with some adjustments needed to diction in order to refine the critical perspective; overall, topic sentences articulate an apparent structural link to the thesis by specifying a single component of the thesis though some topic sentences call for more precise diction to make their link to the thesis stronger; body paragraphs contain adequate selection of evidence along with reasonable associative/interpretive statements, although additional evidence and more precise and frequent associative statements regarding the language and details of the text would make paragraphs more convincing; conclusion ought articulate more clearly the significance of the overall topic; documentation requirements not fully complete.

Style Language and syntax of thesis statement and topic sentences understandable but could include more precise diction; minor coherence problems: re-examine word and logic glue, topic strings, and transitions after the topic sentences; at times, blend quoted material more smoothly, wrapping associations around the evidence; language regarding the organization of paragraphs present but needs to be more explicit; combine some sentences to eliminate wordiness and to provide variety and balance; for clarity, remove vague language and introduce more vivid verbs into some sentences; incorporate more sophisticated associative vocabulary [see ANALYTICAL VOICE chart] and a greater variety of sentence structures; minor problems with grammar, spelling, punctuation, redundancy.

C-,C,C+ / 70,75,78 Acceptable

Content Introduction needs development: additional showing details, a more convincing analogy that ties to the thesis, and/or a clearer transition to the thesis statement; the central idea/opinion of the thesis statement should be narrowed as it is too general or revised as it is unclear or lacks individual insight beyond comments made in class; one or more topic sentences have no connection to the thesis, are redundant, too broad or general in wording, unclearly stated, or merely recall a plot detail, lacking any associative perspective; one or more paragraphs contain inadequate or inappropriate textual support; inadequate, vague, or illogical interpretive-associative commentary in support of thesis; summary of plot prevails rather than analysis of text; some textual references taken out of context; conclusion only summarizes main points and/or needs more concrete discussion of the topic's overall significance; errors in documentation or documentation incomplete.

Style Language and syntax of thesis statements and topic sentences lack concision and precision; coherence issues demand consistent and overall revision in more than one paragraph: transitions after the topic sentences, stronger word and logic glue, tighter topic strings; language indicating the organization of paragraphs unclear; connection to thesis unclear; problems with sentence clarity, redundancy, punctuation, choppy sentences, weak verbs, wordiness, vagueness, spelling, grammar; some awkward incorporation of textual support, inadequate wrapping of associative statements around the evidence; insufficient and/or inappropriate usage of SAT vocabulary; deficient associative language [see ANALYTICAL VOICE chart]; sentence variety lacking.

D-,D,D+,F / 65,67,69,<60 Unacceptable/ Does Not Meet Requirements

Content Major attributes of the showing-telling introduction not present; thesis either not evident or completely lacks a persuasive opinion or is too general; the majority of topic sentences either do not reflect a structural relationship to the thesis or lack a critical perspective on the thesis; the majority of body paragraphs do not exhibit logical development of the topic sentences, either possessing inadequate evidence from the text, providing predominately plot summary, or demonstrating little or no analysis of evidence; ideas unclear; paragraphs do not support the topic sentence; illogical analysis of text; requirements of assignment incomplete; plagiarism present; documentation clearly incomplete or not present.

Style Language and syntax of thesis statement and topic sentences too vague and unclear; significant problems with coherence issues throughout: transitions after topic sentences, word and logic glue, topic strings, language indicating the method of organization; serious spelling, grammar errors; multiple sentences lack clarity because of awkward syntax, vagueness, or wordiness.

SHOWING WRITING RUBRIC

Students receive a copy of this rubric with their revised, graded paper. The teacher circles those items that pertain to the paper.

A–,A / 90,95 Clearly Outstanding

Action verbs in use throughout and in present tense; the paper contains few or no unnecessary "be" verbs; the student has extended the elaboration of each image beyond two sentences; almost no telling or little telling occurs throughout the piece; each sentence shows action or a specific, singular image; the student has extensively revised his or her composition; the first sentence grabs the reader's attention with specific showing detail; sophistication of writing style and vocabulary clearly indicated; grammatical structures are accurately labeled.

B–,B,B+ / 80,85,88 Above Average

Action verbs used primarily; most, if not all, verbs remain in present tense; some "be" verbs could still be eliminated and replaced with action verbs; some places could be extended; the student may be listing new images with each new sentence, though this occurs infrequently; the first sentence attempts to grab the reader's attention, but it could use some additional concrete singular detail; some telling sentences exist, though not many; the paper contains creative ideas but some ideas need more elaboration and showing detail; some wordiness and redundancy need revision; the first draft shows evidence of revision, but additional revision would have added to the quality of this final draft; certain problems with sentence structure, grammar usage, punctuation, and/or capitalization are evident; some evidence of sophisticated writing style and vocabulary emerging; minor problems with required grammatical structures.

C–,C,C+ / 70,75,78 Acceptable

More action verbs needed; writer may have strayed from present tense; avoid reliance on "be" verbs; only relatively minor elaboration of details has been done; sections of the paper contain listing— introducing a new image or detail with each sentence; multiple sections where elaboration needs to be extended; too many plurals and vague words; the paper contains solid ideas and has been completed adequately, but the student's composition needs more development; the student has revised parts of his or her paper, though not extensively; more than three grammatical errors exist.

D–,D,D+,F / 65,67,69,<60 Unacceptable/ Does Not Meet Requirements

The paper contains too many telling phrases or sentences; more substantial revision of the first draft is required; serious errors in grammar exist; the student must see the teacher for help; little revision has been done to the original; numerous "be" verbs and vague, plural words; student has not extended his elaboration of ideas; sentence structure, grammar usage, punctuation and/or capitalization procedures have not been followed.

PEER REVIEW/EDITING ACTIVITIES

Below are four editing activities to use after students have completed a rough draft. All these activities can be easily revised to fit the teacher's classroom context.

Assignment: Partner Review/Editing

Directions:

1. Pick one editing symbol the teacher has either marked on the composition or to which he or she refers during verbal direction-giving in the class.
2. With a partner, write out the revised version of the sentence[s] so that the problem has been corrected.
3. Use Chapter Six of this writing book.
4. Switch and repeat the process with the partner who hasn't made a correction.
5. If you wish, repeat process with different symbol/same or new partner.

Assignment: Partner-Homework Review/Edit (or In-Class Review/Edit)

Directions:

1. The day prior to this assignment, the teacher will require that students bring to class the following day two copies of their composition. This may be a single paragraph, an introduction, a conclusion, or an entire essay.
2. On the day students bring with them two copies of their composition, the teacher will assign each student a partner.
3. For homework tonight, each student will take his or her partner's composition home. (Or this can be entirely for an in-class assignment.)
4. Make an editing sheet. (See p. 251)
5. The student may use the **checklists*** and other aids located throughout this writing book to cover all aspects of the partner's paper. (See below.)
6. Tomorrow each student will have class time to discuss his or her comments with the partner. If a student is absent tomorrow, it is his or her responsibility to make sure the partner's paper with the editing sheet is delivered to school.
7. Each student's editing may be graded based on effort.

> *** Checklists**
> Showing writing revision process p. 47
> Showing-telling introductory paragraph pp. 112
> Thesis statements p. 104
> Topic sentences p. 54+
> Paragraphs pp. 75-76
> Concluding paragraph p. 115
> Transitional glue pp. 68, 107
> Quick Essay Checklist p. 131

Assignment: Partner In-Class Activities for Essays

Day One: Checking essay structure—thesis statements and topic sentences

Directions: Partners should exchange papers, read the thesis statement, and answer the following questions. When both partners are finished answering the questions, jotting their answers on a separate sheet of paper, the partners should discuss the answers.

1. Does the thesis statement include a precise topic + a debatable opinion?
2. Does the thesis merely summarize or only point out an obvious detail or pattern rather than actually argue a position? Explain.
3. Could the reader logically disagree with the thesis statement? (One should be able to disagree if the thesis contains a debatable opinion.
4. Does the diction include vague or abstract words that contain too many meanings, thus preventing a clear focus? Explain.
5. Has the reader provided some specific suggestions for improved diction?

Directions: Partners should read the topic sentences for each paragraph in the body and follow the procedures regarding jotting and discussing listed above.

1. Does each topic sentence clearly help support the argument in the thesis? If not, has the reader offered suggestions?
2. Does the writer include word glue to make the relationship between the thesis statement and topic sentence obvious to the reader? Explain.
3. Is the diction precise and specific? Or does it contain vague and abstract ideas that may be confusing? Has the reader suggested elimination of wordy structures? Explain.
4. Does the topic sentence contain more than one specific idea? Is it too broad? Has the reader suggested that the writer narrow the topic sentence? Explain.
5. Is there a transitional sentence from the topic sentence to the first supporting detail? If not, has the reader suggested one?

Day Two: The introductory paragraph

Directions: Follow each step with a partner.

Step 1: The writer reads the introductory paragraph to the listener.

Step 2: The listener says

A. Why do you think this introduction would grab the attention of most readers?
The writer responds....
B. What do you need to add to the introduction to make it even better, more attention-grabbing?
The writer responds.... The listener suggests....
C. What is your transition sentence(s) from the attention-grabber to the thesis statement?
The writer shows. The listener comments and/or suggests.
D. What is your thesis statement?
The writer shows. The listener comments and/or suggests.
E. What are the sentence structures the teacher is requiring?
The writer shows the listener the highlighted structures.
The listener confirms their existence or points out any problems and suggests solutions.

Step 3: The listener honestly evaluates the introductory paragraph by marking the following numbers on the spaces next to the items mentioned below:

___4 = No improvement needed.
___3 = Needs more work in the following areas:
    ___ • The attention-grabber
    ___ • The transition from attention-grabber to thesis statement
    ___ • The thesis statement's clarity and diction

___ • At least one example of two different sentence structures.

___2 = Needs substantial revision. The writer should review the models on pp. 118–121 and note attention in the areas marked above.

___1 = Little effort shown or the writer may consider meeting with the teacher for additional help.

Step 4: Switch Roles

Day Three: Checking body paragraphs

Directions: Partners should exchange papers, read one body paragraph, and answer the following questions. When both partners are finished answering the questions, jotting answers on a separate sheet of paper, the partners should discuss the answers.

1. Is there a clear transition immediately after the topic sentence? Does the reader understand how the writer is going to organize the information in the paragraph?
2. When the writer includes direct quotations, are these blended as if the words are part of the sentence, or is there an abrupt beginning of quoted material?
3. Is it clear how the textual passages support the topic sentence? Does the writer explain how we should see these details?
4. Is the writer only summarizing details from the story and not explaining why they prove his topic sentence?
5. Is it clear how each sentence helps support the topic sentence?
6. Has the writer provided enough details and commentary to support the topic sentence? Does the reader have suggestions for additional details?
7. Are some sentences too wordy? Are some words too abstract or vague? Has the reader made suggestions for revision?
8. Do some sentences need to be combined, using, for example, a participial phrase, repeat word modifier, analysis modifier, conjunctive adverb, or subordinate clause?
9. Is it clear what the logical and grammatical transitions are? Does the writer use repetition and synonyms for word glue?
10. Are there direct quotations that need further comment and analysis?

Once each partner has worked with the other on one body paragraph, begin the same process with another body paragraph.

Day Four: Checking conclusions

Directions: Partners should exchange papers, read the conclusion, and answer the following questions. When both partners are finished answering the questions, jotting answers on a separate sheet of paper, the partners should discuss the answers.

1. Does the conclusion avoid summarizing the main points of the paper?
2. Does the writer attempt to discuss what is significant about this thesis? Does the writer attempt to relate the thesis to our contemporary culture in an elaborately extensive fashion?
3. Does the writer attempt to relate the thesis to other works of literature?
4. Are there any wordy structures? Vague or confusing statements that could be more precise?
5. Where and how can the writer extend the elaboration of an idea by providing

more concrete detail?
6. Which sentences need combining?

Day Five: Overall evaluation

Directions: After the reader has finished all parts of the writer's composition, the evaluation rubric is used to determine the status of the composition. Once each specific evaluation point that applies to the composition is checked below, the reader will discuss the evaluation with the writer and suggest ways for improving the composition.

4 ____ The thesis statement is clearly stated; diction is impeccable.

____ Introduction includes concrete details and effectively grabs reader's attention.

____ Each topic sentence is clearly stated; diction is impeccable.

____ The writer has a clear transitional sentence from the topic sentence to the first supporting detail.

____ Each topic sentence is supported by extensively elaborated details.

____ Each supporting detail clearly relates in an organized fashion to one another and to the topic sentence.

____ The writer has employed sophisticated diction.

____ Conclusion avoids summary and explains the thesis' relation to other works of literature or a larger community.

3 ____ The thesis statement is clearly stated; diction needs improvement.

____ Introduction's ideas need minor revision, needs to grab attention more vividly.

____ The transitional sentence to the thesis statement may need some revision.

____ Each topic sentence is clearly stated; diction needs improvement.

____ The transitional sentences after the topic sentences need revision.

____ Each topic sentence is supported by details, most sufficiently elaborated.

____ Some details need to be more extensively elaborated.

____ Most details are clearly related to one another and to the topic sentence, though some need additional revision and transitional glue.

____ Conclusion is adequate, but the writer may consider a more elaborated literary or contemporary connection.

2 ____ The thesis statement is not clearly stated; diction needs improvement.

____ Introduction doesn't grab reader's attention or needs a closer tie to the thesis.

____ Some topic sentences are not clearly stated; diction needs improvement.

____ Little extension of elaboration for many details.

____ Transitional sentences after topic sentences needed in many places.

____ Although a few of the details may support the topic, more work needs to be done on making sure they all relate to one another and to the topic.

____ Writer does not employ sophisticated diction.

____ Conclusion contains too much summary.

1 ____ The thesis statement is basically meaningless; diction needs improvement.

____ Unacceptable introduction—no showing details!

____ No transitional sentences, either between the showing introduction and thesis statement or after topic sentences.

____ Most topic sentences are not clearly stated; diction needs improvement.

____ Most topic sentences have less than three supporting details; no elaboration.

____ Although a few of the details may support the topic, much more work needs to be done on making sure they all relate to one another and to the topic.

____ Conclusion incomplete, merely restates thesis statement.

Assignment: Peer review editing workshop (ALTERNATIVE ONE)

Directions

1.   Each student-writer should take a blank sheet of paper and make an editing sheet. (See SAMPLE EDITING SHEET, p. 251)
2.   Student-writers should place their names, or secret numbers, on the editing sheet.
3.   The student-writer turns in to the teacher the editing sheet attached to the composition so that he or she can redistribute compositions to students.
4.   The teacher redistributes the compositions with attached editing sheets.
5.   The student-editor should only place the editing symbol on the student-writer's paper when he or she notices a specific problem. For example, the first student-editor might be exploring places in the text **to extend elaboration.** The first editor to use the symbol **E3** would place this symbol next to the sentence on the student's essay, along with a numerical indication that corresponds with the particular editor. For example, if John is the first editor, he will use **E3–1,** indicating that his comment on the editing sheet corresponds with **E3–1.** Since John is instructed to find at least two places on the student paper to make suggestions, he next might use the symbol **E4–1.** Mary might find another example of **E3** and mark **E3–2,** since she is the second editor to use the symbol **E3.** (See the example on the next page.)
6.   On the editing sheet, student-editors write their names under editor, fill in the letter code, and explain their comments.
7.   Throughout the class period, student-editors will finish editing papers at different times. When one student-editor, for example, finishes editing a paper, he or she should raise his or her hand, and the teacher will provide another paper to edit. During the beginning of the period, one student may have to wait before another paper is available to edit.
8.   At certain times, the teacher may assign a grade to the quality of comments a student-editor makes.
9.   Students need to write two specific suggestions on the editing sheet, which may include an actual sentence revision.
10.   At the end of the period, students will receive their own compositions and editing sheets with several suggestions.
11.   Student-writers should remember that they are not required to follow all suggestions. The teacher hopes that a few comments will prove helpful or at least help the student rethink aspects of the composition.

Sample student composition with editing symbol codes

Dickens shows Scrooge as self-centered and materialistic. Dickens starts by revealing the selfish aspect of Scrooge. For example, Scrooge complains to his nephew that "I live in a world of fools." **E3–1** This pattern continues when Scrooge tells the charity workers that he will donate "nothing." **C** Here Scrooge emphasizes that his practice is not to donate any money for the poor. **E4–1** Instead, Scrooge insists on being "left alone." **E3–2**

Writer's Name_____

Editor	Symbol	Comments
Mike	E3–1	Try something like this: "a comment that shows Scrooge is rude even to members of his own family."
	E4–1	You might talk about the irony of the word "nothing" meaning his soul is full of nothing, too, no compassion.
Sharon	E3–2	This isolation prevents Scrooge from not only making financial commitments to his community but also personal ones. Discuss more.
Sharon	C	These two sentences could be joined by the conjunctive adverb "in fact."

Assignment: Peer review editing workshop (ALTERNATIVE TWO)

This peer editing approach is adapted from *Acts of Teaching: How to Teach Writing* by Joyce Armstrong Carroll and Edward E. Wilson. THE BASIC DIFFERENCE BETWEEN "ALTERNATIVE TWO" AND "ALTERNATIVE ONE" IS THAT THE TEACHER DURING "TWO" DOES NOT TOUCH THE WRITERS' COMPOSITIONS OR EDITING SHEETS DURING THE CLASS PERIOD. Instead, the teacher states what specific detail is to be edited. The students face each other in rows of desks or in two circles of desks. The students on one side of the row or circle never move; the others always move.

1. Student-writers create editing sheets with their names on them (see example above), which remain with their compositions during the period.
2. Students sit across from one another in a long row or two; they exchange papers (composition + editing sheet).
3. The teacher states what one detail, punctuation, structure, or "editing symbol" is to be checked. For example, the teacher may say **E3** or **PrPP**.
4. Once the editors have had sufficient time to look for any errors regarding that detail, they make specific constructive comments on the writers' editing sheets. After papers are returned, the designated "movers" move.
5. Teacher directs new partners to exchange papers, states the detail to be checked, and the editors begin perusing the writers' compositions for the detail, make needed comments on the sheet, and then return the papers.
6. The designated "movers" do so when the teacher signals, and the procedure continues. Only the designated "movers" move throughout the period.

GLOSSARY OF LITERARY TERMS

Allegory   a fictional work where characters and/or setting are personifications of abstract qualities. (*Vanity Fair* in *Pilgrim's Progress; Beauty and Death* in the morality play *Everyman; Beatrice* in *The Divine Comedy.)*

Alliteration   a rhetorical device that repeats the initial identical consonant sounds in succession. *Sure I had drunken in my dreams, / And still my body drank. The Rime of the Ancient Mariner* (Samuel Taylor Coleridge).

Allusion   making a reference to a famous historical, Biblical, mythological, or literary figure or event.

Anadiplosis   repetition of the ending segment at the beginning of another segment. *When I give, I give myself.* (Walt Whitman).

Analogy   a comparison of the similar characteristics of two unlike things.

Anapest   a metrical foot consisting of two unstressed syllables followed by a stressed syllable. *With a leap / and a bound.* (Coleridge).

Anaphora repetition of the beginnings of sentences or clauses. *Let us march to the realization of the American dream. Let us march on segregated housing. Let us march on segregated schools.* (Martin Luther King, Jr.).

Antagonist   the character who is opposed to the protagonist.

Antithesis   juxtaposition of contrasts in parallel structures. That's one small step for a man, one giant leap for mankind. (Neil Armstrong).

Apostrophe   addressing—speaking to—some abstract quality or non-human entity. (Shelley writes, *"O, West Wind, thou art preserver and destroyer.")*

Archetype   derived from Carl Jung, this is a term that refers to a character type, image, setting, or story pattern that can be found in all cultures and from all epochs. *A snake, the temptress, the wise man, the sea, the color red.*

Arrangement the parts of a formal argument, the steps the writer takes to persuade an audience, moving sequentially through the following stages: introduction [exordium], context and background of the topic [narratio], outlining of the main arguments [divisio], the evidence for the main arguments [confirmatio], refuting the opponent's counter-arguments [confutatio], concluding remarks [peroratio]

Assonance   repetition of vowel sounds. *So twice five miles of fertile ground.* (Coleridge).

Asyndeton omitting conjunctions between words, phrases, or clauses. *He has been beaten, tortured, interrogated, manipulated.*

Blank verse   unrhymed lines of ten syllables each (iambic pentameter).
It little profits that an idle king,
By this still hearth, among these barren crags,
Matched with an aged wife, I mete and dole,
Unequal laws unto a savage race. (Tennyson).

Caesura   in poetry, a pause in the line marked either by punctuation (a dash, a comma, a semicolon), internal rhyme, or a blank space. *Featur'd like him, like him with friends possess'd.* (Shakespeare).

Catharsis   the purging of emotion experienced after a tragedy.

Chiasmus   a figure of speech in which a grammatical structure is repeated but in inverse order. *Ask not what your country can do for you, ask what you can do for your country.* (John F. Kennedy)

Closed form   a poem that follows a specific form and metrical pattern. *sonnet, villanelle, sestina.*

Coherence   creating logically consistent and grammatically accurate relationships among sentences and paragraphs in an expository argument.

Colloquial   language that is informal or familiar to a group of people.

Connotation   the meaning of a word other than its strict dictionary definition, the assorted images and ideas associated with a word.

Conceit   a figure of speech, conceit is an elaborate, at times quite intricate, comparison—metaphor or simile—between unlikely objects. (John Donne compares *love* to a *geometric compass* in his poem "A Valediction: Forbidding Mourning.")

Consonance   a rhetorical device used in poetry where the poet repeats the identical consonant sounds typically in the last syllable of words. *That struts and frets.* (Shakespeare).

Couplet   the final two lines of a sonnet linked by rhyme.
For thy sweet love remember'd such wealth brings
That then I scorn to change my state with kings.

Cumulative sentence   a sentence that begins with an independent clause and proceeds to expand the sentence by adding a series of phrases and clauses. *They give you a temper of the will, a quality of the imagination, a vigor of the emotions, a freshness of the deep springs of life, a temperamental predominance of courage over timidity, of an appetite for adventure over love of ease. (General Douglas MacArthur, "Duty, Honor, Country")*

Dactyl   a metrical foot consisting of a stressed syllable followed by two unstressed syllables. *Ever to / come up with / Dactyl tri / syllable.* (Coleridge).

Declarative sentence   a sentence that makes a statement. *I have two new books.*

Denotation   the dictionary definition of a word.

Description   a mode of writing that relies on images to portray a person, place, or thing.

Diction   the individual words chosen by the author.

Doppleganger   a German phrase that asserts that for each person there exists an exact replica of himself, a shadow image. (*Dr. Jekyll and Mr. Hyde).*

Dynamic/Round character   a complex character who changes or develops as a result of the actions of the plot.

Elegy   a poem that reflects upon death or another equally solemn theme.

End rhyme   the final rhyme that occurs at the end of lines in a poem. *eyes / cries, state / fate.*

End-stopped   final punctuation at the end of a poetic line, a line that is not enjambed. *September rain falls on the house.* (Elizabeth Bishop).

Enjambment   occurs when the poet continues the grammatical sentence into the next line.
Once again I see
These hedgerows, hardly hedgerows, little lines. (William Wordsworth).

Epanalepsis   repetition of the beginning at the end of a clause or sentence.
Blood hath bought blood, and blows have answer'd blows. (Shakespeare's *King John*)

Ethos   the impression conveyed by writers and speakers to the audience regarding their own character (their credibility, their trustworthiness, the soundness of their judgment]

Exclamatory sentence   a sentence that expresses a strong or sudden emotion.
I love the absolute phrase!

Exposition   a mode of writing that explains a topic or idea.

Feminine rhyme   rhyme that results from the sound in two or more consecutive syllables, the last syllable being unstressed. *despising-arising.*

Foil   a character whose traits contrast with those of another character in order to accentuate the specific qualities of that other character. *Dr. Watson* and *Sherlock Holmes, Sancho Panza* and *Don Quixote*

Foot   the basic unit used in the measurement of poetry, the foot, contains one stressed syllable and one or more unstressed syllables. *Was this / the face / that launched / a thou / sand ships.* (five feet) (Christopher Marlowe).

Free verse   poetry that has no metrical pattern or regular meter.
All truths wait in all things,
They neither hasten their own delivery nor resist it,
They do not need the obstetric forceps of the surgeon. (Walt Whitman).

Harmartia   a Greek term that refers to the tragic hero's *error in judgment.*

Hubris   a Greek term that means *excessive pride.*

Hyperbole   a figure of speech, hyperbole exaggerates a particular point in order to draw attention to it. *No / this my hand will rather / the multitudinous seas incarnadine, / Making the green one red.* (Macbeth). *I have gray hair. I really do. The one side of my head—the right side—is full of millions of gray hair.* (Holden Caulfield).

Iamb   a metrical foot consisting of an unstressed syllable followed by one stressed. *dis-grace.*

Imagery   the pictures created by words. *I found a dimpled spider, fat and white, / On a white heal-all, holding up a moth.* (Robert Frost).

Imperative sentence   a sentence that gives a command. (*Read the first four chapters of the novel* Crime and Punishment.)

Internal rhyme   one or more words that rhyme within a line of poetry. *The ship was cheered, the harbor cleared.* (*The Rime of the Ancient Mariner.)*

Interrogative sentence   a sentence that asks a question. *What is your favorite?*

Irony   a figure of speech wherein the reality is different from the appearance: VERBAL IRONY occurs when what is meant contrasts with the usual, or literal, meaning of the words stated; SITUATIONAL IRONY occurs when there is a difference between what appears to be true and what is actually true, or between what one expects and what actually happens; DRAMATIC IRONY occurs when the audience has information the character does not possess.

Juxtaposition   the placement of items close together, often for purposes of comparison or contrast.

Language   1. the diction and imagery used by a writer; 2.the types of words or phrases an author uses: *jargon, colloquial, poetic, scholarly, slang.*

Logos   argumentation through an appeal to logical reasoning.

Loose sentence   a sentence that begins with its main idea in the introductory independent clause and follows with less important details. *Wesley walked into the bookstore and purchased* Madame Bovary, *a recommendation made by his English teacher.*

Masculine rhyme   this rhyme results from the final stressed syllable. *state-gate, brings-kings.*

Meter   a regular pattern of rhythm in which the stresses on words occur at apparently equal intervals in time.

Metaphor   a figure of speech, a metaphor is an implied comparison between two unlike objects, our knowledge of the second object in the comparison shedding light upon the first object. To say *Pvt. Walker is a lion when confronted in battle* is to indicate that the characteristics possessed by a lion when attacked are the characteristics Pvt. Walker demonstrates when facing the enemy. To say *The town's businesses are undergoing a dry spell* is to suggest that what a drought means for a landscape is what a lack of paying customers means for a business.

Metonymy   a figure of speech, a metonymy is the substitution of a concept, an attribute, an object for the name of the thing itself; using a word closely associated as a stand-in for the actual word. *The revolutionaries seized the crown, shackled him, and traipsed him before the assembled multitudes outside.* [crown= the king, the head of government.] *She was instructed to stand before the bench and receive her sentence.* [bench - judge]

Mimesis   a Greek term that means the act of imitating reality.

Modes   a form of writing that an author may use in composition: *description, exposition, narration, persuasion.*

Mood   the emotional quality or atmosphere of a setting. *Anxious, foreboding.*

Motif   a reoccurring image, idea, character, or incident.

Narration   a mode of writing that retells events in a logical sequence.

Nemesis   one's enemy.

Ode   an elaborate poem expressed in language dignified, sincere, imaginative, and intellectual in tone.

Onomatopoeia   using words whose pronunciation suggests their meaning. *buzz, sizzle.*

Open form   a poem that is written in free verse; it does not prescribe to an established form or metrical pattern.

Oxymoron   placing together two contradictory words. *Sad joy, wise fool.*

Paradox   a statement that appears contradictory or absurd but may be true. *Time, as we know it, is a very recent invention.* (Aldous Huxley) *Art is a form of lying in order to tell the truth.* (Pablo Picasso).

Parataxis   a series of phrases or clauses without conjunctions. *I eat, I dance, I read.*

Parody   a piece of writing that pokes fun at another serious piece of writing; it is designed to ridicule or criticize the serious work.

Pathetic fallacy   a type of personification in which the author attaches human emotions and responses to nature. *the angry sea, the roses laughing in the sunlight*

Pathos   a Greek term that refers to *emotion, passion, or suffering*; readers of tragedy feel sorrow and pity for the characters; writers may argue by making an appeal to the emotions of their audience.

Periodic sentence   a sentence that begins with a series of phrases or subordinate clauses, and builds toward the independent clause. *If by good luck there had been an ash-tray handy, if one had not knocked the ash out of the window in default, if things had been a little different from what they were, one would not have seen, presumably, a cat without a tail.* (Virginia Woolf *A Room of One's Own.*)

Personification   a figure of speech that attaches human qualities to that which is not human. *The wind stood up and gave a shout.* (James Stephens)

Persuasion   a mode of writing that seeks to alter the reader's point of view on a topic.

Point of view   the perspective from which the story is told—first person, third person limited, third person omniscient, objective; careful readers should always keep in mind that a narrator's point of view is influenced by experiences and ideas that have shaped his or her perspective. [FIRST PERSON POV: the narrator is a character participating in the action of the story. THIRD-PERSON OMNISCIENT POV: the narrator telling the story knows the thoughts and feelings of all the characters involved in the plot. THIRD PERSON LIMITED POV: the narrator telling the story knows the thoughts and feelings of a single character involved in the plot. THIRD-PERSON OBJECTIVE POV: the narrator telling the story is not privy to the thoughts and feelings of any of the characters involved in the plot. *THIRD PERSON NARRATORS ARE USUALLY CONSIDERED TO BE DETACHED OBSERVERS RATHER THAN ACTUAL CHARACTERS INVOLVED IN THE STORY.*]

Polysyndeton   using conjunctions between words, phrases, or clauses. *A man with no hat, and with broken shoes, and with an old rag tied round his head. A man who had been soaked in water, and smothered in mud, and lamed by stones, and cut by flints, and stung by nettles, and torn by briars; who limped, and shivered, and glared, and growled; and whose teeth chattered in his head as he seized me by the chin. (Charles Dickens' Great Expectations)*

Prosody   the study of poetic meter and rhyme.

Protagonist   the main character in a play or story.

Quatrain   a set of four lines in a sonnet.

Rhyme scheme   the pattern, or sequence, in which the end-rhyme sounds occur in a stanza or poem; the pattern of rhyme indicated by the letter assigned to each line. The following sonnet has a rhyme scheme of ABABCDCDEFEFGG.

When in disgrace with Fortune and men's eyes	a
I all alone beweep my outcast state,	b
And trouble deaf heaven with my bootless cries,	a
And look upon myself and curse my fate,	b

Wishing me like to one more rich in hope,   c
Featur'd like him, like him with friends possess'd,   d
Desiring this man's art and that man's scope,   c
With what I most enjoy contented least: d
Yet in these thoughts myself almost despising,   e
Haply I think on thee, and then my state,   f
Like to the lark at break of day arising,   e
From sullen earth sings hymns at heaven's gate;   f
For thy sweet love remember'd such wealth brings   g
That then I scorn to change my state with kings.   g
(William Shakespeare.)

Synecdoche   a figure of speech, synecdoche is the use of a part of something to indicate the whole, or the whole to indicate the part. *Give me a hand with these boxes.* [hand= the person to whom the request for help is made] *Dallas has won five Super Bowls.* [Dallas = the football team Dallas Cowboys]

Sarcasm   often a type of verbal irony, in which, sometimes under the guise of praise, a caustic and bitter expression of strong and personal disapproval is given; these are comments intended to mock or show contempt.

Satire   writing that uses humor and wit to criticize a political or social situation and of which there are two types: **Horatian**—a mild form of satire seeking to create change through sympathetic humor, and **Juvenalian**—a caustic and indignant form of satire, expressing anger at examples of corruption and evil.

Simile   a figure of speech, simile is a direct, or explicit, comparison between two objects using the words *like* or *as. He is like a snake.*

Spondee   a metrical foot that contains two consecutive stresses. *Hum-drum.*

Static/Flat character   an uncomplicated character who changes little, if at all, in the progression of the literary work.

Slant rhyme   approximate rhyme—words used in a rhyming pattern that have some resemblance in sound but are not perfect rhymes. *soul / all   nap / cape*

Sonnet   a fixed form of fourteen lines; the **Shakespearean** sonnet contains three quatrains and a couplet; the **Petrarchan** sonnet contains an octave of eight lines and a sestet of six lines.

Syntax   the order in which words are arranged or grouped within a sentence.

Tone   the writer's attitude toward his subject. *curious, joyful, worried, calm, gracious, comic, profound.*

Tragic flaw   the flaw in the tragic hero's character that precipitates his downfall, known by the Greeks as *hamartia.*

Trochee   a metrical foot consisting of one stressed syllable followed by one unstressed syllable. *Double / double, / toil and / trouble. (*Macbeth)

Trope   any type of figurative language -- a simile, a paradox, a metaphor, irony, hyperbole, etc.

Understatement / Litote   to say something less forcefully than is appropriate. Lady Macbeth, after Duncan's murder, says, *"A little water will wash us of this deed,"* thus suggesting that the crime may be easily disposed of and forgotten. *I have this tiny little tumor on the brain. (*Holden Caulfield)

Unity   the condition in which all sentences in a paragraph support the idea in the topic sentence or all paragraphs in an essay support a thesis statement.

Verse   a line of poetry; poetry that has meter.

Voice   the qualities or personality of the speaker or narrator; a speaker's voice may be *angry, wise, ebullient, etc.* [this definition is distinct from verb voice]

INDEX

EDITING SYMBOLS

A　**Add transitional phrase or sentence: 1)** after initial topic sentence, add a transitional sentence that further clarifies and identifies the path the paragraph intends to take, that is, the organization of material—time, place, idea; **2)** add a phrase or clause acting as a modifier to the end of the topic sentence to further define and specify a general word that appears there; apply this definition to the text; **3)** add a transitional phrase or clause, indicating how you plan to organize the evidence, to the beginning of the sentence that comes after the topic sentence. SEE PP. 189-192.

B　**Blending: 1)** blend text more smoothly with the analysis; **2)** blend needs to be grammatically correct; **3)** explain the text and include it with the writer's words, revealing why this text helps prove the point; **4)** don't blend too early, without first setting up the aspect of the topic sentence the quotation is supposed to support—it is not clear how this supports the topic sentence or previous statement; **5)** first explain the context of the quotation. SEE PP. 192-196.

C　**Combine some sentences.** This helps eliminate wordiness, extend the elaboration of a single idea, eliminate unnecessary breaks in thought and choppy effect. Use participial, infinitive, gerund, absolute, and appositive phrases, as well as subordinate clauses to combine. SEE PP. 196-198.

give another sentence

E　**Extend the elaboration of an idea: 1)** the writer needs to elaborate and incorporate more textual support; **2)** the writer is missing some important textual examples; **3)** the writer should extend the elaboration of details, commenting further on this idea before moving to the next; **4)** elaboration is vague or merely restates the evidence. SEE PP. 198-202.

engage more senses ←

keep this image going!

EV　**Textual evidence doesn't provide clear support** for the writer's position or previous statement. Reread the text carefully.

G/P　**Fix any grammatical or punctuation errors!** If the writer doesn't understand the error, see the teacher. **RO, CS, //, SV, SF, PA** SEE PP. 150-153 AS WELL AS **PUNCTUATION RULES** FOR CLAUSES AND PHRASES THROUGHOUT CHAPTER 5: ADVSC 127, ADJSC 128, NSC 129 CP/CP-C 130, PrPP/PaPP 131 AbP 133, GP 134, ADV-IP 134 ADJ-IP 135, N-IP 135 AP 136.

IP　**Improving introductory paragraphs: 1)** the analogy for the introduction is not effective; too many aspects of the situation re-created are not applicable to the paper's thesis; **2)** not all of the showing details in the introduction are necessary; remove those that are not associated with the concepts in the thesis; **3)** the writer needs to interpret and comment on the details created in the introduction, highlighting specifically these associations seen as similar to the thesis. SEE PP. 202-204.

L　The student **merely lists details** without elaborating each image or explaining why these details/quotations provide support for the topic sentence. SEE PP. 205-207.

O　**Off-topic: 1)** evidence doesn't support the topic sentence; **2)** not completely off-topic, but either the writer is slipping into plot summary or failing to adequately explain how evidence supports topic. SEE PP. 208-210.

P   **Paragraph needs overall revision: 1)** the organization (time, place, idea) of main points supporting topic sentence needs to be identified or emphasized more clearly (pp. 60 - 64); **2)** these sentences do not provide complete coherence; check logic and word glue, and topic string; **3)** paragraphs could use more textual support and analysis—look for additional examples; **4)** tie to thesis needs to be stronger. SEE PP. 210-214.

S   **Summarizing** here rather than explaining how these details support the topic sentence. This problem is similar to listing. SEE PP. 215-216.

SH   **Show concrete images** rather than tell these details. The reader can't see any images. Showing text includes direct excerpts from the literary text along with the writer's elaborated analysis. SEE PP. 38-39, 216-217.

T   **Transitions weak: 1)** check word and logic glue between sentences (pp. 68-70); **2)** revise transition so there is closer link between these sentences; **3)** transition could be less wordy; **4)** maintain topic focus. SEE PP. 217-220.

TH   **Thesis needs revision: 1)** make minor adjustments in style and clarity; **2)** thesis contains only a topic, not an opinion; **3)** the idea in the thesis is unclear or too general (see chapter three). SEE PP. 224-225.

TS   **Revise the topic sentence: 1)** need stronger focus so that all sentences can clearly connect to main sentence; this will help coherence; **2)** topic sentence contains an example, a plot detail rather than an organizing idea + aspect of thesis (102-103); **3)** connect the topic sentence to thesis more clearly, perhaps adding actual words or synonyms from the thesis; **4)** this might be too broad or too vague—not sure the reader will understand the meaning; **5)** diction is imprecise. SEE PP. 220-223.

V   **Vague: 1)** this comment needs to be more specific, precise; avoid plurals; **2)** this comment does not really say anything. SEE PP. 225-227.

W   **Wordy structures: 1)** this phrase is unnecessary; do not write, "In chapter one it says, 'Hester stands still'"; instead, blend text with the writer's analysis—see **B1**; **2)** use fewer words; **3)** beware piling adjectives or adjective phrases one after another—either eliminate unnecessary adjectives or reposition some in participial phrases; **4)** remove redundant words within the sentence. SEE PP. 227-230.

~   **Redundant:** you've already mentioned this.

WC   **Word** here is **not the best choice.** Language is jargon or colloquial. SEE P. 231.

X   **Revise: 1)** cut the sentence or phrase; **2)** revise for clarity and conciseness. See pp. 231 - 233.

VT: verb tense ←

◯   **Vivid verbs: 1)** revise this "be" verb with a more active verb; **2)** avoid the passive verb in this context. SEE P. 234.

[ ]   **Vary** some of these **sentence beginnings.** SEE PP. 233-234.

CPSIA information can be obtained
at www.ICGtesting.com
Printed in the USA
LVOW04s0006080717

540642LV00026B/957/P

9 780985 384906